Three Dimensions of Poetry

Three Dimensions of Poetry

AN INTRODUCTION

BY

Vincent Stewart

Lock Haven State College

CHARLES SCRIBNER'S SONS · NEW YORK

Printed in the United States of America
SBN 684-41453-8
Library of Congress Catalog Card Number 79-92877

ACKNOWLEDGMENTS

ANGUS & ROBERTSON LTD.—for "The Dosser in Springtime" from *Collected Poems
1936–1967* by Douglas Stewart.

ATHENEUM PUBLISHERS—for "The Tunnel" from *Reasons for Moving* by Mark Strand.
   Copyright © 1964, 1968 by Mark Strand. Reprinted by permission of Atheneum
   Publishers. This poem appeared originally in the *Partisan Review.*

MARVIN BELL—for "The All Girls Drill Team" and "For My Sister, Contemplating
   Divorce" from *Things We Dreamt We Died For.* Copyright © 1966 by Marvin
   Bell. For "Travel." Copyright © 1967 by Marvin Bell. This poem appeared
   originally in *Poetry.*

WILLIAM BLACKWOOD & SONS LTD.—for "Milking Kraal" and "Lament for a Dead
   Cow" by Dr. F. Carey Slater.

CHATTO AND WINDUS LTD.—for "For a Lamb," "Where Are Those High and Haunting Skies," "Indian Pipe," and "Sestina" from *Collected Poems* by Richard
   Eberhart.

CITY LIGHTS BOOKS—for "Just as I used to say/love comes harder to the aged" from
   Pictures of the Gone World by Lawrence Ferlinghetti. Copyright © 1955 by
   Lawrence Ferlinghetti. For "Xochitepec" and "Sestina in a Cantina" from
   Selected Poems of Malcolm Lowry. Copyright © 1962 by Margerie Lowry. Re-
   printed by permission of City Lights Books.

CATHERINE BREESE DAVIS—for "After a Time."

DELACORTE PRESS—for "Morels" and "Dachshunds." Reprinted from *The Tin Can
   and Other Poems* by William Jay Smith. Copyright © 1962 by William Jay
   Smith. A Seymour Lawrence Book-Delacorte Press. Used by permission of the
   publisher.

REUEL DENNEY—for "To the Roman Bridge on Michigan Avenue."

J. M. DENT & SONS LTD.—for "A Refusal to Mourn the Death, by Fire, of a Child in
   London," "Poem in October," and "Do Not Go Gentle into that Good Night"
   from *Collected Poems* by Dylan Thomas. Reprinted by permission of the Trustees

iv

for the copyrights of the late Dylan Thomas and J. M. Dent & Sons Ltd. For "The Flute Man" from *No Voyage and Other Poems* by Mary Oliver. Reprinted by permission of J. M. Dent & Sons Ltd.

JAMES DICKEY—for "The Performance."

DOUBLEDAY & COMPANY, INC.—for one haiku from *An Introduction to Haiku* by Harold G. Henderson. Copyright © 1958 by Harold G. Henderson. Reprinted by permission of Doubleday & Company, Inc. For "The Way Through the Woods," copyright 1910 by Rudyard Kipling, from *Rewards and Fairies* by Rudyard Kipling. Reprinted by permission of Mrs. George Bambridge and Doubleday & Company, Inc. For "Highway: Michigan," copyright 1940 by Theodore Roethke; "My Papa's Waltz," copyright 1942 by Hearst Magazines, Inc.; "Elegy for Jane," copyright 1950 by Theodore Roethke; "The Yak," copyright 1952 by Theodore Roethke; "The Waking," copyright 1953 by Theodore Roethke; "Snake," copyright © 1955 by Theodore Roethke; "Reply to a Lady Editor," copyright © 1957 by Theodore Roethke; "The Harsh Country," copyright © 1959 by Beatrice Roethke as Administratrix of the Estate of Theodore Roethke; "In a Dark Time," copyright © 1960 by Beatrice Roethke as Administratrix of the Estate of Theodore Roethke; and "The Thing," copyright © 1963 by Beatrice Roethke as Administratrix of the Estate of Theodore Roethke; all from *The Collected Poems of Theodore Roethke.* Reprinted by permission of Doubleday & Company, Inc.

FABER AND FABER LTD.—for "The Whitsun Weddings" and "Afternoons" from *The Whitsun Weddings* by Philip Larkin. For "Preludes" from *Collected Poems 1909–1962* by T. S. Eliot. For "Considering the Snail" and "Rastignac at 45" from *My Sad Captains* by Thom Gunn. For "Order to View" and "Coda" from *Collected Poems* by Louis MacNeice. All reprinted by permission of Faber and Faber Ltd., publisher.

FARRAR, STRAUS & GIROUX, INC.—Reprinted with the permission of Farrar, Straus & Giroux, Inc. from *For the Union Dead, Imitations* and *Life Studies* by Robert Lowell. "For the Union Dead" copyright © 1960 by Robert Lowell. "Water" copyright © 1962 by Robert Lowell. "Scream," "Mouth of the Hudson," and "July in Washington" copyright © 1964 by Robert Lowell. From *Imitations:* "Ballad for Dead Ladies" copyright © 1958, 1959, 1960, 1961 by Robert Lowell. From *Life Studies:* "Skunk Hour" copyright © 1958 by Robert Lowell. For "A Sick Child" from *Complete Poems* by Randall Jarrell. Copyright © 1949, 1969 by Mrs. Randall Jarrell.

HARCOURT, BRACE & WORLD, INC.—for "Advice to a Prophet," © 1959 by Richard Wilbur. Reprinted from his volume, *Advice to a Prophet and Other Poems* by permission of Harcourt, Brace & World, Inc. First published in *The New Yorker* Magazine. For "Junk," © 1961 by Richard Wilbur. Reprinted from his volume, *Advice to a Prophet and Other Poems* by permission of Harcourt, Brace & World, Inc. For "Ballad for the Duke of Orleans," © 1961 by Richard Wilbur. Reprinted from his volume *Advice to a Prophet and Other Poems* by permission of Harcourt, Brace & World, Inc. First published in *The New Yorker* Magazine. For "Sonnet," © 1956 by Richard Wilbur. Reprinted from his volume, *Things of this World,* by permission of Harcourt, Brace & World, Inc. For "Museum Piece" from *Ceremony and Other Poems,* copyright, 1948, 1949, 1950, by Richard Wilbur. Reprinted by permission of Harcourt, Brace & World, Inc. For "because you take life in your stride(instead" from *95 Poems,* © 1958 by E. E. Cummings. Reprinted by permission of Harcourt, Brace & World, Inc. For "mr u will not be missed," copyright, 1944, by E. E. Cummings. Reprinted from his volume, *Poems 1923–1954,* by permission of Harcourt, Brace & World, Inc. For "Preludes" from *Collected Poems 1909–1962* by T. S. Eliot, copyright, 1936, by Harcourt, Brace & World, Inc.; copyright, © 1963, 1964, by T. S. Eliot. Reprinted by permission of the publishers. For "Concord," "The Holy Innocents," and "Death from Cancer" from *Lord Weary's Castle,* copyright, 1944, 1946, by Robert Lowell. Reprinted by permission of Harcourt, Brace & World, Inc.

HARPER & ROW—for "The Pawnbroker" from *The Privilege* by Maxine Kumin. Copyright © 1964 by Maxine W. Kumin. For "Old Mary" from *Selected Poems* by Gwendolyn Brooks. Copyright © 1959 by Gwendolyn Brooks. Reprinted by permission of Harper & Row, Publishers.

HARVARD UNIVERSITY PRESS—for ten poems by Emily Dickinson. Reprinted by permission of the publishers and the Trustees of Amherst College from Thomas H. Johnson, Editor, *The Poems of Emily Dickinson*, Cambridge, Mass.: The Belknap Press of Harvard University Press. Copyright, 1951, 1955, by The President and Fellows of Harvard College.

HOLT, RINEHART AND WINSTON, INC.—for "Loveliest of Trees," "To an Athlete Dying Young," "Reveille," and "On the Idle Hill of Summer" from "A Shropshire Lad" —Authorized Edition—from *The Collected Poems of A. E. Housman*. Copyright 1939, 1940, © 1959 by Holt, Rinehart and Winston, Inc. Copyright © 1967 by Robert E. Symons. Reprinted by permission of Holt, Rinehart and Winston, Inc. For "The Chestnut Casts his Flambeaux" from *The Collected Poems of A. E. Housman*. Copyright 1922 by Holt, Rinehart and Winston, Inc. Copyright 1950 by Barclays Bank Ltd. Reprinted by permission of Holt, Rinehart and Winston, Inc. For "A Cabin in the Clearing" and "Questioning Faces" from *In the Clearing* by Robert Frost. Copyright 1951, © 1962 by Robert Frost. Reprinted by permission of Holt, Rinehart and Winston, Inc. For "Mending Wall," "'Out, Out—,'" "Stopping by Woods on a Snowy Evening," "Provide, Provide," "After Apple-Picking," "Fire and Ice," "Acquainted with the Night," and "In Divés' Dive" from *Complete Poems of Robert Frost*. Copyright 1916, 1923, 1928, 1930, 1939 by Holt, Rinehart and Winston, Inc. Copyright 1936, 1944, 1951, © 1956, 1958 by Robert Frost. Copyright © 1964, 1967 by Lesley Frost Ballantine. Reprinted by permission of Holt, Rinehart and Winston, Inc.

HOUGHTON MIFFLIN COMPANY—for "The Flute-Man" from *No Voyage* by Mary Oliver. For "You, Andrew Marvell" from *Collected Poems* by Archibald MacLeish. Copyright © 1962 by Archibald MacLeish. Reprinted by permission of the publisher, Houghton Mifflin Company.

JOHN JOHNSON—for "Kanheri Caves" and "Jason" by Dom Moraes.

MARGOT JOHNSON AGENCY—for "The Iron Characters" from *The Next Room of the Dream* by Howard Nemerov.

ALFRED A. KNOPF, INC.—for "The Yak," by Hilaire Belloc. For "Miriam Tazewell," "The Tall Girl," and "Bells for John Whiteside's Daughter." Copyright 1924 by Alfred A. Knopf, Inc. and renewed 1952 by John Crowe Ransom. Reprinted from *Selected Poems* by John Crowe Ransom, by permission of the publisher. For "Domination of Black," "The Snow Man," "The Emperor of Ice-Cream," "Sunday Morning," "Life is Motion," "Peter Quince at the Clavier," and "Thirteen Ways of Looking at a Blackbird." Copyright 1923 and renewed 1951 by Wallace Stevens. Reprinted from *The Collected Poems of Wallace Stevens* by permission of Alfred A. Knopf, Inc. For "Autumn Refrain." Copyright 1936 by Wallace Stevens. Reprinted from *The Collected Poems of Wallace Stevens* by permission of Alfred A. Knopf, Inc. For "Study of Two Pears" and "Woman Looking at a Vase of Flowers." Copyright 1942 by Wallace Stevens. Reprinted from *The Collected Poems of Wallace Stevens* by permission of Alfred A. Knopf, Inc.

LITTLE, BROWN AND COMPANY—for "Pit Viper" and "The Skindivers" from *White Paper* by George Starbuck, by permission of Atlantic-Little, Brown and Co. Copyright © 1960, 1961, 1962, 1963, 1964, 1965, 1966 by George Starbuck. For "The Science of the Night" from *Selected Poems 1928–1958* by Stanley Kunitz, by permission of Atlantic-Little, Brown and Co. Copyright, 1953, by Stanley Kunitz.

LIVERIGHT PUBLISHING CORPORATION—for "To Brooklyn Bridge," "National Winter Garden," "Repose of Rivers," "Voyages I," and "Royal Palm" from *Complete Poems of Hart Crane*. Permission by Liveright, Publishers, 386 Park Ave., N.Y., N.Y. Copyright 1933 by Liveright Publishing Corp.

PHILIP LEVINE—for "Lights I Have Seen Before."

MCCLELLAND AND STEWART LTD.—for "Slug in Woods" from *Selected Poems* by Earle Birney, reprinted by permission of The Canadian Publishers, McClelland and Stewart Limited, Toronto.

THE MACMILLAN COMPANY—for "The Lake Isle of Innisfree" and "The Song of the Wandering Aengus." Reprinted with permission of The Macmillan Company from *Collected Poems* by William Butler Yeats. Copyright 1906 by The Macmillan Company renewed 1934 by William Butler Yeats. For "The Three Hermits." Reprinted with permission of The Macmillan Company from *Collected*

Larkin. Reprinted from *The Whitsun Weddings,* by Philip Larkin, by permission of Random House, Inc. For "Afternoons." From *The Whitsun Weddings,* by Philip Larkin. © Copyright 1964 by Philip Larkin. Reprinted by permission of Random House, Inc. For "Bearded Oaks." Copyright 1942, © 1966 by Robert Penn Warren. From *Selected Poems: New and Old, 1923–1966,* by Robert Penn Warren. Reprinted by permission of Random House, Inc. For "Eidolon." From *Selected Poems: New and Old, 1923–1966,* by Robert Penn Warren. © Copyright 1966 by Robert Penn Warren. Reprinted by permission of Random House, Inc. For "The Three Companions." Copyright 1934 and renewed 1962 by W. H. Auden. Reprinted from *Collected Shorter Poems 1927–1957,* by W. H. Auden, by permission of Random House, Inc. For "As I Walked Out One Evening" and "In Memory of W. B. Yeats." Copyright 1940 by W. H. Auden. Reprinted from *Collected Shorter Poems 1927–1957,* by W. H. Auden, by permission of Random House, Inc. For "If I Could Tell You." Copyright 1941 by W. H. Auden. Reprinted from *Collected Shorter Poems 1927–1957,* by W. H. Auden, by permission of Random House, Inc. For "Fish in the Unruffled Lakes." Copyright 1937 and renewed 1965 by W. H. Auden. Reprinted from *Collected Shorter Poems 1927–1957,* by W. H. Auden, by permission of Random House, Inc.

THE RYERSON PRESS—for "Ice." Reprinted from *Selected Poems of Charles G. D. Roberts* by Charles G. D. Roberts, by permission of The Ryerson Press, Toronto. For "The Blue Heron." Reprinted from *The Leather Bottle* by Theodore Goodridge Roberts, by permission of The Ryerson Press, Toronto. For "How One Winter Came in the Lake Region." Reprinted from *Collected Poems* by Wilfred Campbell, by permission of The Ryerson Press, Toronto.

CHARLES SCRIBNER'S SONS—for "Richard Cory" and "The House on the Hill" from *The Children of the Night* by Edwin Arlington Robinson (1897) and "Miniver Cheevy" (Copyright 1907 Charles Scribner's Sons; renewal copyright 1935 Ruth Nivison) from *The Town down the River* by Edwin Arlington Robinson, reprinted with the permission of Charles Scribner's Sons. For "The Subway" which is reprinted with the permission of Charles Scribner's Sons from *Poems* by Allen Tate. For "Water Island" (Copyright © 1960 Howard Moss) and "A Swim Off the Rocks" (Copyright © 1962 Howard Moss) which first appeared in *The New Yorker,* which are reprinted with the permission of Charles Scribner's Sons from *Finding Them Lost and Other Poems* by Howard Moss.

THE SOCIETY OF AUTHORS—For "Loveliest of Trees," "To an Athlete Dying Young," "Reveille," "On the Idle Hill of Summer," and "The Chestnut Casts His Flambeaux." Reprinted by permission of The Society of Authors as the literary representative of the Estate of the late A. E. Housman, and Messrs. Jonathan Cape Ltd., publishers of A. E. Housman's *Collected Poems.*

THE SWALLOW PRESS INC.—for J. V. Cunningham "4," *To What Strangers, What Welcome.* Swallow Press, Chicago, Illinois. For Alan Stephens "The Vanishing Act," *The Sum.* Swallow Press, Chicago, Illinois. For Maxine Cassin "Annals," *Touch of Recognition.* Swallow Press, Chicago, Illinois.

THE UNIVERSITY OF CHICAGO PRESS—for "Considering the Snail" and "Rastignac at 45." Reprinted from *My Sad Captains and Other Poems* by Thom Gunn by permission of The University of Chicago Press. © 1961 by The University of Chicago Press.

THE UNIVERSITY OF NORTH CAROLINA PRESS—for "Desert Fox" and "An Alice for Annie" from *The Day I Stopped Dreaming About Barbara Steele and Other Poems* by R. H. W. Dillard. Reprinted by permission of The University of North Carolina Press.

THE VIKING PRESS, INC.—for "To a Giraffe" from *Tell Me, Tell Me* by Marianne Moore. All Rights Reserved. Reprinted by permission of The Viking Press, Inc.

A. P. WATT & SON—for ten poems (see The Macmillan Company) by William Butler Yeats. Reprinted from *The Collected Poems of W. B. Yeats* by permission of M. B. Yeats and The Macmillan Company of Canada. For "The Way Through the Woods" from *Reward and Faries* by Rudyard Kipling. Reprinted by permission of Mrs. George Bambridge and Macmillan & Company Ltd.

WESLEYAN UNIVERSITY PRESS—for "Silent in America: 5." Copyright © 1964 by Philip Levine. Reprinted from *Not This Pig,* by Philip Levine, by permission of Wesleyan University Press. For "Anniversaries," "A Dream Sestina," "Varia-

Table of Contents

Part II: Poems for Study

Note: Poems marked with an asterisk (°) are included and discussed in the chapters
in Part I.

Preface

The design of this book is the result of what I have learned, both in teaching poetry and in trying to understand the poems that I read. Essentially, this is, I hope, the book for which I have been searching, a textbook which will not only offer the student some insight into the nature of poetry, but which will also offer him a systematic approach to the enjoyment of new poems.

As I began organizing my ideas for this textbook, there seemed to be several principles that would have to be followed. First, there should be a sufficient number of poems analyzed to demonstrate the myriad possibilities of poetry and of poetic analysis. To this end twenty-four poems are analyzed in Part I. Second, there should be exercises which both guide the student and point up for him the principles introduced in the text. Whereas the exercises in most textbooks seem constructed to point out the eccentricities of particular poems, the "Questions for Study" in Part I are designed to point up certain principles relevant to all poems. Third, there should be enough poems for study for the student sufficiently to test the principles he has learned. The 249 poems in Part II, which the instructor may use as he wishes, are included for this purpose. Fourth, it is important that the poems used in this kind of study be poems that are immediately approachable by the student, for the objectives of this textbook are not to explore the history of poetry or to define any particular school, period, or type of poetry. To avoid irrelevant digression into problems of literary or language history, about fifty percent of the poems in this textbook are by twentieth-century poets; older poems have been given modern spellings and punctuation according to the following principles:

1. Modern spelling conventions are followed except where obvious puns might be obscured.

2. Modern punctuation conventions are followed except where a felicitous ambiguity might be eliminated.

3. Modern capitalization conventions are followed except where there are obvious personifications.

Fifth, it is imperative that the student be offered a well-defined and well-ordered theory of poetry on which he can build as his experience broadens. This textbook is based on just such a theory, a theory concerning the nature of poetry itself, not the eccentric manifestations of poetry. There is here no discussion of lyric, ballad, narrative, or dramatic monologue, for these are not primary matters, and there are overriding principles which are common to all of these various kinds of poems. Nor is there any consideration of verse drama, for as verse it is like any poetry and as drama it involves considerations which are irrelevant here. The primary consideration in this book is the study of the genre itself; the study of the various ways in which the genre manifests itself is another thing altogether.

Most importantly, my theory rejects as an over-simplification the analysis which divides poetry into two elements: 1) the material, or content, of the poem and 2) the structure, or apparatus, of the poem. The failure of this kind of analysis is that it does not account for the fact that the content of any poem is of two kinds—literal and thematic—and that the thematic content is the result of the interworking of the literal content and the structure. The literal content may be thought of as what the poem says; the thematic content may be thought of as the implication of what the poem says. Although any division of the aspects of poems is at best artificial, it is the analyst's job to find the most accurate and useful division. I propose, therefore, a tri-part analysis which examines: 1) the literal content of the poem; 2) the structure of the poem; and 3) the thematic content of the poem.

Chapter 1 is a preface to the study of poetry in which several preliminary critical problems are discussed: 1) What is a poem? 2) What relation does the historical and intellectual milieu in which a poem is written have to the poem? 3) How does the fact that a poem may be written as an expression of belief in certain ideas current at the time it is written, or as a reaction against those ideas, influence the success of the poem as poem? 4) How much of the thematic content of the poem can be attributed to the poet's conscious comment on the world? Chapter 2 discusses the literal or paraphrasable content of the poem, and deals with such matters as the objective correlative, the metaphor, and imagery. Chapters 3–4 discuss the way the poet shapes his poem in order to shape his readers' reactions. There are several minor innovations in these chapters: 1) the concept of the "illusion of the random"—the illusion the poet creates as he makes his poem seem to be an inevitable sequence of words rather than the carefully arranged sequence that it is; 2) the discussion of accentual verse which attempts to make some sense out of those poems which, following the earliest English poetry, lie in a kind of twilight zone between metrical verse and *vers libre* (or that verse with no fixed recurrent rhythmical pattern); 3) the analysis of syllabic verse, an increasingly popular form among modern poets; and 4) the attempt to offer some objective basis for the analysis of the prosody of free verse. There is a discussion of selected fixed forms (including the sonnet) to characterize the general problem of fixed forms, and there are discussions of traditional metrics, of sound devices like rhyme and alliteration, and of the structure of poems which follow no fixed forms. Chapter 7 is concerned with the universal implications of the literal content of the poem. There are discussions of how irony can affect the thematic content and of how the reader's reaction to the poem can be affected by his own body of experience and attitudes. Chapter 8 applies the principles discussed previously to a single poem, Robert Frost's "Acquainted with the Night," showing the student how what he has learned fits into a cogent theory that offers him a systematic procedure for dealing with poems. So that this can be a useful handbook for the student to use in the future, the glossary defines terms that are not discussed at length elsewhere. The note "For the Instructor" lists poems which may be particularly useful examples for class discussion. An index of authors, titles, and first lines aids easy reference.

To provide a certain flexibility, this book is written so that the materials do not have to be taken up in the order in which they are presented, but can be arranged and adapted to meet the needs of the instructor.

An author always needs to acknowledge more debts than he ever has the space to mention, but a few obvious debts can be partially paid here. I am grateful to Dr. Rhodes Dunlap and Dr. Swen Armens of the graduate English faculty of the University of Iowa, who allowed me to begin speculating about matters of poetic theory in their classes; to Donald Justice, Paul Engle, and the members of the Iowa Poetry Workshop, who sharpened my perceptions; to Mrs. Martha Finney of the University of Massachusetts at Boston, who listened during many hours of discussion; to the Departments of English at Northeast Missouri State College and Virginia Polytechnic Institute who gave me the opportunity to try out my ideas in the classroom; to my colleagues at Virginia Polytechnic Institute who have patiently listened and made suggestions; to my colleagues at Scribners; and to my wife, Judith, who has simply been patient.

Lock Haven, Pennsylvania   VINCENT STEWART

For My Parents

I

Three Dimensions
of Poetry

1

The Nature of the Poem

The study of poetry has fascinated scholars for hundreds of years. Those who have delighted in counting and classifying have found much to whet their appetites in poetry. They have counted such things as types of lines, types of rhythms, types of rhymes, types of stanza forms, and types of poems. Too often their discussions have sounded like those of that medieval scholar who could find nothing better to worry about than the number of angels who can dance on the point of a needle. This ridiculous argument about how many bodiless bodies can dance on the area-less area is no more silly than many of the endless discussions of poetry that students have had to endure. The fact is that there are several considerations which have proved fruitless.

In the first place, it is impossible to formulate an abstract definition of what poetry is; the ludicrous results that have always followed such attempts is the proof. We learn from Wordsworth, for example, that poetry is "emotion-packed language," but this is a term as vague as those angels on the point of that needle. Emily Dickinson with her statement that poetry is what "takes the top of your head off" proves that good poets are no more successful in formulating an abstract definition of poetry than are bad critics. Finally what result are endless definitions of such poetic types as lyrics, epics, narratives, and the like. But these get us no closer to an idea of what distinguishes that class of literary objects called "poems." We are left where we started.

Others, having decided that the search for a generalization about poetry itself is fruitless, have turned to the study of the reactions of readers of poems. They have handed copies of poems to groups of readers, carefully noted each reader's response, and compiled long lists of statements about these responses. They have tallied the scores of those poetic devices that produce pleasure in readers, and they have tallied the scores of those poems which lead their readers into philosophical speculation. And they have discovered that they are still trying to catch hold of those fuzzy angels. They have gotten no closer to the poem itself.

One consideration that does prove fruitful is the question of what a poet does when he creates a poem, for we can define objectively that the poet does more than just string a group of words together in a particular sequence. The poet looks out at the world in which he lives and sees that the objects in that world have relationships he had not noticed before. He takes that perception and forms it into an idea for a poem. For example, one day he may look out and see the shadows shrinking around the trees as the sun moves higher and realize that as the shadows shrink the light grows; he has an idea for a poem. As he works that idea around in his head or on paper, he begins to shape it and to shape the language in which it will be expressed; the product of this process is a poem. In the course of working out the poem, the poet brings to bear on his perception all of his own ideas, opinions, and experiences so that his poem not only defines some fresh perception of the world, but also his particular attitude toward that perception. And if the part of the world about which he writes is representative of some larger part, the poem begins to have larger and, possibly, universal implications.

So it is that in poetry a part is extended into the whole, and a contained idea begins to have implications far greater than its beginnings. This is why we read poems: we not only have our emotions aroused as we are entertained by poems, but we also have the opportunity to share the particular perceptions of poets. Perhaps this will be demonstrated by a poem which has interested a great many readers.

The Canonization

For God's sake hold your tongue and let me love,
    Or chide my palsey or my gout;
My five gray hairs or ruined fortune flout;
    With wealth your state, your mind with arts improve;
        Take you a course; get you a place;
        Observe his honor or his grace;
Or the king's real or his stampèd face
    Contemplate; what you will, approve,
    So you will let me love.

Alas, alas, who's injured by my love?
   What merchants' ships have my sighs drowned?
Who says my tears have overflowed his ground?
   When did my colds a forward spring remove?
      When did the heats which my veins fill
      Add one more to the plaguey bill?
Soldiers find wars, and lawyers find out still
   Litigious men, which quarrels move,
   Though she and I do love.

Call us what you will, we are made such by love;
   Call her one, me another fly.
We're tapers too, and at our own cost die,
   And we in us find the eagle and the dove.
      The Phoenix riddle hath more wit
      By us; we two, being one, are it.
So to one neutral thing both sexes fit;
   We die and rise the same, and prove
   Mysterious by this love.

We can die by it, if not live by love,
   And if unfit for tombs and hearse
Our legend be, it will be fit for verse;
   And if no piece of chronicle we prove,
      We'll build in sonnets pretty rooms;
      As well a well-wrought urn becomes
The greatest ashes, as half-acre tombs,
   And by these hymns, all shall approve
   Us canonized for love:

And thus invoke us: You, whom reverend love
   Made one another's hermitage,
You, to whom love was peace that now is rage,
   Who did the whole world's soul contract and drove
      Into the glasses of your eyes
      (So made such mirrors, and such spies,
That they did all to you epitomize)
   Countries, towns, courts; beg from above
   A pattern of your love!

—JOHN DONNE

There are some obvious barriers between this poem and the modern reader. The language of the seventeenth century is not that of the twentieth century, and the words in seventeenth-century poems are not always used as they are in the twentieth century. But when we find out that the king's "stampèd face" refers to his picture on coins, that "the plaguey bill" refers to the list of those who died during those times when the plague attacked London, and that to the seventeenth-century reader *die* could mean to achieve climax during sexual intercourse as well as to cease living, the poem begins to make more sense to us and we begin to understand why it has inspired so much attention.

At the beginning of the poem the speaker addresses someone who has apparently spoken slightingly of the speaker's love for his lady. The speaker is defensive and in the first stanza he lists the things that the critic can do rather than tease him about his love. The critic can, the speaker says, insult his palsey, his gout, his age, or his poor luck. The critic can make money, or improve himself with art, or take some action and obtain some position, or watch some official ("his honor") or some nobleman ("his grace") or the king in the flesh or on coins. The speaker doesn't care what the critic does, just so he is left to love in peace. All of this is to say, "You can say anything you like about me or anybody else, but don't pry into my love life."

To continue his argument, the speaker asks a series of ridiculous questions in the second stanza, to prove that he and his lover are not hurting anybody else by being in love. Do they sink any ships or flood anybody's land? When they are cold, do they hold spring back, or does their hot blood make anybody sick? Do they keep soldiers from fighting or lawyers from arguing suits? The implication is, of course, that they don't bother anybody else, so why should anybody bother them?

Then at the beginning of the third stanza the speaker says that whatever he and his lover are called, they are made that by their love. They are like flies, or like candles that consume themselves in their own flames. Of course, if we know the secondary meaning of *die* in the seventeenth century, line 21 begins to take on new meaning. He says that he and his lover are both fierce ("the eagle") and meek ("the dove"). He says that they are the answer to the riddle of the Phoenix: What is two things at the same time it is one thing? With this the speaker becomes bolder and takes the offensive in the argument; he ceases to defend himself and his lover and begins to argue for the merits of their love. He says that their love is like something magical since it is a neutral thing that fits both sexes, that he and his lover *die* (in its second meaning) and rise by their love.

The lovers would, in fact, rather die if they can't live and love.

And if anyone thinks that their story will not be fit for a funeral, it will be fit for poems. If they don't make the history books ("chronicle") they will be put into sonnets, and that will be just as good, because a beautiful urn is as good a resting place as a huge tomb. And by those poems everybody will declare that the lovers are made saints by their love. Since the lovers are saints, in the last stanza the speaker offers a prayer that others can pray to them. Others can pray that the lovers—who were each other's refuge, to whom love was both peace and rage, who became the symbols of everything in the world and encompassed whole nations, cities, and courts— might give them the plan of their love.

What the poem has to offer us, then, is a new perception of lovers as people who are able by the force of their love to transform the world around them. And the exaggeration of the lover's claim is calculated to arouse our laughter, even if it is understanding laughter. The question that is apt to appear at this point is "If that's what he meant, why didn't he just come out and say it?" But notice that when we did just come out and say it, it took us many more words than it took Donne and our account is not nearly so interesting. As a matter of fact, *how* Donne says it is just as important as *what* he says.

In traditional terms, the form of Donne's poem is as essential to its character as is its content. Traditionally critics have separated the form from the content of a poem for purposes of analysis; this is a dichotomy which is supposed to be helpful in the analysis of poetry. But if this is not a true representation of the poem, if the poem is one whole instead of two parts, how can such a separation be truly useful? A look at a poem by Walt Whitman may provide some answers.

When I Heard the Learn'd Astronomer

When I heard the learn'd astronomer,
When the proofs, the figures, were ranged in columns before me,
When I was shown the charts and diagrams, to add, divide, and
    measure them,
When I sitting heard the astronomer where he lectured with much
    applause in the lecture-room,
How soon unaccountable I became tired and sick,
Till rising and gliding out I wander'd off by myself,
In the mystical moist night-air, and from time to time,
Look'd up in perfect silence at the stars.

                    —WALT WHITMAN

It is easy to sum up this poem. The speaker is obviously dissatisfied with the attempt of the scientist to rationally and systematically explain the universe; he goes outside and finds a much more satisfactory explanation in a sort of mystical communion with the universe. But how do we know that the poet is serious in writing the poem? After all, is it not common sense that the scientist can explain the universe much better than an ignorant man who just silently looks up at the stars? How do we know that the poem is not ironical or satirical? These questions may seem even harder to answer if we demand that the answer come from the poem itself and not from what we know of Whitman in other poems, if we ask how the poem itself directs the reader's attention.

The answer lies in the form of the poem, in the syntactical, semantical, and musical relationships of the words. The poem is in what is usually called *free verse;* that is, we can find no pattern in the lines: no specific number of syllables per line, no specific number of stresses per line. This does not mean, however, that there are no patterns in the poem, but in a poem like this one those patterns are dictated by the necessities of what the poet is saying rather than by any traditional verse form. And we must believe that the poet is controlling the sound of the poem, if for no other reason, because he insists that we say the one-syllable *learn'd* instead of the two-syllable and more common *learnèd.* As readers we must trust the rhythm that the poet dictates.

As we look further, we find more evidence of plan in the form of the poem. The eight lines break into two distinct four-line parts. The first four lines comprise a compound introductory clause which sets up the condition from which the speaker wants to escape. As the speaker becomes more and more bored the lines become longer. The items in series in lines 2 and 3 reflect the lists of the astronomer, and the fact that these dependent clauses cannot make a complete thought reflects the unsatisfactory nature of the scientist's explanations.

Lines 5 through 8 comprise the independent clause which completes the sentence. As the speaker goes out into nature to find the explanation which can satisfy him, the thought is completed, and to add to the effect the lines themselves become shorter. When the poem and the problem are at last resolved in line 8, the line is a simple, plain one. Thus is the sense of the poem represented in its form; thus are the false complexities of the scientist (false, at least, according to the poem) contrasted with the simplicity of the speaker's solution.

We can see that in this poem the content and the form combine to make a rational statement of an anti-intellectual position. The poem indicates that science, with its catalogues, classifications, and reductions to lists and formulas, is unable to approach the truth which lies in nature and in communion with natural things. When the tedium of the astronomer's talk is contrasted with the mystical experience the speaker has when he gazes at the stars themselves, there is a strong implication that expounding astronomers are not needed when communion with nature reveals mystical truths no science can reveal.

These observations should indicate something to us about how we should study poems. Robert Frost has said that poetry "begins in delight and ends in wisdom." The order of the items in that statement is significant, for although poetry does offer us wisdom, it must first of all offer us delight. Literary criticism and analysis are really nothing more than an attempt to find out what it is about poems that makes them delight us. For if a critic is honest he will admit that he believes those poems greatest which he enjoys most. The first part of our job when we begin to study poetry is to find out what those things are which make poems delightful.

THE POEM AS POEM

There are several ways we can look at a poem. We may consider it simply as an aesthetic object, a work of art to be looked at and entertained by. We may consider the poem as a fresh perception which is offered to us by the poet, a new way of looking at the world. Or we may consider the poem a new experience, one more experience to add to our store and bring to bear on future experiences. Actually the poem is all this and more. As our anaylsis of "When I Heard the Learn'd Astronomer" has demonstrated, the poem is actually a threefold entity.

Certainly the poem is a new experience in looking at the world, for when we get a chance to see the world as we never have seen it before, we have experienced one of the greatest delights of poetry. But the poem also offers us a formal experience, for we must be affected by the way the poet has arranged his poem, by the way he has introduced us into his own world. Finally, the poem offers us some comment, some rational statement about the world. Unless we take account of all three of these aspects, we have not considered the whole poem.

But still we have not answered our very first question: What is a poem? How are we to define what we mean when we speak of a *poem,* if we reject all definitions of poetry as ludicrous? There is one definition that we have not tried, a simple and straightforward definition. If we compare a page of poetry with a page of prose, there is a striking contrast. The prose has a straight right margin, while the poetry has a ragged right margin. The first thing we notice is that the poem is broken into lines and perhaps stanzas, while the prose is broken into paragraphs. The simplest distinctions are often the best, and the simplest definition of poetry is this one: *A poem is a discourse arranged in lines.*

We cannot, nevertheless, accept our definition without testing it, without finding out if the line truly does distinguish poetry. Toward making such a test, we will try out Whitman's poem as prose.

> When I heard the learned astronomer, when the proofs, the figures, were ranged in columns before me, when I was shown the charts and diagrams, to add, divide, and measure them, when I sitting heard the astronomer where he lectured with much applause in the lecture-room, how soon unaccountable I became tired and sick, till rising and gliding out I wandered off by myself, in the mystical moist night-air, and from time to time, looked up in perfect silence at the stars.

The poem is not at all the same in this form. In the first place its two-part division is not nearly so evident when it is printed in this way. In the second place, the device of having the lines grow longer in the first part, and then having a series of four short lines in the second part is not evident at all. Finally, when the poem is written this way, the sentence, which is quite clear when we get it bit by bit in lines, becomes over-long and awkward.

It becomes clear, therefore, that the line is the basis of the poem, the integral part of the poem's form. It becomes clear as well that no aspect of the poem can be omitted from consideration if we are to understand the whole poem.

THE POEM AS IDEA

There is one important question that always arises in any discussion of poetry: What capacity does a poem have to make meaningful statements about human activity in general? Sometimes, in fact, we might be led to believe that the only function that a poem has is to make philosophical statements. Too often the English teacher has but one question to ask: What is the theme of the poem? As we have seen in "The Canonization" and in "When I Heard the Learn'd Astronomer," a poem certainly can (and almost always does) make some statement about the human condition. But rarely is this statement so simplistic that it can be condensed into a single statement of theme. Rather, the statement of the poem is the result of the complex intertwining of literal content and form and is only meaningful in terms of the poem as a whole.

There are, for example, endless verbal complexities to be considered in poetry. Since poems usually try to use a minimum of words, each word is often required to perform several functions. In the poem by Donne the word *die* works two ways to enrich the texture of the statements. Since the data for the poem consists of human experiences which become symbols for the human condition in general, we must understand the particular human experience before we can see whatever universal implications that experience may have.

Poets seldom set out to compose a poem which will express a particular philosophical point of view. Rather the poet sees a scene, or an action, or perceives a particular relationship and gets an idea for a poem. Or the poet may even set out to work out a particular formal problem. But in the course of working out his idea or problem, the poet cannot avoid having all of his past experiences and his own beliefs come to bear on his material. Consequently, poems usually quite legitimately express personal outlooks and a part of our enjoyment of poetry results from such expressions.

Poetry is capable of a kind of rational statement possible in no other form of discourse. In the first place, poetry is built on the world of human experience, rather than on the world of ideas, so that poems deal more immediately with experiences with which we can identify than does the philosopher as he juggles his abstract concepts and syllogisms. In the second place, the language of poetry is so highly structured that we receive the statement of a poem in a disciplined manner that is equalled by no other literary form.

THE POEM AS HISTORY

Poetry has traditionally been associated with history, to the point sometimes that teachers argue that a knowledge of history is necessary to the student of poetry. Often the study of poetry is treated as the study of the history of ideas, with no attention to the fact that the primary purpose of reading poems is entertainment. Certainly, poems do represent an important part of cultural history, and, as we have noted, poems offer us a special view of ourselves and our problems at particular times, but it is unfortunate when the study of poetry is reduced to nothing more than the study of history.

It is true that certain historical information is often necessary for us to enjoy a poem. As in the case of "The Canonization," we often have to do some historical study to discover exactly what the words in a poem mean. When a poem comes from a much earlier period, it often contains words which are no longer used or words whose meanings have changed in the intervening years. If this is the case, then certainly some historical data is necessary to a successful reading of the poem. Sometimes, too, poems refer to events and to persons familiar to readers at the time in which the poem was written, but which must be explained to readers of a later period.

The sort of historical information which is needed to understand the words of a poem is a valuable and legitimate addition to the student's apparatus for studying the poem. But it is unfortunate when a poem's relation to history becomes the basis for judging whether or not the poem is a good one, for the history of the poem is merely information which is preliminary to evaluation.

THE POEM AS THE VOICE OF THE POET

A kind of statement that is often made about poems is one which indicates that the poem is an attempt by the poet to work out some system of philosophy. Sometimes, teachers even make their most important concern the question, "What is the poet trying to say in this poem?" This concern ignores the fact that poets seldom set out to *say* anything in the sense of making a philosophical statement; most often poets are trying to make vivid a perception or work out a formal problem and in the course of writing the poem do, incidentally, *say* things.

The poet's interest as he is writing his poem is in the creation of a poem, in the same way that a painter is interested in creating a painting. This interest is a narrow one, one which involves only the poet. It is only after the act of creation that the poet begins to be concerned about readers, and no one will deny that most poets are very concerned that their poems be read. Even Emily Dickinson, who for the most part kept herself and her poems hidden from the world, had a few friends to whom she regularly showed her writings.

There are many explanations which are advanced by psychologists for the poet's desire to expose what he has created principally for himself. Perhaps it is merely that the poet wishes to expose to the world what he has done so that others may share his delight in it. More likely, however, he wishes to expose his creation to readers so that they may praise and admire his accomplishment. After all, poets are just as susceptible to a need for approval as are other people.

But if we accept the premise that the poet's primary purpose is not to communicate some philosophical position, we must accept the position that what a poem *says* may not necessarily represent the opinion of the poet. Consequently, we are on much safer ground when we assign the ideas in a poem, not to the poet, but simply to the "speaker" in the poem. The speaker is approachable and definable, while the poet is behind the poem, hidden by his own manipulation of language and experience.

We must always be careful before we assign a philosophical position to a poet simply because we find that position reflected in a poem. Poets are not often philosophers who systematically develop schemes to explain the universe; rather, they are keen observers who may in the course of observing make profound comments. It is impossible to define a poet's position from a single poem; rather, such a position can only be determined by examination of a poet's body of poems and the body of his non-poetic writing.

So it is that poems are wholes in which all parts must work toward one end, in which all interpretation must come out of the whole. Criticism and analysis cannot afford to ignore any aspect of the poem; consequently, we will define three dimensions of poems so that we can study poems whole. There is the *sensory dimension,* including the literal content, the concrete, objective content of the poem; there is the *formal dimension,* including the structure, the music, the manipulation of the language; and there is the *rational dimension,* through which the meaning of the poem and its comment on the world emerge.

QUESTIONS FOR STUDY

NOTE: These questions may be applied to any of the poems in Part II.

1. Would you like to have information about any matter discussed in the poem which is not given in the poem? What effect would such information have on your reaction to the poem?
2. Do you like the poem? If you do, try to pinpoint the source of your delight. If you do not, try to pinpoint where the poem fails for you.

2

The Sensory Dimension

When we read poems, the first aspect of the poem that we notice is that which most immediately appeals to our senses. This is what the poem can literally present, what its surface conveys to us before we try to find any deeper meaning; this is the content that can be paraphrased, that can be "summed up." When we first read the poem we are not interested in what it "means"; we are interested in what it says. As we read and re-read the poem we may become interested in what the poem may mean, but if its objective, or concrete, content is uninteresting to us, we are uninterested in finding out what the poem means.

The objective content of the poem consists of some sort of experience. This experience may range from the very intellectual to the physical. In any case, it is the ability of the poem to involve us in that experience that attracts our interest. To be forced to undergo the sometimes arduous task of analysis and interpretation from the outset usually detracts from the pleasure of any reader; therefore, the poem must entertain the reader at first with its literal content. And the reader can only be entertained when he is involved in what he is reading.

The most immediate means of involving a reader in a poem is sense imagery. When the poem leads us to see, hear, feel, smell, and taste things, or to imagine that we do, we are much more likely to respond to what the poem says, for we are much more likely to be able to become involved in the poem. Such appeals to the senses are out of the real world that we know, the world we live in every day, and the poem can be pleasurable for us merely by arranging some of the details of that world in a particular order. The result is that we may read the poem and be surprised that the poet has been able to describe an experience we have all had in a way we could never describe it ourselves. But the effectiveness of the poet's description will result, in large part, from his ability to involve us in the experience he is describing.

To demonstrate how important concrete expression is in a poem, we will examine two much-anthologized poems by two distinguished English poets. First, read the following poem.

London, 1802

Milton! thou should'st be living at this hour:
England hath need of thee: she is a fen
Of stagnant waters: altar, sword, and pen,
Fireside, the heroic wealth of hall and bower,
Have forfeited their ancient English dower
Of inward happiness. We are selfish men;
Oh! raise us up, return to us again;
And give us manners, virtue, freedom, power.
Thy soul was like a Star, and dwelt apart:
Thou hadst a voice whose sound was like the sea:
Pure as the naked heavens, majestic, free,
So didst thou travel on life's common way,
In cheerful godliness; and yet thy heart
The lowliest duties on herself did lay.

—WILLIAM WORDSWORTH

This poem does two things at once. It is both a comment on the condition of London in the year 1802, as indicated in the title, and a eulogy to Milton. London's condition is indicated by the statement of her great need of a man like Milton to cure her moral disintegration. The speaker in the poem makes clear from the beginning what his attitude toward the London of 1802 is. The London of 1802 has stagnated, has forfeited its happiness, because it is selfish and has forgotten the traditional virtues. Milton is established as an exemplar of the kind of men the London of 1802 needs. The speaker's feelings are powerful ones and if this poem fails to arouse its reader powerfully it is not because of any weakness inherent in the subject matter.

We must look to the expression of the emotion in the poem to find its failure. In the first place, the disintegration of London is not revealed to us; it is told to us. We are instructed to take an attitude rather than led to take an attitude. The words which describe are abstract words which carry judgments with them. Take, for example, the verb *forfeited*. When the speaker says that England has *forfeited* its power, there is the immediate parallel statement that England is at fault, since *forfeited* carries that meaning. In addition, look at the many vague terms. What exactly, we might ask, is "the heroic wealth of hall and bower" or "inward happiness"? What does the speaker mean by "manners," "virtue," "freedom," or "power"? These are terms that can have many meanings, depending on who is using the terms. We might also ask for some specifications about "soul . . . like a star," "naked heavens," "majestic," "free," "life's common way," or "cheerful godliness." The poem is ineffectual because it is abstract and vague.

In contrast look at another poem about London written just a few years earlier.

London

I wander thro' each charter'd street
Near where the charter'd Thames does flow,
And mark in every face I meet
Marks of weakness, marks of woe.

In every cry of every Man,
In every Infant's cry of fear,
In every voice, in every ban,
The mind-forg'd manacles I hear.

How the Chimney-sweeper's cry
Every black'ning Church appalls,
And the hapless Soldier's sigh
Runs in blood down Palace walls.

But most thro' midnight streets I hear
How the youthful Harlot's curse
Blasts the new born Infant's tear,
And blights with plagues the Marriage hearse.

—WILLIAM BLAKE

Here the judgment is left, for the most part, to the reader; the speaker merely presents the evidence. To be sure, the case is a loaded one, but we are allowed to arrive at our own judgment, even if the judgment that can be arrived at from the evidence that is presented is thoroughly predictable. And if we are led toward that judgment, it is part of the pleasure of reading poetry to be so led. The speaker presents a list, or catalogue, of sounds which are the concrete expressions of the "Marks of weakness, marks of woe." There are abstractions in the poem ("mind-forg'd manacles," for example), but these abstractions are made concrete by the evocation of the sounds we have all heard or can imagine hearing: men wailing, babies crying, boys weeping, and soldiers sighing. These sounds become emblems of the weakness and woe that characterize London as far as the speaker is concerned.

The subjects of these two poems are similar, but one poem is obviously more effective than the other. The failure of "London, 1802" and the success of "London" are both in the literal contents of the poems, in what we call the *sensory dimension,* because those poems which are most successful on this level are those which most effectively involve the senses of the reader, as do the sounds in "London." To see further just how a poem may operate in the sensory dimension, let us look at a familiar one by T. S. Eliot.

Preludes

I

The winter evening settles down
With smell of steaks in passageways.
Six o'clock.
The burnt-out ends of smoky days.
And now a gusty shower wraps
The grimy scraps
Of withered leaves about your feet
And newspapers from vacant lots;
The showers beat
On broken blinds and chimney-pots,
And at the corner of the street
A lonely cab-horse steams and stamps.

And then the lighting of the lamps.

II

The morning comes to consciousness
Of faint stale smells of beer
From the sawdust-trampled street
With all its muddy feet that press
To early coffee-stands.

With the other masquerades
That time resumes,
One thinks of all the hands

That are raising dingy shades
In a thousand furnished rooms.

III

You tossed a blanket from the bed,
You lay upon your back, and waited;
You dozed, and watched the night revealing
The thousand sordid images
Of which your soul was constituted;
They flickered against the ceiling.
And when all the world came back
And the light crept up between the shutters
And you heard the sparrows in the gutters,
You had such a vision of the street
As the street hardly understands;
Sitting along the bed's edge, where
You curled the papers from your hair,
Or clasped the yellow soles of feet
In the palms of both soiled hands.

IV

His soul stretched tight across the skies
That fade behind a city block,
Or trampled by insistent feet
At four and five and six o'clock;
And short square fingers stuffing pipes,
And evening newspapers, and eyes
Assured of certain certainties,
The conscience of a blackened street
Impatient to assume the world.

I am moved by fancies that are curled
Around these images, and cling:
The notion of some infinitely gentle
Infinitely suffering thing.

Wipe your hand across your mouth, and laugh;
The worlds revolve like ancient women
Gathering fuel in vacant lots.

—T. S. ELIOT

This poem describes a city at different times of the day, and in the course of the description an attitude that is not exactly favorable is revealed. We can see how this attitude is developed and how interest is maintained through a close study of how the poem operates in the sensory dimension.

THE OBJECTIVE CORRELATIVE

The term *objective correlative* was introduced by T. S. Eliot to explain how works of art operate to produce emotional reactions in readers. The theory is that concrete experiences are correlatives, or equivalents, of emotions, so that what the successful poem does is to present a concrete experience which is the objective correlative of the emotion the poem is attempting to promote in the reader. (See the Glossary for Eliot's statement.)

"Preludes" presents a series of objective correlatives. The first section is an evening scene in which refuse and trash lie around amid the smells of cooking. The days are smoky, and the blinds and chimney pots are broken. It must be cold, for the cab-horse steams and stamps. It is a dismal scene and the emotion that is evoked is one of despair. The second scene is a morning one; it is a scene which matches the first: a morning of "stale smells" and "muddy feet," a time of masquerades instead of openness, a time of "dingy shades/In a thousand furnished rooms" (with all of the loneliness and cheapness connoted by *furnished room*). Once again there is the objective correlative of despair. The third scene pictures a woman who cannot sleep, waking continually to "The thousand sordid images," until dawn, when the sounds of day come in the window, and all the woman has to do is to take the curling papers from her hair and hold "the yellow soles of feet" in her "soiled hands." This is indeed the picture of despair. The fourth scene is a personification of "The conscience of a blackened street" and the objective correlative would give way to abstraction if the abstraction were not made specific by its comparison to a man in the midst of the five o'clock traffic, being trampled by people going home from work, an "Infinitely suffering thing." This comparison, of which we will say more later, maintains the objective correlative of despair. Finally, the speaker addresses the reader, telling him to make what amounts to a cynical gesture, for despite the fact that there is all of this despair, the world goes on, like old women going round and round vacant lots scrounging for fuel to warm themselves.

By no means have we explained the whole poem when we have outlined the objective correlative in the poem, but we have, at least, arrived at some notion of why the poem produces the emotional reaction that it does. Nor have we, in this short space, completely explained the objective correlative itself: we have only said what it is; we have not said how it is what it is. We must move on to the foundations of the objective correlative, the metaphor and the image.

THE METAPHOR

A metaphor is, essentially, a comparison. It says, implicitly or explicitly, that one thing is like another thing. "A fog strolled complacently down the street" says that the fog is like a man strolling down the street. "He came charging in like a herd of buffalo" says that the impression that he gave as he charged in is like the impression one would have of a charging herd of buffalo. Sometimes the comparison is simply assumed, as in the metaphor about the fog, and the one thing is treated as if it *is* another thing; other times the comparison may be made explicit with connecting words such as *as if, like, than,* or *similar to* (such metaphors are often referred to as *similes*). Metaphors can serve a great many purposes. They can clarify a difficult concept by pointing out its similarities to some concrete experience. They can describe and they can serve to heighten interest. The metaphors in "Preludes" do all of these things.

The first section opens with a metaphor in the line "The winter evening settles down" where the evening is compared to a person or an animal which settles itself. Metaphors are also used in lines 4 and 5, where days are compared to fires which burn out and the shower is compared to someone who can wrap things around you. These metaphors all serve to describe the kind of reaction the speaker has to the evening, day, and shower; the metaphors tell the reader what these things "seem like" to the speaker. The same kind of metaphor appears in line 14, at the beginning of the second section, where the morning is compared to someone who wakes up, and this metaphor works in the same way as those in the first section. A slightly different metaphor appears in Part II, lines 5 and 6 where in the phrase "the other masquerades/That time resumes," time is compared to someone who carries out a deception. There is a kind of oblique moral judgment implied in this metaphor, so that it is more than merely descriptive. The fact that time must resume masquerades rather than presenting a true face to the world implies that the practical necessities of life in the world require compromises. In the third section there are several metaphors—line 6 (thoughts compared to movie-type images), line 7 (the coming of dawn compared to someone's returning), and line 11 (the street compared to a person)—all of which serve to clarify the concepts that are being developed. Section four also contains metaphors; in addition, as previously noted, the entire section is a metaphor. In line 1 the soul is compared to something that can be stretched across the skies and in line 2 the skies are compared to a light that fades where the horizon is marked by city buildings. In lines 10 and 11 thoughts ("fancies") are compared to something that can be curled around something else, to which images are compared. In addition the "he" of the section is a metaphor for "The conscience of a blackened street/Impatient to assume the world." This would indeed be an abstract concept if it were not made concrete by the metaphor. Then in the last two lines of the poem the world is explicitly compared to old crones "Gathering fuel in vacant lots," a comparison which makes concrete the loneliness and futility described in the poem.

These metaphors get the poem over otherwise insurmountable barriers of abstraction and vagueness. But their purpose is not purely utilitarian; they also make the poem more interesting to read. Another of the joys of poetry is to discover a striking metaphor strikingly put.

THE IMAGE

We have said that the objective correlative is a concrete experience which is the equivalent of some emotion. But it is obvious that in one sense when we read poems the only concrete experience we are having is the experience of reading the poem. Reading a poem is an act of the imagination and the job of the poem is to make us imagine the concrete experiences which become objective correlatives. The poem does this by leading us to recall concrete experiences we have had in the past or by leading us to imagine what it would be like to undergo a particular experience. The tool for this process is the sense image; by evoking our memories of sensory experiences— smells, sounds, sights, tastes, textures—the poem builds for us mental concrete experiences. The objective correlative in "Preludes" is built in just such a manner.

The first line calls up a kind of complex of sense images, for when we think of a winter evening settling down we immediately think of the feelings and smells of winter evenings. In the first section there are images of smell ("smell of steaks"), sight (the passageways of tenements, the end of the day, the rain, the leaves and old newspapers, the broken blinds and the chimney-pots, the cab-horse steaming and stamping, and the streetlights being lighted), feeling (the rain and the cold of winter), hearing (the rain beating and the horse's snorting and stamping). Immediately we can imagine exactly what it would be like to be abroad on such a day; the poem has given us the concrete experience. A similar experience of morning is offered in the second section. Once again there are several kinds of images: smell (beer and coffee), sight (the street covered with trampled sawdust, the muddy feet of pedestrians, the shades going up in the windows, and the myriad furnished rooms), hearing (the sounds of people going about in the morning), taste (beer and coffee). Once again we can imagine what it would be like to be out at such a time. We could go through the entire poem in this manner, noting every image, but there are one or two images that are of special interest. In the last four lines of Part III, where we see the woman sitting on the edge of her bed, she is described to us by the careful choice of just two aspects of her appearance: the curlers in her hair and the yellow feet held in dirty hands. From these two details it is not hard for us to project a whole woman, and we draw from our own experiences with people a type which we place in this situation. Then there are the "ancient women/Gathering fuel in vacant lots." The sight image of old women, bent and arthritic, bending over in trash-filled vacant lots to get fuel to warm themselves makes the metaphor a powerful one, for we are able to draw either on our actual experiences or on our experiences from movies and television to have an image of the poverty and despair that is pictured in the poem.

Unless we can have this kind of sensory experience the objective correlative in the poem is unlikely to be effective, and we are therefore unlikely to have a meaningful emotional experience in reading the poem. Obviously, however, it is not necessary that the poet describe in detail every aspect of the experience; the selection of a few telling details can create the whole picture.

How the poem operates in the sensory dimension, then, is of primary importance to its success or failure. It would be a serious mistake, however, to assume that when we have described the operation in the sensory dimension we have completely described the poem, for the way it is put together and the conclusions we draw from internal evidence and from the speaker's attitude toward that evidence are just as important as the literal content.

NOTE: These questions may be applied to any of the poems in Part II.

1. Summarize the objective or literal content of the poem. For what emotion is this the objective correlative?
2. What metaphors are developed in the poem?
3. What images are developed in the poem? How effectively do these images evoke the concrete experience?
4. Are you interested in the literal content of the poem? If so, try to pinpoint why. If not, try to pinpoint where the literal content fails.

3

The Formal Dimension
The Rage for Order

Within each of us is what Wallace Stevens has called "a rage for order." We take the natural world in which we live and continually reorder it to suit our predilections toward order. We divide our nations into city and country. We divide our cities into streets and blocks and neighborhoods. We divide our blocks and neighborhoods into lots and houses, and we divide our houses into rooms. We put our clothes into drawers and we put our papers into files. We place our books in ranks on shelves and we put our dishes and eating utensils into cupboards. We drive on the right-hand side of the highway and we mark intersections so that the automobiles moving in one direction stop while those moving in the other direction pass by. We define working areas for ourselves, in our rooms and in our basements and at our places of business. Every aspect of our lives is pervaded by our desire for order. Most of this order serves very useful purposes; it makes our lives easier by making things easy to find and by giving us an orderly means of making decisions (for example, when we approach an intersection in our automobile).

But not all of the order that we impose on ourselves is purely utilitarian. We order our entertainments as much as we order our more pragmatic activities. We play our games according to rules and in our sports each player usually has specific responsibilities. We watch movies in which there are well-ordered plots and in which lives must be lived out within a specified time. We plan parties to which a specific number of people are invited to arrive at a specific time. This rage for order does, in fact, extend to every corner of our lives.

But at the same time we like to create the illusion of spontaneity. We like to pretend that we impose less order than we do on the world.

We like to arrange our furniture and decorations so that they appear to be carelessly thrown into their places; girls like to arrange their hair so that it seems to have just fallen that way. We are constantly striving to make arrangements of our lives that *appear* to be random, that have the same illusion of randomness that we see in nature. This paradox of structure together with the illusion of randomness is nowhere more evident than in poetry, as the following poem will illustrate.

Variations on a Theme from James

"large, loose, baggy monsters"

1

It's not a landscape from too near.
Like sorrows, they require some distance
Not to bulk larger than they are.
The risk is, backing off too far.
Once we have found a middle ground,
The warts, the pimples disappear.
There's but a shagginess remains,
An olive or a purple haze,
Which has at least that saving grace
Of average faces, average hills,
A nice, unshaven atmosphere.

2

Whatever goats are climbing there,
Being all invisible,
Animate objects of a will
Contemplative without desire,
Suffer no vertigo at all,
But climb until *our* spirits tire,
Or dine forever, or until
The speculative garbage fail,
Tin cans and comic books, which small,
Imaginary campers there
Forgot against this very hour.

3

Such art has nature in her kind
That in the shaping of a hill
She will take care to leave behind

Some few abutments here and there,
Something to cling to, just in case.
A taste more finical and nice
Would comb out kink and curl alike.
But O ye barbers at your trade,
What more beguiles us? Your coiffures?
Or gold come waterfalling down?

—DONALD JUSTICE

One of the first things we notice about this poem is that the quotation from Henry James, "large, loose, baggy monsters," is not really integral to understanding the poem. It is merely a starting point for the speaker, who muses on matters of perception. When James uses the phrase he is discussing the Russian novelists, particularly Tolstoy and *War and Peace,* and the phrase represents James's view of the form of those sprawling novels. The speaker in this poem takes a great leap away from novels and begins talking about mountains, which might also very well be viewed as "large, loose, baggy monsters."

In the first section the speaker is obviously looking at some mountains from a distance, and he finds that his perception of the mountains is changed drastically according to where he stands. If he stands too close, the mountains seem so large that he can see them only in parts, rather than as a whole. When we think of "landscapes" we normally think of paintings of landscapes, and from up close the mountains do not look like a painting. But if he backs "off too far" a different problem arises; he cannot see any of the details of the mountains; the scene is just one great blur. What he has to find is a middle ground, where he can see the details, including flaws, as well as the whole.

Having found a vantage point from which to view the mountains, in the second section the speaker muses about what he cannot see on the mountains and imagines what may be up there. He imagines goats, and he imagines the litter that campers have left. Obviously, since these imaginary goats can have no physical sense of tiring, it is his spirit that can tire from this imaginary activity. All of the activity here is in the mind of the speaker; it is an activity that he is imposing on what he is seeing.

In the third section the speaker begins to muse on the aesthetic implications of what he has been saying, and he concludes that art is like nature when it does not present a picture in which there are no flaws but rather when it leaves a few imperfections, "Some few abutments here and there." The speaker notes that there are tastes which prefer to order and control everything, but he questions these tastes, asking which is more beautiful, "What more beguiles us?", perfect hair-dos with every hair in place, or blond hair falling naturally, "gold come waterfalling down."

THE STRUCTURE OF REALITY

Donald Justice's poem is both a discussion and an illustration of the principles with which this chapter deals. What Justice's poem presents is the problem of how to handle reality in art: Should an artist present nature just as it is, or should he impose an artificial structure and order on it to create logically organized works of art? One might think from the last three lines of the poem that the answer would be negative:

> But O ye barbers at your trade,
> What more beguiles us? Your coiffures?
> Or gold come waterfalling down?

But a qualification of this response is implied within the poem, for art is involved with "the shaping of a hill," and shaping, or structuring, necessitates the application of some principle of order. Further those goats and campers which are created in the speaker's imagination are "Animate objects of a will," a will which must exert itself to find the proper "middle ground."

A fact that cannot be escaped is that a poem exists in space and time. There are limits to how much *can* be included in a poem, so details must be selected that produce a desired total effect. In any experience there are, for example, pleasant and unpleasant details. One may go to a party and eat good food, stub a toe, have good conversation, and be slapped by a beautiful girl. The details which are selected to be included in an account of the party govern the listener's impression of the evening. If one tells only of the good food and good conversation, then the party will appear as a pleasant experience, but if one tells only of the toe-stubbing and the face-slapping, then the party will appear as an unpleasant experience. If one wished to appear objective, he would include all these details. In any case, the effect of the account is produced by the selection of details.

In the same way the effect of poems is dependent upon the selection of details. Whenever a poet writes a poem he has at hand an almost infinite number of details that he could include, and the nature of his poem forms as he decides which details he will include. Therefore, all poems are the result of the shaping intelligence of the author, even if that shaping consists of no more than choosing some details instead of others.

The selection of details also reveals much about who is speaking in the poem. In "Variations on a Theme from James," the fact that the speaker is concerned with finding the right perspective from which to view the landscape indicates that he is a person who is sensitive to art, to finding the right position from which to see the most beautiful picture. The speaker becomes even clearer in the second section when we learn that he is a person with an active imagination, who is able to visualize imaginary events on the hills. Finally, we learn in the third section that he is a person who is explicitly concerned with the critical questions of what art should and should not do.

Therefore the selection of details determines to a large part two important aspects of the poem: 1) the general effect, or tone, of the poem and 2) the character of the speaker in the poem. If a reader's reaction is in any part the result of his sense of a "voice" in the poem, then that reaction is shaped by the selection of details. The poem is, then, the result of a very important shaping and structuring, even though the structure created may not always be obvious.

THE ILLUSION OF THE RANDOM

When we go to hear a concert, we do not expect to hear the musician simply play whatever notes come to mind; we expect him to play a specified piece and to play it well. But what we call playing well is being able to perform a difficult *planned* piece of music with as much apparent ease as if he were improvising. In other words, we want the appearance of spontaneity, but we want the perfection of practice. The same sort of thing is true in poetry. We know that poems are the result of the manipulation of language by a poet; we know that poets revise poems and shape them to produce the effects they seek. Nevertheless, we want poems to *seem* as if they are spontaneous, as if the words could reasonably occur in no other order. What we want, in other words, is for poems to seem unplanned and natural, for the words to have the illusion of the random.

A good example of the illusion of the random is "Variations on a Theme from James." As our examination of the poem from two viewpoints has shown, it is a carefully organized poem which makes a very rational point about the nature of art. The poem is, however, written in such a manner that it seems to be simply the random musing of a sensitive speaker. Starting with a view of some mountains he wonders about what is the best place from which to see the mountains. He decides that the ideal viewpoint is a middle ground. As he thinks about the mountains, he begins to wonder about what he cannot see on them. He imagines that there are goats on the mountains, and he imagines that campers have spoiled the natural setting with garbage that he cannot see. These musings lead him to thinking about the treatment of nature in art and to the idea that art should imitate nature in not making the picture too ordered.

The poem follows a probable thought process, so that as we read it we are not aware of its careful organization. It is only on a second look that we see its detailed organization, and that is what we expect of poems—the illusion of the random.

So it is that all poems are the result of a structuring, an important part of which is the selection of details. The selection of details reveals the characteristics of the speaker in the poem, and is responsible for the tone or effect of the poem. But although poems are carefully structured and organized, we also expect them to appear unplanned and natural, to give an illusion of the random.

QUESTIONS FOR STUDY

NOTE: These questions may be applied to any of the poems in Part II.

1. What does the selection of details reveal about the speaker? What is his attitude toward his subject matter?
2. How much does the selection of details affect your reaction to the poem? What other details might have been included? What effect would other details have produced?
3. How is the poem made to seem spontaneous? What in the poem produces the illusion of the random? If the poem does not have the illusion of the random, how does that affect your reaction to the poem?

4 ∿

The Formal Dimension
The Windows of Structure
The Line

When we read poems we are, in a sense, being controlled by the poems we are reading. We see the world as it is pictured by the poem, and we have no choice but to look through the eyes of the speaker of the poem. Imagine a room about twenty feet long, with two small windows at either end; imagine that there is a tree outside about midway between the windows; imagine that there has been a freakish storm and the half of the tree facing the left window has been denuded of leaves. If we look through the window on the left we see a tree that looks dead and lifeless, like a tree in winter. If we look through the window on the right we see a tree full of leaves, in the full life of spring. But in each case we are seeing the same tree, only we are seeing it through different windows. A poem is like a window: it directs our vision of its subject so that we see only a particular perception of the world.

There are essentially two factors which control what we see when we look through a window. The first is the angle from which we look through the window. If we stand far to one side we will see something different from what we will see if we stand directly in front of the window. The aspect of the poem that we have called the sensory dimension corresponds to the angle from which we look through the window, except that the poet has directed what we see by his selection of details instead of by simply allowing a limited viewing area as a window does. The second is the actual physical frame of the window, which may be of different sizes and of different shapes. The physical form of the poem, the construction of the lines and the sounds employed, corresponds to the physical frame of the window, in that this language construct is the medium through which the content of the poem is presented, just as the framework of the window is the medium through which we view a scene. The part of the frame that we are considering in this chapter is the line.

Lines in English poetry are constructed on four bases: accentual, syllabic, accentual-syllabic, and random. Each of these kinds of lines has particular considerations which are peculiar to it, so that we will take each up in order, but there are two aspects of the English language that are basic to any consideration of lines in poetry: accents and syllables. The syllable is not difficult for English speakers to identify; we can all easily hear how many different parts there are in a word. But the accent as it is meaningful in poetry requires a fuller explanation. As an example, take the word *committee*. This word has three syllables: *com-mit-tee*. When we speak this word aloud, we give the most energy to or put the most stress on the middle syllable *mit: com-mít-tee*. But the matter is not that easy; syllables in English do not divide neatly into stressed and unstressed syllables. If we listen to how we pronounce *committee* again we will hear that we give slightly more stress to the first syllable than to the last. If we use ´ as the mark for the syllable with the most stress, ` as the mark for the syllable with the next to the most stress, and ˆ as the mark for the syllable with the least stress, we would mark *committee* as follows: *còm-mít-têe*. For the purposes of analyzing lines of poetry we are only interested in putting syllables into two categories; accented and unaccented. In the case of *committee* the middle syllable has more stress than the other two, so that (using - for unaccented and / for accented) we would mark *committee* as follows:

$$- \quad / \quad -$$
com-mit-tee

Let us now analyze the sentence "The man bit the dog" to see how it might operate as a line of poetry. Depending on the context in which the sentence appears, it may be pronounced in several ways. If it is a simple prose statement, it is pronounced "Thê màn bít thê dòg." As a line of poetry it would be marked

$$- \quad - \quad / \quad - \quad /$$
The man bit the dog.

Although *bit* and *dog* do not have equal stress here, each has more stress than the syllables around it, so that each has poetic accent. In different contexts the poetic accent would change. If the sentence is in answer to the question "Who bit the dog?" the pronunciation would be "Thê mán bìt thê dòg." As a line of poetry this would be marked

\-   /   -   -   /

The man bit the dog.

Still another context is in answer to the question "What did the man bite?" The response would be "Thê màn bìt thê dóg." As a line of poetry this would be marked

\-   /   /   -   /

The man bit the dog.

In any case we read lines of poetry in their contexts, as they would be spoken in any English conversation, to determine where the accents lie. Hopefully, once we have trained our ears we no longer have to do a detailed analysis of stresses to determine where the accents are; we simply learn to hear them.

THE ACCENTUAL LINE

The oldest kind of line in English is the accentual line. Old English poetry, such as *Beowulf*, is all accentual. By *accentual line* we mean that *there is a recurrent pattern of the number of accents in the line, but there is no recurrent pattern of the number of syllables in the line.* This pattern can best be seen by looking at an example.

Junk

> *Huru Welandes*
> > *worc ne geswiceð*
> *monna ænigum*
> > *ðara ðe Mimming can*
> *heardne gehealdan.*[1]

> An axe angles
> > from my neighbor's ashcan;
> It is hell's handiwork,
> > the wood not hickory,

[1]This means: "Indeed, Wayland's handiwork, the sword Mimung, which he made, will never fail any man who knows how to use it properly." (Wilbur's translation.)

The flow of the grain
                    not faithfully followed.
The shivered shaft
                    rises from a shellheap
Of plastic playthings,
                    paper plates,
And the sheer shards
                    of shattered tumblers
That were not annealed
                    for the time needful.
At the same curbside,
                    a cast-off cabinet
Of wavily-warped
                    unseasoned wood
Waits to be trundled
                    in the trash-man's truck.
Haul them off! Hide them!
                    The heart winces
For junk and gimcrack,
                    for jerrybuilt things
And the men who make them
                    for a little money,
Bartering pride
                    like the bought boxer
Who pulls his punches,
                    or the paid-off jockey
Who in the home stretch
                    holds in his horse.
Yet the things themselves
                    in thoughtless honor
Have kept composure,
                    like captives who would not
Talk under torture.
                    Tossed from a tailgate
Where the dump displays
                    its random dolmens,
Its black barrows
                    and blazing valleys,
They shall waste in the weather
                    toward what they were.
The sun shall glory
                    in the glitter of glass-chips,
Foreseeing the salvage
                    of the prisoned sand,

And the blistering paint
              peel off in patches,
That the good grain
           be discovered again.
Then burnt, bulldozed,
            they shall all be buried
To the depth of diamonds,
             in the making dark
Where halt Hephaestus
          keeps his hammer
And Wayland's work
        is worn away.

—RICHARD WILBUR

If we analyze the first ten lines of this poem according to the number of accents and syllables, we can see what kind of pattern develops.

```
 -  /  /  -
An axe angles
                  -   -   /  -  /  -
                  from my neighbor's ashcan;
```
(10 syllables)

```
 - -  /   / -  -
It is hell's handiwork,
                  -  /   -  /  - -
                  the wood not hickory
```
(12 syllables)

```
 -  /   -  -   /
The flow of the grain
                  -  /  - - /  -
                  not faithfully followed.
```
(11 syllables)

```
 -  /   -    /
The shivered shaft
               /-   -   -  /  -
               rises from a shellheap
```
(10 syllables)

```
 -  /  -  /   -
Of plastic playthings,
                  /  -  /
                  paper plates,
```
(8 syllables)

```
  -    -    /    /
And the sheer shards
                    -    /    -    /    -
                    of shattered tumblers
                                        (9 syllables)


  -    -    /  -    /
That were not annealed
                    -    -    /    /    -
                    for the time needful.
                                        (10 syllables)
  -    -    /    /  -
At the same curbside,
                    -    /  -  /  - -
                    a cast-off cabinet
                                        (11 syllables)


  -  /   - -    /
Of wavily-warped
                    -  /    -      /
                    unseasoned wood
                                        (9 syllables)


  /    -  -  /    -
Waits to be trundled
                    -  -    /    -    /
                    in the trash-man's truck.
                                        (10 syllables)
```

There is clearly a recurrent pattern of four accents per line, although the number of syllables varies from eight to twelve. Since the number of accents is constant while the number of syllables is not, the poem is readily identifiable as accentual. When the number of syllables is so infinitely variable, the line is almost never like the preceeding line, so that there is little chance that the rhythm might become sing-song or monotonous. Nevertheless, the poem is given a rhythmical consistency by the recurrence of the four accents in each line.

THE SYLLABIC LINE

An increasingly popular line among modern poets is the syllabic line, where *there is a recurrent pattern of the number of syllables in the line, but there is no recurrent pattern of the number of accents in the line.* This is a deceptively simple line form, because it seemingly allows the poet to break a prose statement into any arbitrary system of "lines," but the following poem demonstrates that the same rigorous discipline is required for syllabic poems as for any other kind:

Poem in October

It was my thirtieth year to heaven
Woke to my hearing from harbour and neighbour wood
   And the mussel pooled and the heron
       Priested shore
    The morning beckon
With water praying and call of seagull and rook
And the knock of sailing boats on the net webbed wall
    Myself to set foot
      That second
   In the still sleeping town and set forth.

My birthday began with the water-
Birds and the birds of the winged trees flying my name
   Above the farms and the white horses
      And I rose
   In rainy autumn
And walked abroad in a shower of all my days.
High tide and the heron dived when I took the road
    Over the border
      And the gates
  Of the town closed as the town awoke.

A springful of larks in a rolling
Cloud and the roadside bushes brimming with whistling
   Blackbirds and the sun of October
      Summery
   On the hill's shoulder,
Here were fond climates and sweet singers suddenly
Come in the morning where I wandered and listened
    To the rain wringing
      Wind blow cold
  In the wood faraway under me.

Pale rain over the dwindling harbour
And over the sea wet church the size of a snail
   With its horns through mist and the castle
      Brown as owls
   But all the gardens

Of spring and summer were blooming in the tall tales
Beyond the border and under the lark full cloud.
    There could I marvel
        My birthday
  Away but the weather turned around.

  It turned away from the blithe country
And down the other air and the blue altered sky
  Streamed again a wonder of summer
        With apples
    Pears and red currants
And I saw in the turning so clearly a child's
Forgotten mornings when he walked with his mother
    Through the parables
      Of sun light
  And the legends of the green chapels

  And the twice told fields of infancy
That his tears burned my cheeks and his heart moved in mine.
  These were the woods the river and sea
       Where a boy
    In the listening
Summertime of the dead whispered the truth of his joy
To the trees and the stones and the fish in the tide.
    And the mystery
      Sang alive
  Still in the water and singingbirds.

  And there could I marvel my birthday
Away but the weather turned around. And the true
  Joy of the long dead child sang burning
      In the sun.
    It was my thirtieth
Year to heaven stood there then in the summer noon
Though the town below lay leaved with October blood.
    O may my heart's truth
      Still be sung
  On this high hill in a year's turning.

                        —DYLAN THOMAS

The most obvious thing about the lines in this poem is that they are
of different lengths; therefore we cannot expect to find a single
recurring pattern like four accents in the line in every line of the
poem. But we also notice that each of the stanzas includes just ten

lines, so that what we may find is that matching lines in each stanza are the same (that is, all the first lines may be the same; all the fifth lines may be the same, and so forth.) For a start, then, let us look at the number of syllables in the lines. Without bothering to go through the poem line by line here, we can soon learn that matching lines in each stanza do have the same number of syllables; in fact the poem is constructed on the following pattern:

> 9 syllables
> 12 syllables
> 9 syllables
> 3 syllables
> 5 syllables
> 12 syllables
> 12 syllables
> 5 syllables
> 3 syllables
> 9 syllables

However, just because there is a syllabic pattern, this does not mean that there may not be an accentual pattern also. In order to check out that possibility, let us look at the accents in the first, second, fourth, and fifth lines of each stanza. The first lines vary in number of accents:

/   -   -   /   -   /   -   /   -
It was my thirtieth year to heaven

  -   /   -   - /   -   -   /   -
My birthday began with the water-

-   /   - - /   - - /   -
A springful of larks in a rolling

  -   /   - - -   /   -   /   -
Pale rain over the dwindling harbour

  -   /   - /   -   -   /   /   -
It turned away from the blithe country

  -   -   /   -   /   - /   - -
And the twice told fields of infancy

  -   /   -   -   / -   -   /   -
And there could I marvel my birthday

The accents vary from three to four, and although some lines might be read a bit differently it would require great distortion to read all the lines with the same number of accents. The same holds true for the second lines of each stanza:

/ - - / - - / - - / - /
Woke to my hearing from harbour and neighbour wood

/ - - / - - / - / - - /
Birds and the birds of the winged trees flying my name

/ - - / - / - / - - / -
Cloud and the roadside bushes brimming with whistling

- / - - / - / - / - - /
And over the sea wet church the size of a snail

- / - - - / - - / - - /
And down the other air and the blue altered sky

- - / - - / - - / - - /
That his tears burned my cheeks and his heart moved in mine.

- / - - / - - - / - - /
Away but the weather turned around. And the true

These lines have either four or five accents, and again it would require distortion to read the lines as the same. We can see variations in the fourth lines.

/ - /
Priested shore

- - /
And I rose

/ - -
Summery

/ - /
Brown as owls

- / -
With apples

- - /
Where a boy

- - /
In the sun.

And in the fifth lines:

```
 -  /   -  /   -
The morning beckon

 -  / - /   -
In rainy autumn

 -   -   /   /   -
On the hill's shoulder,

 -  / -   / -
But all the gardens

 /    -   -  /  -
Pears and red currants

-   -  / - -
In the listening

/   -   -  / -
It was my thirtieth
```

All this should make it clear that the only consistent recurrent pattern is the number of syllables per line. When the number of accents is so infinitely variable, again there is little chance that the rhythm might ever become sing-song or monotonous, although the recurrent pattern of the number of the syllables in the line gives the poem a rhythmical consistency.

THE ACCENTUAL-SYLLABIC LINE

The vast majority of poems in English have been written in what has been traditionally called *meter;* however, to keep our terms consistent, we will call these poems and their lines *accentual-syllabic.* By this term we mean that *there is a recurrent pattern of the number of accents and the number of syllables in the line, and for the most part the unaccented and accented syllables alternate in a recurrent pattern.* Accentual-syllabic lines are classified according to the patterns of alternation of accented and unaccented syllables, so that we will want to examine lines of each of the four main types: iambic, anapestic, trochaic, and dactylic. Since poems are classified according to the pattern in the bulk of their lines, we will apply these same terms to poems.

If the movement in a line is from one unaccented syllable to one accented syllable (-/) we say the line is iambic. A line can contain any number of iambic units. We describe the line in terms of the type of unit and of how many of the units appear in each line. The terms we use to describe the number of units per line are derived from Greek:

1 unit:	mono-meter
2 units:	di-meter
3 units:	tri-meter
4 units:	tetra-meter
5 units:	penta-meter
6 units:	hexa-meter
7 units:	hepta-meter

To see how accentual-syllabic lines work, let us examine an iambic poem.

The Holy Innocents

Listen, the hay-bells tinkle as the cart
Wavers on rubber tires along the tar
And cindered ice below the burlap mill
And ale-wife run. The oxen drool and start
In wonder at the fenders of a car,
And blunder hugely up St. Peter's hill.
These are the undefiled by woman—their
Sorrow is not the sorrow of this world:
King Herod shrieking vengeance at the curled
Up knees of Jesus choking in the air,

A king of speechless clods and infants. Still
The world out-Herods Herod; and the year,
The nineteen-hundred forty-fifth of grace,
Lumbers with losses up the clinkered hill
Of our purgation; and the oxen near
The worn foundations of their resting-place,
The holy manger where their bed is corn
And holly torn for Christmas. If they die,
As Jesus, in the harness, who will mourn?
Lamb of the shepherds, Child, how still you lie.

—ROBERT LOWELL

If we count the syllables we will discover that every line in this poem has ten syllables, so that we can move at once to an examination of the accents.

```
/ -    -   /   -  / - /  -   /
Listen, the hay-bells tinkle as the cart

/   -   -  /  -  /  -/   -   /
Wavers on rubber tires along the tar

-  /  -   /  -/  -   / -   /
And cindered ice below the burlap mill

-  /   -  /  -  / -   /  -    /
And ale-wife run. The oxen drool and start

-   /  - / -  /  - / - /
In wonder at the fenders of a car,

-   /  -  /  - / -   / -   /
And blunder hugely up St. Peter's hill.
```

First of all, it is easy to see that there is, for the most part, a regular alternation of unaccented and accented syllables, except at the beginnings of the first and second lines. Further, there is a ratio of five accents for every ten syllables, so that we can expect the accents to each be paired with one unaccented syllable. If we divide the lines into two-syllable units, with one accent in each unit, the pattern is like the following:

```
/ - : - / : - / : - / : - /
/ - : - / : - / : - / : - /
- / : - / : - / : - / : - /
- / : - / : - / : - / : - /
- / : - / : - / : - / : - /
- / : - / : - / : - / : - /
```

There are five units in each line; traditionally these units are called *feet*, so that we would say that there are five feet in each line. In these six lines all of the feet except two are iambic feet (the first foot in the first line and the first foot in the second line are trochaic feet), so that the primary movement in the poem is iambic. Consequently, we would say that this poem is written in *iambic pentameter*. Since accentual-syllabic lines have an ideal exact pattern, it is possible to pick out variations from that pattern. In this case the two trochaic feet which are substituted for iambic feet in the first two lines are rhythmical variations.

ANAPESTIC:

If the movement in a poem is from two unaccented syllables to one accented syllable (--/) we say the poem is anapestic. For example here is an anapestic poem:

The Yak

As a friend to the children commend me the Yak;
  You will find it exactly the thing;
It will carry and fetch, you can ride on its back,
  Or lead it about with a string.

The Tartar who dwells on the plains of Thibet
  (A desolate region of snow)
Has for centuries made it a nursery pet,
  And surely the Tartar should know!

Then tell your papa where the Yak can be got,
  And if he is awfully rich
He will buy you the creature—or else he will not.
  (I cannot be positive which.)

—HILAIRE BELLOC

There are either eleven or twelve syllables in the first and third lines of each stanza and eight or nine syllables in each of the second and fourth lines of each stanza. As we will learn a variation of one syllable often occurs in accentual-syllabic lines as a result of rhythmical variations. Therefore, it is still necessary to analyze the accents to see the pattern.

$$- - / - - / - - / - - /$$
As a friend to the children commend me the Yak;

$$- - / - - / - - /$$
You will find it exactly the thing;

$$- - / - - / - - / - - /$$
It will carry and fetch, you can ride on its back,

$$- / - - / - - /$$
Or lead it about with a string.

Once again there is a regular alternation of unaccented and accented syllables, but in this case there are two unaccented syllables between each accent, so that we will divide these syllables into feet consisting of three syllables each.

```
- - / : - - / : - - / : - - /
      - - / : - - / : - - /
- - / : - - / : - - / : - - /
      - / : - - / : - - /
```

In this case there are four feet in the first and third lines and three feet in the second and fourth lines, so that we would say that the first and third lines are anapestic tetrameter and the second and fourth lines are anapestic trimeter. Here, as in "The Holy Innocents" there is rhythmical variation. An iambic foot is substituted at the beginning of the fourth line. This is a very common sort of variation in anapestic poems.

TROCHAIC:

If the movement in the poem is from one accented syllable to one unaccented syllable (/-) we say the poem is trochaic. For example, here is a trochaic poem:

Indian Pipe

Searching once I found a flower
By a sluggish stream.
Waxy white, a stealthy tower
To an Indian's dream.
This its life supreme.

Blood red winds the sallow creek
Draining as it flows.
Left the flower all white and sleek,
Fainting in repose.
Gentler than a rose.

Red man's pipe is now a ghost
Whispering to beware.
Hinting of the savage host
Once that travelled there.
Perfume frail as air.

—RICHARD EBERHART

After finding there are either seven or eight syllables in the first and third lines of each stanza and five or six syllables in the second, fourth, and fifth lines of each stanza, the next step is to analyze the accents:

```
  /   -   / - / - / -
Searching once I found a flower
```

```
  / - / - /
By a sluggish stream.
```

```
  / - /   - / - / -
Waxy white, a stealthy tower
```

```
  / - / -   /
To an Indian's dream.
```

```
  / - /  - /
This its life supreme.
```

Here there is the same sort of alternation that there was in the iambic poem, except that the lines all start on accented syllables instead of unaccented syllables; this is how we distinguish trochaic poems from iambic poems. If we mark the feet, we can see that the line is different from an iambic line:

```
/ - : / - : / - : / -
      / - : / - : /
/ - : / - : / - : / -
      / - : / - : /
      / - : / - : /
```

Notice that in the second, fourth, and fifth lines the last syllable is left off. This is a common sort of variation in trochaic poems, a kind of variation which is found in most of the lines of this poem. There are two other lines with variations in "Indian Pipe":

```
/  - : / -  - : /   - :  /
Left the flower all white and sleek
```

```
/  - - : /  - : /
Whispering to beware
```

The first line has a dactylic foot (which we will discuss next) substituted for the second trochaic foot, and the second line has a dactylic foot substituted for the first trochaic foot. Nevertheless, we can definitely say that the first and third lines of each stanza are trochaic tetrameter and the second, fourth, and fifth lines of each stanza are trochaic trimeter.

DACTYLIC:

If the movement in the poem is from one accented syllable to two unaccented syllables (/--) we say the poem is dactylic. The following is a poem that is mostly dactylic:

Annals

This was the year of the blackbird.
That was the year of the swallow.
Time is a bird on the wing.
Today is an owl in a hollow.

Tomorrow will be for a robin.
Yesterday's only a lark.
But the evenings of Spring are to me
Three nightingales singing at dark.

—MAXINE CASSIN

Not much can be concluded from a count of syllables alone, since three lines have seven syllables, two lines have eight syllables, and three lines have nine syllables. We will have to look at the pattern of accented syllables and unaccented syllables.

/ - - / - - / -
This was the year of the blackbird.

/ - - / - - / -
That was the year of the swallow.

/ - - / - - /
Time is a bird on the wing.

- / - - / - - / -
Today is an owl in a hollow.

In this poem there is a regular alternation with two unaccented syllables between each two accented syllables, and this does seem to be just like the anapestic poem except that the lines begin on the accented syllables instead of the unaccented syllables.

```
/ - - : / - - : / -
/ - - : / - - : / -
/ - - : / - - : /
(-) / - - : / - - : / -
```

Here we see something that dactylic poems have in common with trochaic poems; one or both unaccented syllables are often dropped from the last foot. Another variation is the extra syllable at the beginning of the fourth line. The first line of the second stanza also has that extra syllable at the beginning.

```
(-) / -    - :/   - -: / -
Tomorrow will be for a robin
```

The pattern completely changes, however, in the last two lines from dactylic trimeter to anapestic trimeter:

```
-   -   / : -   -   / : - - /
But the evenings of Spring are to me
```

```
-   / : -   -   / : - - /
Three nightingales singing at dark.
```

There are many ways to vary and to arrange accentual-syllabic lines so that the rhythm does not fall into a monotonous sing-song. The job for the reader is to constantly listen for the rhythms that are built into the poem, so that he can read the poem properly.

THE RANDOM LINE

The form that is identified with English poetry since Walt Whitman, and especially with twentieth-century American poetry (although the form is actually not at all new), is what has been called variously "free verse" or "*vers libre.*" For our purposes we will use the term *the random line. The line is random when there is no recurrent pattern of either syllables or accents.* It is a mistake to assume that there is no structure to these lines, as the following poem will illustrate:

For My Sister, Contemplating Divorce

Our father
married for good, we know now.
Not so

the rest of us, we know now.
Like the escapee
who says breaking out can't be
done, our parents
warned us not to
be too quick to
grow up. We thought
their great heights
gave them sickness.
And went ahead.
If my first wife was wife
not for two years
it was not for not
trying. Nor could mother
be accused of giving
her second husband
no chance. Foolishness
occurs to us,
has run so far in our family
before and after
long marriages. Now welcome to
the fold, black wooly Ruby.
How do we know
how we're doing
until we do, do, do?
Everyone tries. Who's to say
twelve years has been
too long to?

—MARVIN BELL

There is obviously some kind of rationale at work in the breaking
of the lines in this poem. The only question is to identify just what
that rationale is.

In order to see just what effect the line breaks have in this poem,
let us read it as normal prose:

Our father married for good, we know now. Not so the rest of
us, we know now. Like the escapee who says breaking out
can't be done, our parents warned us not to be too quick to
grow up. We thought their great heights gave them sickness.
And went ahead. If my first wife was wife not for two years
it was not for not trying. Nor could mother be accused of
giving her second husband no chance. Foolishness occurs to
us, has run so far in our family before and after long mar-

riages. Now welcome to the fold, black wooly Ruby. How do
we know how we're doing until we do, do, do? Everyone
tries. Who's to say twelve years has been too long to?

As we read this passage we find that there are places where the sound
stops for a moment. Linguistically these points are defined as "junctures." The first juncture occurs in the first sentence between *good*
and *we*. Usually, but not always, junctures occur at marks of punctuation. It would seem natural to break the lines at these points of
juncture:

Our father married for good,
we know now.
Not so the rest of us,
we know now.
Like the escapee
who says breaking out can't be done,
our parents warned us
not to be too quick to grow up.
We thought their great heights gave them sickness.
And went ahead.
If my first wife
was wife not
for two years
it was not
for not trying.
Nor could mother be accused of
giving her second husband no chance.
Foolishness occurs to us,
has run so far in our family
before and after long marriages.
Now welcome to the fold,
black wooly Ruby.
How do we know
how we're doing
until we do, do, do?
Everyone tries.
Who's to say
twelve years has been too long to?

Most readers will agree that the second version is duller than the
first. When we look at the two versions we can see very quickly that
most of the line breaks in Marvin Bell's poem do not occur at normal

points of juncture. When a line break occurs where there is no juncture, the result is what we call *tension,* because a tension is set up between the normal patterns of speech and the imposed patterns of the poem. In "For My Sister, Contemplating Divorce" these points of tension occur at the ends of lines 1, 3, 6, 7, 8, 9, 10, 11, 14, 16, 17, 18, 19, 20, 23, 24, 30.

The important point, however, is that these points of tension are not without their function. An examination of the first twelve lines, in which there are seven points of tension, will demonstrate some of the ways that points of tension can function in a poem.

> Our father
> married for good, we know now.

The line break after *father* forces the reader to concentrate for an instant on the reference to the father and places the phrase "married for good" in a position of emphasis, so that the father's fidelity is underscored.

> Not so
> the rest of us, we know now.

The line break after *so* emphasizes the negative phrase and sets up "the rest of us" in contrast to the father.

> Like the escapee
> who says breaking out can't be
> done, our parents
> warned us not to
> be too quick to
> grow up. . . .

The line break after "can't be" introduces the possibility of reading the clause "who says breaking out can't be" as complete, emphasizing the impossibility of breaking out, an impossibility which is emphasized further by the appearance of *done* finishing out the phrase "can't be done" at the beginning of the next line. This line break and the one after *parents* set up the phrase "done, our parents" with the possibility of "our parents are finished" in addition to the literal meaning of the sentence. The same thing happens when the tensions set up the phrase "warned us not to" as a unit, and the phrase "be too quick to" as a unit.

> . . .
> grow up. We thought
> their great heights
> gave them sickness.

The tensions here set up "grow up we thought" as a unit, with the possibility of "we thought we could grow up." And the line "their great heights" is emphasized by the tension before it, so that the irony of considering the mature adult height as a flaw is made sharper. Thus, tension can play an important part in the statement of the poem.

Tension of this sort occurs in accentual, syllabic, and accentual-syllabic poems, too, but in poems written in the random line tension becomes an organizing principle, just as iambic pentameter is an organizing principle of many accentual-syllabic poems.

There are, then, four types of lines in English poetry: 1) the accentual line, 2) the syllabic line, 3) the accentual-syllabic line, and 4) the random line. Each line requires its own kind of analysis, and the variety of poetry written in English requires that the sophisticated reader be familiar with all of the characteristics of lines. Another element that enters into the structure of lines in English poetry is tension, and although tension occurs in all kinds of poems, it becomes particularly important in poems written in the random line.

QUESTIONS FOR STUDY

NOTE: These questions may be applied to any of the poems in Part II.

1. Is the poem written in the accentual line, the syllabic line, the accentual-syllabic line, or the random line?
2. If the line is accentual, what is the recurrent pattern of the number of accents in the line? If the line is syllabic, what is the recurrent pattern of the number of syllables in the line? If the line is accentual-syllabic, what is the recurrent pattern of the number of feet in the line and are those feet predominately iambic, trochaic, dactylic, or anapestic?
3. Which lines have tension and how does that tension function?

5

The Formal Dimension
The Windows of Structure
The Stanza

In the last chapter we used the metaphor of a window to describe the importance of the structure of a poem in shaping the poem as an art object to which a reader reacts. We then compared the lines to the frame of the window. Now let us carry that metaphor a bit further and say that the lines of a poem are like the individual pieces of wood which are used to construct the frame of a window. As these pieces have to be organized and put together before they can be called a window-frame, lines of poetry have to be arranged and linked before we have a complete poem. These pieces of wood might be put together so that there is one great space of one square pane, or they might be put together so that there are many small spaces for many small diagonal panes. The character of the window and the perception of the viewer will be determined by the way that those pieces are put together and arranged. In the same way, the character of the poem and the perception of the reader is determined by how the lines are arranged and linked, by the stanza form.

Stanzas in English poetry may be formally fixed, so that the poet follows a predetermined pattern in writing his poem, or they may be as loosely defined as are paragraphs in prose, where the writer simply makes a new stanza or a new paragraph whenever he arrives at a new division of thought. We may, in fact, divide stanza forms into two main types: 1) those which are purely structural, based on an arrangement of sounds and lines with no necessary reference to divisions of thought, and 2) those which are purely topical, with no necessary reference to the arrangement of lines and sounds.

THE STANZA AS FIXED STRUCTURE

The predetermined fixed forms in the tradition of English poetry come from many sources. Many, such as the familiar ballad stanza, might be called "folk" forms since they have arisen spontaneously in an oral tradition of poems passed by word-of-mouth from one generation to another. We are all familiar with the ballad stanza, the homely fourteener of hymns and folk songs, as in the familiar hymn "Amazing Grace":

> When we've been there ten thousand years,
> Bright, shining as the sun,
> We'll have more days to sing God's praise
> Than when we first begun.

This stanza form is known as a "fourteener" because each two lines are made up of fourteen syllables, to form a tetrameter line followed by a trimeter line. Many others, like some of those we will examine, have been devised by poets of many countries to pose problems and challenges that the poet can solve. There are far too many such forms for us to examine them all; there are too many, in fact, for them all to be listed in the Glossary. But we can examine a few fixed forms to see the kinds of problems that they pose for poets.

LIMERICK

One of the most familiar of all forms is the limerick. It is so much a part of our lives that we seldom stop to think of it as a complicated poetic form. Limericks are included in our drinking songs, in television commercials, in popular magazines on their humor pages. As we shall see, however, the limerick places rather severe requirements on the technical competence of the poet. This is illustrated by the following popular limerick:

Real Estate

> There was a young lady of Wantage
> Of whom the town clerk took advantage.
>   Said the county surveyor,
>   "Of course you must pay her.
> You've altered the line of her frontage."
>
> —ANONYMOUS

One of the most obvious aspects of this poem is its strong accentual-syllabic line. No subtlety of ear is required to scan the poem:

```
 -     / : -    -   / : - -    / : -
There was a young lady of Wantage
```

```
 -    /  : -    -      /  : - -   / : -
Of whom the town clerk took advantage.
```

```
  -    -   / : -   -  /: -
Said the county surveyor,
```

```
  -    /  :  -    -    / : -
"Of course you must pay her.
```

```
 -    / : -    -   /  : - -   /  : -
You've altered the line of her frontage."
```

All but four of the thirteen feet in the poem are anapestic. This indicates one of the first characteristics of the limerick: it is almost always either anapestic or dactylic. Secondly, it almost always consists of two trimeter lines followed by two dimeter lines followed by one trimeter line. The trimeter lines rhyme with each other and the dimeter lines rhyme with each other. A third characteristic is indicated by the unaccented syllables at the ends of the lines. The rhymes consist of two syllables and end on an unaccented syllable. This is the typical rhyme of light verse. We noticed when we studied accentual-syllabic lines that anapestic and dactylic lines are particularly suited to funny poems. Limericks, then, typically use two of the most common devices of light verse to create their mood. One final point that may be considered is that the limerick finishes in a very short time; its shortness, coupled with the distinctive rhythm and rhyme, make it eminently memorizable. This may be the reason for its great popularity.

JAPANESE FORMS

Two other short forms which have gained wide use in twentieth-century American poetry have a long tradition in Japan. The Japanese court custom was that every educated and cultured person wrote short poems to commemorate all occasions. Today, there are contests every year in Japan for which the Emperor himself writes poems.

HAIKU. The oldest and most well-known of these two short poems is the haiku.

The New and the Old

> Railroad tracks; a flight
> of wild geese close above them
> in the moonlit night.
> —SHIKI
> translation by Harold G. Henderson

This very small poem has several stringent requirements. First, there is the structure. A haiku consists of three lines, the first with five syllables, the second with seven syllables, and the third with five syllables. All haiku are, therefore, syllabic. This means that the poet has no more than seventeen syllables to say what he has to say. In those few syllables he must present an image, indicate a season of the year, and present some emotion. In this haiku there is the image of geese flying over railroad tracks, indicating that the season is late autumn; the fact that all there is are the railroad tracks and the geese portrays an emotion of loneliness. Thus, "The New and the Old" contains all of the elements of haiku. The haiku is, certainly, a limited form, but to be successful, a haiku must be very skillfully written.

TANKA. Another Japanese form which is merely an extension of the haiku is the tanka. For example, look at the following poem:

Tanka

> Pine tree, standing there
> beside my low house of stone,
> I consider you
> and am standing face to face
> with men out of other times.
> —THE PRIEST HAKUTSU
> English version by Vincent Stewart

Notice that the form merely adds two lines of seven syllables each to the base form of the haiku, resulting in one line of five syllables, followed by one line of seven syllables, followed by one line of five syllables, followed by two lines of seven syllables each. The other requirements of the tanka are much the same as those of the haiku, except that tanka writers do not follow the rules as stringently as do haiku writers. For instance, in this tanka, there is no indication of a particular season. The tanka does, also, give the poet fourteen more syllables with which to work.

Many of the forms which are found in English poetry come out of the traditions of French and Italian poetry. These forms are, for the most part, fairly complicated because they were developed in a tradition of courtly love poetry in which frills and embellishments were considered as important as content.

VILLANELLE. The villanelle, a highly structured form, has attracted many poets, particularly in recent years.

After a Time

After a time, all losses are the same.
One more thing lost is one thing less to lose;
And we go stripped at last the way we came.

Though we shall probe, time and again, our shame,
Who lack the wit to keep or to refuse,
After a time, all losses are the same.

No wit, no luck can beat a losing game;
Good fortune is a reassuring ruse:
And we go stripped at last the way we came.

Rage as we will for what we think to claim,
Nothing so much as this bare thought subdues:
After a time, all losses are the same.

The sense of treachery—the want, the blame—
Goes in the end, whether or not we choose,
And we go stripped at last the way we came.

So we, who would go raging, will go tame
When what we have we can no longer use:
After a time, all losses are the same;
And we go stripped at last the way we came.

—CATHERINE DAVIS

The first thing we notice about "After a Time" is that certain lines are repeated several times; this is the most important feature of the villanelle form. If we look more closely we see that the same two lines are repeated. This repetition follows a very exact pattern. The villanelle always has nineteen lines arranged in five stanzas of three lines each, ending with a stanza of four lines. The first line of the first stanza is the third line of the second and fourth stanzas. The third line of the first stanza is the third line of the third and fifth stanzas. The first line of the first stanza is the third line of the last stanza, and the third line of the first stanza is the fourth line of the last stanza. These repeated lines pose a problem for the poet: how to keep the repetition from becoming monotonous. Unless the two repeated lines carry much force, there can be no excuse for their repetition. In "After a Time" there are two principal ideas. The first is that time reduces all disappointments to the same level, expressed in the line "After a time, all losses are the same," so that what seem to be very important disappointments will not seem so later. The second is that we leave the world alone and without friends or possessions, as we entered it: "And we go stripped at last the way we came." So the repeated lines in "After a Time" do carry the kind of force necessary to support the villanelle form.

SESTINA. The sestina also runs the risk of monotony, but for a different reason.

Sky Full of Dead

After the noise and spasm of battle, a lull
Invaded the thinned camp, and all the soldiers,
Turning their blackened faces to the sky
And the small hills they had held, that held their dead,
Lay down with the guns that bartered wounds for lives.
The sun was down, and the hills were cold and blue.

The sun went down and the hills got cold and blue
Only after battles, it seemed. The usual lull
Was an endless noon haze when they wielded their lives
Against the grain of boredom. The toil of soldiers
Hardened their hands and clothes. There were no dead,
And even the sniper's fire became the sky.

They dozed and hungered for battle. The daily sky
Was the true enemy, dressed in illusive blue,
A smiling magician who could transform the dead
Or make a dream come true in the hot lull—
Lullabyes, hallucinations, blood of soldiers!
His reveries loosened the foothold of their lives.

Invisible, then not, then dead, alive
And breathing on our bread, the four-faced sky
Turned us against our will, to become soldiers,
Deploying beneath a sky that is never blue
And brilliant as it was in the ideal lull
Of childhood, when no one could be dead.

Now past the hammocks swinging with the dead,
We hunt among the blasted trees for the lives
We have never led, for the spasms that would lull
Frayed nerves to sleep, that would eclipse the sky—
And perhaps, when we woke, we should find it blue
And the air cold, and we no longer soldiers.

Others may hope to make their peace. We soldier,
And watch, at night, in the mud, the naked dead
Bodies change and blaze in chalky blue
Under the frozen moon, that tugs at our lives
And our blood struggling and beating toward the sky.
Star-rise and moon-rise are only another lull.

Shadows of tall soldiers loom in the sky
In the midnight lull, and shoulder their massive lives.
They are blue hills malignant with the dead.

—ROBERT MEZEY

The first thing that we notice about this poem is that the same six words appear at the ends of the lines in each of the first six stanzas. The words are *lull, soldiers, sky, dead, lives,* and *blue.* The repetition of these words is according to a pattern: 123456, 615243, 364125, 532614, 451362, 246531. The last stanza contains only three lines, and each line contains two of the six words: 23, 15, 64. The sheer complexity of manipulating these six words through a thirty-nine line poem makes this a difficult form. As in the villanelle the repetition makes monotony a problem. As in the villanelle, one possibility to relieve monotony is to make the words so important that they demand repetition. This is a poem about the horrors of war, so all of the words are an integral part of that horror. *Sky* and *blue* together emphasize the irony of death under a beautiful sky, but one that is "the true enemy" and one that is "full of dead." *Soldiers, dead,* and *lives* are obviously important in war, and *lull* provides a contrast to the violence. There are other ways, moreover, that monotony is avoided. The words are used in different contexts: in the first stanza *lull* is a resting time, and in the third stanza it is "the hot lull." The words are used as different parts of speech: in the first five stanzas *soldier* is used as a noun, and in the sixth stanza, in the phrase "we soldier," it is used as a verb. The words acquire special force at the ends and beginnings of stanzas; the word that ends one stanza becomes the end word for the first line of the next stanza. The sestina is a difficult form, but used by a good craftsman it can be a powerful form.

SONNET. By far the most famous form we have borrowed from the medieval Italian poets is the sonnet. This fourteen-line form has become, in the minds of many, the ideal. Although there are many variations on the sonnet, sonnets are still written in the original Italian or Petrarchan pattern.

The Subway

Dark accurate plunger down the successive knell
Of arch on arch, where ogives burst a red
Reverberance of hail upon the dead
Thunder like an exploding crucible!
Harshly articulate, musical steel shell
Of angry worship, hurled religiously
Upon your business of humility
Into the iron forestries of hell:

Till broken in the shift of quieter
Dense altitudes tangential of your steel,
I am become geometries, and glut
Expansions like a blind astronomer
Dazed, while the worldless heavens bulge and reel
In the cold revery of an idiot.

—ALLEN TATE

The most important characteristic of the Italian sonnet is that it is organized in two parts, the first of eight lines and the second of six. The eight-line part is known as the "octet" and the six-line part is known as the "sestet." Normally the octet sets up a situation or poses a question to which the speaker reacts in the sestet. In the poem "The Subway" the octet describes the subway in nightmarish terms as something frightening. It is a very emotional description, in which the cold iron of the subway becomes something alive. Then, in the sestet the speaker reacts to the nightmarish experience. He finds himself reduced and dazed, thrown into "the cold revery of an idiot."

The other principal form of the sonnet is the English sonnet, in which the octet is extended for twelve lines and the sestet is reduced to two lines, as in the following:

Only the Moonlight

He'd never married, so when he got sick
I went up after work. We talked awhile
About the new men and how long they'd stick.
When I got up I told him with a smile

That what he'd always needed was a wife
To nurse and cheer him up, to cook and share.
He turned and cried, "God, but I hate this life!—
The waking in the night and no one there,

"Only the moonlight with you in your bed,
Only that canned stuff on the kitchen shelf.
Single, I wanted peace, and got instead
This lonely hell of living by yourself."

And when he died he screamed with his last breath,
Being too terribly alone with death.

—PAUL ENGLE

In this sonnet the first twelve lines set up the picture of the lonely man on his deathbed. We know the speaker is sympathetic, because he takes the trouble to visit and because he listens to the dying man's troubles. The reaction of the speaker in the couplet at the end is not one of sympathy, however, but one of confirmation and summation of the dying man's condition: "Being too terribly alone with death." The effect of the couplet at the end of an English sonnet is usually one of a quick summation of the entire poem.

In English, sonnets are normally iambic pentameter and rhymed. (We normally use letters, a different letter for each rhyme, to show rhyme patterns.) The usual rhyme pattern of the Italian sonnet is *abbaabba, cdecde,* but as we have already seen there can be some variation from that pattern for the rhyme pattern of "The Subway" is *abbaacca, defdef.* The usual rhyme pattern of the English sonnet is *abab, cdcd, efef, gg;* "Only the Moonlight" is an example of this pattern. As in the Italian sonnet, however, there can be variations of this pattern. Occasionally, one will even find the two basic patterns combined in some way.

The above by no means exhaust the possibilities of fixed forms in English poetry. Sometimes the poet may create his own fixed form for the purpose of just one poem. The important aspect, nevertheless, about a fixed form is that it is a structure of language imposed on the content of the poem.

THE STANZA AS PARAGRAPH

Instead of following a specific predetermined structure in a poem, the poet can allow content to limit the stanzas, as in the following well-known poem by Wallace Stevens:

Thirteen Ways of Looking at a Blackbird

I

Among twenty snowy mountains,
The only moving thing
Was the eye of the blackbird.

II

I was of three minds,
Like a tree
In which there are three blackbirds.

III

The blackbird whirled in the autumn winds.
It was a small part of the pantomime.

IV

A man and a woman
Are one.
A man and a woman and a blackbird
Are one.

V

I do not know which to prefer,
The beauty of inflections
Or the beauty of innuendoes,
The blackbird whistling
Or just after.

VI

Icicles filled the long window
With barbaric glass.

The shadow of the blackbird
Crossed it, to and fro.
The mood
Traced in the shadow
An indecipherable cause.

VII

O thin men of Haddam,
Why do you imagine golden birds?
Do you not see how the blackbird
Walks around the feet
Of the women about you?

VIII

I know noble accents
And lucid, inescapable rhythms;
But I know, too,
That the blackbird is involved
In what I know.

IX

When the blackbird flew out of sight,
It marked the edge
Of one of many circles.

X

At the sight of blackbirds
Flying in a green light,
Even the bawds of euphony
Would cry out sharply.

XI

He rode over Connecticut
In a glass coach.
Once, a fear pierced him,
In that he mistook
The shadow of his equipage
For blackbirds.

XII

The river is moving.
The blackbird must be flying.

It was evening all afternoon.
It was snowing
And it was going to snow.
The blackbird sat
In the cedar-limbs.

—WALLACE STEVENS

This poem contains thirteen random thoughts about blackbirds. Some are different sightings of blackbirds, some are sights which remind one of blackbirds, some are philosophical comments on blackbirds. Importantly, there is no predetermined form that these thoughts must take. No two of the thirteen numbered stanzas are alike; each takes the form that its content demands. Some stanzas are as short as two lines, some are as long as six lines. The stanzas are developed as paragraphs are in prose, according to the demands of content. Here, then, the stanza form is totally governed by what is being said.

There are two possibilities in poetry as far as stanza form is concerned: 1) the stanza form may be a structure of language (rhythm, rhyme, etc.) which is imposed on the content of the poem, or 2) the stanza form may be developed according to the organization of the content. In some cases, as we have seen in the sonnets, the content may be developed to fit into a predetermined structure of language.

QUESTIONS FOR STUDY

NOTE: These questions may be applied to any of the poems in Part II.

1. Is there a fixed predetermined stanza form? If so, is this a traditional fixed form like the sonnet, villanelle, etc.? Are there any variations from the predetermined form?
2. How are content and stanza form merged? Does the organization of the content complement the organization of the stanzas?

6

The Formal Dimension
The Sounds of Structure

When we defined poetry as discourse arranged in lines, we were saying, by implication, that poetry makes a more conscious use of the sounds of language than does prose. For the line to have the effect on a discourse that we described in Chapters 1 and 4, it must be heard. Poetry is an oral art, and sound is an integral part of any poem, whether we hear it read to us by someone else or read it aloud ourselves or hear it spoken by the voice inside our heads as we read it silently.

In Chapters 4 and 5 we discussed how the groups of sounds we call words can be manipulated and structured, but we have not yet discussed how the individual sounds which comprise those words can be formed and shaped into the structure of the poem. Word sounds become significant in a poem when they are repeated. The *b* in *bad* is not significant in the phrase "the bad wolf," but it begins to become significant when *big* is added and the phrase becomes "the bad wolf is big." The significance of the repetition of the *b* is increased when that repetition is emphasized by placing the words together as in "the big bad wolf." In the same way, the sentence "the children play every morning" becomes much more interesting when it is changed to "the children play every day" and the *a* sound is repeated in *day* and *play*. Notice, too, in this last example that we must listen to the sounds of the words; we cannot be misled by spelling. The *y* in these words is irrelevant because it is not pronounced; for example, the same *a* sound occurs in *baste* and *waste*, although these words are spelled differently than *day* and *play* and end in an *st* sound. Further, in these words the final *e* is irrelevant because it is not pronounced. Note also the identical sounds of *waste* and *waist*. To see exactly how such sound repetitions can work in a poem, consider the following:

Rastignac at 45

Here he is of course. It was his best
trick always: when we glance again toward
the shadow we see it has consist-
ed of him all along, lean and bored.

We denounced him so often! Yet he
comes up, and leans on one of the bars
in his dark suit, indicating the
empty glass as if we were waiters.

We fill it, and submit, more or less,
to his marvellous air of knowing
all the ropes debonair weariness
could care to handle, of "everything

that I know I know from having done,
child, and I survive." What calmly told
confidences of exploration
among the oversexed and titled,

or request for a few days' loan, are
we about to hear? Rastignac tell us
about Life, and what men of your
stamp endure. It must be terrible.

It is. To the left of his mouth is
an attractive scarlike line, not caused
by time unhelped. It is not the prize,
either, of a dueller's lucky thrust.

But this: time after time the fetid
taste to the platitudes of Romance
has drawn his mouth up to the one side
secretly, in a half-maddened wince.

We cannot help but pity him that
momentary convulsion; however,
the mere custom of living with it
has, for him, diminished the horror.

—THOM GUNN

The two kinds of sound repetition that we find in poems, rhyme and alliteration, are both present in this poem. A detailed examination of how these devices are used in "Rastignac at 45" should reveal the principles of sound repetition in poetry.

RHYME

The first and most obvious kind of sound repetition in poetry is rhyme. *Rhyme is the repetition of the final sounds of lines.* For example, in the lines

> Hickory, dickory, dock,
> The mouse ran up the clock,

the final sounds of the end words, made up of the vowel sound *ah* and the consonant sound *k*, match; this is an example of rhyme. As we examine "Rastignac at 45" we will discover three types of rhyme: true rhyme, assonance, and consonance.

TRUE RHYME:

True rhyme occurs when the final consonant sounds and the final vowel sounds which precede them are the same, or when there are no final consonant sounds and the final vowel sounds are the same. In the first stanza the second and fourth lines end with "toward" and "bored." In both cases the final consonant sounds are *rd* and the vowel sound which precedes them is *o;* this is therefore a case of true rhyme. The first and third lines of the second stanza end in "he" and "the"; in neither case is there a final consonant and the final vowel sound is *e* in both cases. This is also a case of true rhyme. Other examples of true rhyme are "less" and "-ness" in the third stanza and "done" and the *shun* of the last syllable of "exploration" in the fourth stanza.

ASSONANCE:

Assonance occurs when the final consonant sounds differ, but the final vowel sounds which precede them are the same. There is only one example of assonance in "Rastignac at 45." The second and fourth lines of the fifth stanza end in "us" and "terrible." The vowel sound in "us" is *uh*. The final syllable of "terrible" is actually pronounced *buhl*. Therefore, although the final consonant sounds differ, the final vowel sounds which precede them are the same. Other examples of assonance are bait-lake, beg-let, pitch-sit, and boat-hope.

CONSONANCE:

Consonance occurs when the final consonant sounds are the same, but the final vowel sounds which precede them differ. Most of the rhymes in "Rastignac at 45" are examples of consonance. The first and third lines of the first stanza end with "best" and "consist"; both of these words end in the consonant sounds *st*, but the final vowel sound in "best" is *eh* and that in "consist" is *ih*. In the sixth stanza there is one case of a near-rhyme that is not quite perfect consonance, in the second and fourth lines, which end in "caused" and "thrust." The first ends in *sd* and the second in *st*. If you listen carefully you will hear that the only difference between *d* and *t* is that the vocal cords are producing sound when we say *d* and *t* is whispered. These two sounds are, therefore, very close. Other examples of consonance are "bars" and "waiters" in the second stanza, "told" and "titled" in the fourth stanza, "are" and "your" in the fifth stanza, "is" and "prize" in the sixth stanza, "fetid" and "side" and "Romance" and "wince" in the seventh stanza, and "that" and "it" and "however" and "horror" in the eighth stanza.

Rhyme can occur in the poem according to a pattern, or it can simply occur randomly, according to no particular pattern. In "Rastignac at 45" the rhyme does occur according to a pattern; the rhymes in each stanza follow the pattern *abab*.

ALLITERATION

Alliteration occurs whenever there are repetitions of sounds within lines. Usually alliteration occurs randomly, according to no particular pattern, as in the first three lines of "Rastignac at 45" where the *s* sounds are repeated:

> Here he is of course. It was his best
> trick always: when we glance again toward
> the shadow we see it has consist- . . .

In these same lines there are other examples of alliteration: "Here he," "It was his," "always: when we," and "glance again."

Sometimes, however, alliteration may occur according to a pattern. This is the case in "Junk," which we examined in Chapter 4, in which at least three of the four accented syllables in each line alliterate with each other:

An axe angles
>   from my neighbor's ashcan;

It is hell's handiwork,
>   the wood not hickory,

The flow of the grain
>   not faithfully followed.

The effect of this kind of alliteration is to make the already heavy accentual pattern even heavier. This is a dangerous device, one which could rather quickly become monotonous.

Alliteration can produce very musical effects in poetry, but it can also sometimes be so strong that the alliteration is the only thing that the reader hears. One must be aware both of the possibilities and of the dangers.

The two ways that poetry uses the individual sounds which make up words are rhyme and alliteration. Rhyme can be of three kinds: true rhyme, assonance, and consonance, and it can be either patterned or random. Alliteration can produce a very subtle effect or it can produce a very marked effect, according to the needs of the poem.

QUESTIONS FOR STUDY

NOTE: These questions may be applied to any of the poems in Part II.

1. Does rhyme occur in the poem? Is that rhyme true rhyme, assonance, or consonance? Is the rhyme patterned or random? What is the effect of the rhyme?
2. Does alliteration occur in the poem? Is the alliteration subtle or marked? What is the effect of that alliteration?

7

The Rational Dimension

Until now, we have been discussing aspects of the poem which are, for the most part, provable. That is, the elements of the sensory dimension and the formal dimension are discovered by looking into the poem and finding out what is actually there. To say, however, that to have discovered these elements is to have totally described the poem is to say that the poem is something that exists completely independent of its readers. For the fact is, we must admit, that different readers will react differently to the same poem and will find different statements about the world in the same poem. By maintaining that only one reaction to or one interpretation of a poem is correct we would unfortunately restrict the possibilities of the poem; yet to say that all reactions and all interpretations are correct is to admit total anarchy. As Donald Justice says in "Variations on a Theme from James," which we discussed in Chapter 3,

> Once we have found a middle ground,
> The warts, the pimples disappear.

What we must find when analyzing is a middle ground from which we can operate both responsibly and freely.

Any reader brings a highly individualized set of attitudes, prejudices, and past experiences with him to a poem. Emerson quotes the proverb "He that would bring home the wealth of the Indies, must carry out the wealth of the Indies." If we apply this proverb to the reading of poetry, we must admit that each reader carries out a different wealth. What we must find, then, is some controlling principle which will guide us as we read a poem like this one:

Mending Wall

Something there is that doesn't love a wall,
That sends the frozen-ground-swell under it,
And spills the upper boulders in the sun;
And makes gaps even two can pass abreast.
The work of hunters is another thing:
I have come after them and made repair
Where they have left not one stone on a stone,
But they would have the rabbit out of hiding,
To please the yelping dogs. The gaps I mean,
No one has seen them made or heard them made,
But at spring mending-time we find them there.
I let my neighbour know beyond the hill;
And on a day we meet to walk the line
And set the wall between us once again.
We keep the wall between us as we go.
To each the boulders that have fallen to each.
And some are loaves and some so nearly balls
We have to use a spell to make them balance;
'Stay where you are until our backs are turned!'
We wear our fingers rough with handling them.
Oh, just another kind of out-door game,
One on a side. It comes to little more:
There where it is we do not need the wall:
He is all pine and I am apple orchard.
My apple trees will never get across
And eat the cones under his pines, I tell him.
He only says, 'Good fences make good neighbours.'
Spring is the mischief in me, and I wonder
If I could put a notion in his head:
'*Why* do they make good neighbours? Isn't it
Where there are cows? But here there are no cows.
Before I built a wall I'd ask to know
What I was walling in or walling out,
And to whom I was like to give offence.
Something there is that doesn't love a wall,
That wants it down.' I could say 'Elves' to him,
But it's not elves exactly, and I'd rather
He said it for himself. I see him there
Bringing a stone grasped firmly by the top
In each hand, like an old-stone savage armed.
He moves in darkness as it seems to me,
Not of woods only and the shade of trees.

He will not go behind his father's saying,
And he likes having thought of it so well
He says again, 'Good fences make good neighbours.'

—ROBERT FROST

What happens in this poem is clear. The speaker goes out with his neighbor to repair the fence that runs between their farms. This experience causes the speaker to wonder about the necessity of having a fence. He muses that there is something in nature that doesn't like walls, because the wall is always being torn down by unseen forces. Further he does not see why there needs to be a wall to separate his apple orchard from his neighbor's pine trees. The neighbor, on the other hand, merely quotes the old proverb, "Good fences make good neighbors." The speaker tries to insert some doubt about the wisdom of this proverb into the neighbor's thinking, but to no avail, for the neighbor just repeats the proverb.

The question is, does this poem speak merely of the wall running between the pine trees and the apple orchard, or does it speak as well of walls in general? Does this poem concern merely the relationship between these two particular men, or does it concern the general problem of human relationships? Certainly, it is a common practice to look in poems for meanings which go beyond the surface content of the poem, but we must recognize the dangers inherent in searching for meaning. There is always the possibility that we will make of the poem something that it is not and thus not really read the poem we have before us. There is also the danger that we will become so involved in interpretation that we will fail to fully enjoy the poem, that we will make of it merely a philosophical document.

We must, therefore, adopt some principle which will keep us from violating the poem, from making it something which it is not. The most sensible premise we can adopt is that any interpretation we advance must be supported by evidence from the poem. We cannot bring information drawn from sources other than the poem to bear on the act of interpretation. Matters of history or of the biography of the author are relevant only if they are mentioned explicitly in the poem. In Chapter 1, in discussing "The Canonization" by John Donne, we discovered that the phrase "the plaguey bill" refers to the list of those who had died that was published in London during the times of plague; this is a piece of historical information, but we are justified in considering it because it is brought up by its explicit mention in the poem.

In our search for meaning, then, in "Mending Wall," we must be sure that we remain constrained by what is actually *in* the poem. We must be certain that we are true to the poem.

THE EXTENSION OF THE OBJECTIVE CORRELATIVE

In Chapter 2 we discussed the objective correlative; we said that the objective correlative is a concrete experience which renders objectively the emotion the poem is attempting to promote in the reader. We have already described the experience to which we react in "Mending Wall." This experience is a very specific one, involving only two people: the speaker and his neighbor. It may very well be, however, that the experience of these two particular people may be like the experiences of many people and therefore what is true for these two particular people may be true for people in general. Consequently, if there is in the poem any statement about the need or lack of need for walls between these two people, there may be a statement about the need or lack of need for walls in the world at large.

Clearly the speaker in the poem is not in complete sympathy with wall building. In the first part of the poem he demonstrates that there is a force in nature which works against walls, which is essentially antithetical to walls. In the second part of the poem he tries to cast doubt on the neighbor's proverb, "Good fences make good neighbors." Finally, when the neighbor cannot be shaken in his belief about fences, the speaker describes him as a savage:

> . . . I see him there
> Bringing a stone grasped firmly by the top
> In each hand, like an old-stone savage armed.

The neighbor building a wall is like a primitive, uncivilized and unaffected by the progress man has made in human relationships. The speaker goes further:

> He moves in darkness as it seems to me,
> Not of woods only and the shade of trees.

He moves in a darkness that is not a darkness of nature, but is, rather, a darkness of the spirit, a darkness of the man himself. The speaker, then, sees the building of walls as a thing antithetical to civilization, antithetical to human progress.

THE EXTENSION OF IRONY

Thus far we have simply been discussing the attitude of the speaker in the poem as he himself pictures it. We have been concerned with seeing the world through the speaker's eyes. But we, as readers, are in a fortunate position; we can see more than the speaker sees. We can, as objective observers, examine what he says in the light of the situation in which we see him. The term *irony* as it is used in poetry refers to what the reader can see that the speaker and the participants in the poem cannot see because of their personal involvement. We must, therefore, examine this poem to see if there are elements which we, because of our detached position, can see.

In the first place, despite his feelings about fences, the speaker obviously goes out each year to repair the fence, justifying it to himself:

> Oh, just another kind of out-door game,
> One on a side. It comes to little more.

The speaker spends most of his energy in the poem attempting to refute his neighbor's proverb, "Good fences make good neighbors," but the only time, so far as we can tell from the evidence in the poem, that the speaker and his neighbors do come together as good neighbors is when they meet to repair the fence. So, in the sense that it brings them together regularly, maintaining a good fence does make these two men good neighbors. Therefore, the irony of the poem is that while the speaker is protesting walls, the evidence that the reader sees would tend to indicate that perhaps the speaker is negating his own argument. Finally, the neighbor has the last word in the poem, for the last words are, "Good fences make good neighbors."

THE EXTENSION OF THE READER INTO THE POEM

One further step in interpretation is necessary. We are each the product of what and where we are and have been. We each possess certain attitudes and prejudices which will affect how we interpret the poems we read. A boy who has spent his life in the city is apt to be less receptive to arguments based on nature than is a boy who has been raised in a rural area. Similarly, a girl with strong religious convictions is unlikely to be receptive to a poem which speaks of views in opposition to those convictions. A man whose political position is such that he favors an essentially internationalist position might find a political interpretation in "Mending Wall," and say that the poem indicates that the walls between countries should be broken down, that we should strive for a world in which there are no national boundaries. Conversely, a man who takes an opposite political stance is not likely to find such an interpretation in the poem, and may reject the poem because he does find such an interpretation being made. It is not that we should avoid having such personal reactions to poems; it is that we should always be aware of what our own personal attitudes and orientations are, so that we can sensibly interpret our own reactions to poems.

This dimension is properly called rational because it requires from the reader more than just an experience of the poem; it requires from him a rational act of the mind; it requires from him interpretation. Three steps must be taken when interpreting: 1) extending the objective correlative by finding out whether or not the particular concrete experience in the poem has any relationship to experience in general, 2) finding out whether or not there are any poetic ironies in the poem, and 3) assessing the affect on interpretation of one's own particular attitudes and orientations.

QUESTIONS FOR STUDY

NOTE: These questions may be applied to any of the poems in Part II.

1. What are the larger implications of the particular experiences which are described in the poem? Does the poem say anything about life in general?
2. Is there any poetic irony in the poem? Is there anything that you as the reader can see that the speaker or the participants in the poem cannot see?
3. How have your own attitudes affected your reaction to this poem? How are your attitudes involved in how you react to this poem?

8

The Critic and the Poem

In the preceding chapters we have examined the aspects of poetry separately, and to some extent we have been doing it an injustice, for no poem can be explained by examining only one of the ways in which it works. A poem's total effect on its reader is determined by many factors, and only when we have examined all of those factors can we have a sensible idea of how a particular poem works. The "Questions for Study" at the end of each chapter point toward explaining particular aspects of the poem, but we must ask *all* of these questions of a poem before we can understand it in any significant sense. It would be inappropriate, then, to end this discussion of poetry without putting at least one poem through all of its paces. Therefore, let us read the following poem, which has been praised by critics, and apply each question to it, to see exactly what it is that the critics have praised.

Acquainted with the Night

I have been one acquainted with the night.
I have walked out in rain—and back in rain.
I have outwalked the furthest city light.

I have looked down the saddest city lane.
I have passed by the watchman on his beat
And dropped my eyes, unwilling to explain.

I have stood still and stopped the sound of feet
When far away an interrupted cry
Came over houses from another street,

But not to call me back or say good-bye;
And further still at an unearthly height,
One luminary clock against the sky

Proclaimed the time was neither wrong nor right.
I have been one acquainted with the night.

—ROBERT FROST

Would you like to have information about any matter discussed in the poem which is not given in the poem? What effect would such information have on your reaction to the poem? There are no obscure references in the poem. All of the objects and places described are familiar. The only piece of information that one might ask for is the specific location of the experience described in the poem. But such information would not be likely to have any effect on the reader's reaction, since the important thing is that the speaker reacts as he does, and he reacts in this place as he would in any other place under similar circumstances.

Do you like the poem? If you do, try to pinpoint the source of your delight. If you do not, try to pinpoint where the poem fails for you. This is a very moving poem. It is delightful, not in the sense that it produces laughter or great joy, but in the sense that it very clearly captures a kind of experience we have all had, the experience of finding oneself alone at night and feeling somehow a profound communion with the universe. The poem describes clearly the experience of communing with night itself.

Summarize the objective or literal content of the poem. For what emotion is this the objective correlative? In this poem someone describes a walk he took late at night. It was a rainy night and the speaker walked out past the city limits. He looked down the deserted city streets and once he passed by an officer going about his rounds, but he avoided speaking to the officer. Once he heard a cry in the distance and stopped to listen, but the cry was not for him. Finally at some height, as on a tower, he saw an illuminated clock and looked to it for information, but the time according to the clock "was neither wrong nor right." At the end of the poem the speaker repeats that he has "been one acquainted with the night."

This experience is the objective correlative for a complicated set of emotions. First, there is a sense of exhilaration in the perception of communion with the night and in the recognition of a kind of knowledge about the nature of the universe. Then there is the loneliness, the isolation, that comes with this knowledge.

What metaphors are developed in the poem? There are almost no metaphors developed in this particular poem. The speaker does describe the clock as a proclaimer, and to the extent that this is a personification of the clock, this is a metaphor. There is a sense, also, in which one can consider the entire poem a metaphor, for one might view the speaker's experience on this particular night as a metaphor for human experience in general; this point was developed under the rational dimension.

What images are developed in the poem? How effectively do these images evoke the concrete experience? The images in this poem are of several kinds. The general image of night, and of darkness, is introduced in the first line, and the second line begins to suggest the quality of the night by introducing the image of rain, which appeals to both the sense of sight and the sense of touch. The image of darkness is developed by the speaker's statement that he has "outwalked the furthest city light." The visual image of a dark city, lonely and deserted, is helped by the image of "the saddest city lane," and the picture of the speaker's passing the watchman is a sharp detail. Sound images are developed in the third stanza: the image of the sound of feet on an otherwise silent street and the image of a single cry in the distance. Finally, there is the image which dominates the poem, the image of the lighted clock which rises above everything else and is the most visible object in the poem. These few images result in an excellent evocation of the experience because each is so sharp that the reader is compelled to fill in the gaps to produce an entire picture in his imagination.

Are you interested in the literal content of the poem? If so, try to pinpoint why. If not, try to pinpoint where the literal content fails. The literal content of "Acquainted with the Night" is interesting, in the first place, because it deals with a familiar kind of experience, one with which almost any reader can identify, and it makes that experience important. Further, it is interesting because it is developed in such precise concrete detail that the reader has a clear experience with which to identify.

What does the selection of details reveal about the speaker? What is his attitude toward his subject matter? In the first place, the speaker does not select the most obvious details; he notices subtle things, like his awkwardness on passing the watchman. He is a sensitive man, responsive to the world around him, as his response to the distant cry shows. If he were not a sensitive, responsive person, he would ignore the cry, but he must stop to see if he should respond to it. He takes his relationship to his world seriously; hence his concern about what the clock proclaims.

How much does the selection of details affect your reaction to the poem? What other details might have been included? What effect would other details have produced? The details in this poem are all calculated to produce a feeling of loneliness and isolation; they all emphasize the darkness, the speaker's separation from the city, his lack of connection with other human beings. Other common details of the night might have been included, like lighted windows and people driving home late at night, but the inclusion of such details would have diluted the effect of loneliness and would have produced a very different kind of poem.

How is the poem made to seem spontaneous? What in the poem produces the illusion of the random? If the poem does not have the illusion of the random, how does that affect your reaction to the poem? "Acquainted with the Night" is written in a very conversational tone; the words are simple. The poem consists of a series of simple statements which follow logically, one on the other, so that the reader can imagine the speaker talking to him.

Is the poem written in the accentual line, the syllabic line, the accentual-syllabic line, or the random line? The first line of the poem can be read two ways, so that the problem is to find the best reading. It could be read as a perfect iambic line:

$$- \; / \quad - \; / \; - \; / \; - \; / \quad - \quad /$$
I have been one acquainted with the night.

It could be read with a trochee at the beginning of the line:

$$/ \quad - \quad - \; / \; - \; / \; - \; / \quad - \quad /$$
I have been one acquainted with the night.

The first reading poses several problems. The natural inclination is to put the stress on *I*, on the subject of the sentence; to put the stress on *have* is, also, to make the statement sound like that of the petulant child who cries "I *have!*" The second pattern, therefore, would seem appropriate for the first five lines and the seventh line. All of the other lines, except for the last which repeats the first, are consistantly iambic:

$$- \quad / \quad - \; / \quad - \; / \; - \; / \; - \; /$$
And dropped my eyes, unwilling to explain.

Because every line has five accents and ten syllables, and because the iambic pattern predominates, the poem is accentual-syllabic. The effect of the variations in the pattern in the early lines is to give the sentences weight, as if they are carefully considered.

If the line is accentual, what is the recurrent pattern of the number of accents in the line? If the line is syllabic, what is the recurrent pattern of the number of syllables in the line? If the line is accentual-syllabic, what is the recurrent pattern of the number of feet in the line and are those feet predominately iambic, trochaic, dactylic, or anapestic? The essentially iambic pattern has already been noted, and since there are five iambic feet in each line the metrical pattern of the poem is iambic pentameter.

Which lines have tension and how does that tension function? There are only two cases of tension in this poem. The first is in the third stanza:

> When far away an interrupted cry
> Came over houses from another street . . .

The line-break after *cry*, where normally one would go on from the subject to the verb with no break, emphasizes the word *cry*, which is the most important image in the stanza. The tension is further emphasized by the alliteration of the *k* sounds in *cry* and *came*. The second case is in the fourth stanza:

> One luminary clock against the sky
> Proclaimed the time was neither wrong nor right.

The line-break after *sky*, where there would normally be no pause, emphasizes both the image of the clock standing out against a dark sky and the message of the clock in the next line, which is the climax of the poem.

Is there a fixed predetermined stanza form? If so, is this a traditional fixed form like the sonnet, villanelle, etc.? Are there any variations from the predetermined form? The poem has fourteen lines and consists of twelve lines followed by a couplet. Thus, at first glance it seems to be an English sonnet. But the content of the poem does not break into the neat twelve lines followed by a summary couplet of the English sonnet. Instead, the content breaks into thirteen lines of development followed by the clinching repetition of the first line. There is a further variation of traditional sonnet practice. This sonnet is written in a form called *terza rima*. The three-line stanzas each rhyme *aba*, and the *b* rhyme of the stanza becomes the *a* rhyme of the next stanza, so that the pattern becomes *aba, bcb,* etc. The pattern is neatly ended in this poem by returning to the first rhyme in the middle line of the fourth stanza and then ending with a couplet which uses the initial rhyme.

How are content and stanza form merged? Does the organization of the content complement the organization of the stanzas? The variation of usual sonnet form mentioned above suits the content organization of this poem. The *terza rima* form produces an ongoing effect, with the lines closely linked together by the rhyme pattern. Thus, the first thirteen lines are closely unified by the *terza rima* pattern, as they are by the content organization. The clinching last line is not only a neat way to fill out the pattern; it also emphasizes what has been said in the poem.

Does rhyme occur in the poem? Is that rhyme true rhyme, assonance, or consonance? Is the rhyme patterned or random? What is the effect of the rhyme? Every line in the poem rhymes with at least two other lines, and the rhymes are all true rhyme: night-light-height-right-night, rain-lane-explain, beat-feet-street, and cry-by-sky. There is the further rhyme of night-light-height-right-night and beat-feet-street by consonance. The effect of the strong true rhyme in this poem is often to emphasize the images: night, rain, city light, city lane, the sound of feet, an unearthly height, and against the sky.

Does alliteration occur in the poem? Is the alliteration subtle or marked? What is the effect of that alliteration? A subtle random alliteration does occur in this poem. The alliteration of "cry/Came" has already been noted. Alliteration occurs most noticeably in "I have stood still and stopped the sound of feet," a pattern which contrasts significantly with the *k* sound at the beginning of "cry," in the next line. The effect of alliteration in this poem is primarily to make the texture of the language fluid and melodious.

What are the larger implications of the particular experiences which are described in the poem? Does the poem say anything about life in general? Insofar as the experience that the speaker undergoes is an experience which anyone could undergo, the poem is certainly universal. The significant point in the poem, however, is that the clock proclaims a time that is neither wrong nor right. The only answer that the universe gives, then, is a purely relativistic answer. There are no absolutes; there are no definitely universal statements. The night, then, is a metaphor for the uncertainty that the speaker feels when faced with relativism.

Is there any poetic irony in the poem? Is there anything that you as the reader can see that the speaker or the participants in the poem cannot see? The most obvious irony is that the clock, to which we look for guidance, which we expect to structure our lives, ultimately offers no guidance at all. The clock cannot tell us if the time is wrong or right; time is found to be useless as a basis for order.

How have your own attitudes affected your reaction to this poem? How are your attitudes involved in how you react to this poem? This is not a poem in which personal prejudices are apt to be greatly involved, except that someone who takes an absolutist view of the universe, someone who believes that universal statements can be made, is likely to reject the conclusion of the poem. Still, that person can participate in the experience with the night; it is on that experience that the poem centers.

With this much information at hand, a reader can intelligently assess *how* the poem works. The reader is prepared to say *why* the poem does or does not succeed for him. This is not to say that such a detailed analysis is necessary to read or enjoy the poem. Such analysis is only useful when a reader wants to criticize a poem, to discover how and why it works. The hope is, of course, that the reader of this book will have made the principles discussed here so much a part of his equipment for reading poems that he will not have to think separately of the various aspects of a poem as he reads; he will be simply an intelligent and sophisticated reader responding to poems.

NOTE: These questions are compiled from the "Questions for Study" in Part I.

This Systematic Approach to Poems is intended as a guide for the study of poems, as an organized approach to each poem.

I. The Nature of the Poem
   A. Would you like to have information about any matter discussed in the poem which is not given in the poem? What effect would such information have on your reaction to the poem?
   B. Do you like the poem? If you do, try to pinpoint the source of your delight. If you do not, try to pinpoint where the poem fails for you.

II. The Sensory Dimension
   A. Summarize the objective or literal content of the poem. For what emotion is this the objective correlative?
   B. What metaphors are developed in the poem?
   C. What images are developed in the poem? How effectively do these images evoke the concrete experience?
   D. Are you interested in the literal content of the poem? If so, try to pinpoint why. If not, try to pinpoint where the literal content fails.

III. The Formal Dimension
   A. The Rage for Order
      1. What does the selection of details reveal about the speaker? What is his attitude toward his subject matter?
      2. How much does the selection of details affect your reaction to the poem? What other details might have been included? What effect would other details have produced?
      3. How is the poem made to seem spontaneous? What in the poem produces the illusion of the random? If the poem does not have the illusion of the random, how does that affect your reaction to the poem?
   B. The Windows of Structure
      1. The Line
         a. Is the poem written in the accentual line, the syllabic line, the accentual-syllabic line, or the random line?
         b. If the line is accentual, what is the recurrent pattern of the number of accents in the line? If the line is syllabic, what is the recurrent pattern of the number of syllables in the line? If the line is accentual-syllabic, what is the recurrent pattern of the number of feet in the line and are those feet predominately iambic, trochaic, dactylic, or anapestic?
         c. Which lines have tension and how does that tension function?
      2. The Stanza
         a. Is there a fixed predetermined stanza form? If so, is this a traditional fixed form like the sonnet, villanelle, etc.? Are there any variations from the predetermined form?
         b. How are content and stanza form merged? Does the organization of the content complement the organization of the stanzas?

C. The Sounds of Structure
   1. Does rhyme occur in the poem? Is that rhyme true rhyme, assonance, or consonance? Is the rhyme patterned or random? What is the effect of the rhyme?
   2. Does alliteration occur in the poem? Is the alliteration subtle or marked? What is the effect of that alliteration?

IV. The Rational Dimension
   A. What are the larger implications of the particular experiences which are described in the poem? Does the poem say anything about life in general?
   B. Is there any poetic irony in the poem? Is there anything that you as the reader can see that the speaker or the participants in the poem cannot see?
   C. How have your own attitudes affected your reaction to this poem? How are your attitudes involved in how you react to this poem?

FOR THE INSTRUCTOR

Since this book has grown out of an attempt to find a textbook that would complement the approach that I use in the classroom, perhaps a word about that approach would be helpful. The teaching of the material included in Part I of this book has, it seems to me, one basic purpose—to provide the student with the apparatus he needs to explain his reactions to poems. This material, then, should be gotten through as quickly as possible, so that the class can proceed to its real business, discussing poems. The consideration of each chapter, therefore, is a two-part procedure:

> 1) Assign a chapter to read overnight (Chapter IV might need to be sub-divided), and ask the students when they come to class what parts of the chapter need clarification. Hopefully, these will be few.

> 2) Consider several poems from Part II in terms of the "Questions for Study" at the end of the chapter. This process can be continued until it is clear that the students understand the concepts introduced in that chapter. This step may stretch over more than one class period.

After all eight chapters have been studied in this manner, the class is ready simply to consider poems and to discover how well they work. As an aid to the teacher in planning step two of this process, I have indicated in the following outline some poems that I have found useful at various points in the study of poetry. I have included only 54 poems in this outline, believing that the majority of the poems should be left free and uncompromised by any classified listing for independent student analysis. The teacher is, of course, sure to find other poems that he would prefer to use at various points.

Chapter 1: The Nature of the Poem
   A Narrow Fellow in the Grass, page 162
   Dover Beach, page 156
   How One Winter Came in the Lake Region, page 176
   mr u will not be missed, page 221
   You, Andrew Marvell, page 219

The glossary and Part I have also been designed so that the teacher can, if he wishes, simply begin with poems and consider the material in Part I only as it is occasioned by the consideration of individual poems. What is important, finally, is not what pedagogical method the teacher chooses, but that he and his students study and enjoy studying the poems.

II

Poems for Study

SIR THOMAS WYATT

They Flee from Me, That Sometime Did Me Seek

They flee from me, that sometime did me seek,
   With naked foot stalking within my chamber:
Once have I seen them gentle, tame and meek,
   That now are wild, and do not once remember,
   That sometime they have put themselves in danger
To take bread at my hand; and now they range
Busily seeking in continual change.

Thankéd be Fortune, it hath been otherwise
   Twenty times better; but once especial,
In thin array, after a pleasant guise,
   When her loose gown did from her shoulders fall,
   And she me caught in her arms long and small,
And therewithal so sweetly did me kiss,
And softly said, "Dear heart, how like you this?"

It was no dream; for I lay broad awaking:
   But all is turn'd now, through my gentleness,
Into a bitter fashion of forsaking;
   And I have leave to go of her goodness;
   And she also to use new fangleness.
But since that I unkindly so am served:
How like you this, what hath she now deserved?

WILLIAM STEVENSON

Jolly Good Ale and Old

I cannot eat but little meat,
   My stomach is not good;
But sure I think that I can drink
   With him that wears a hood.
Though I go bare, take ye no care,
   I nothing am a-cold;
I stuff my skin so full within
   Of jolly good ale and old.
      Back and side go bare, go bare;
      Both foot and hand go cold;

But, belly, God send thee good ale enough,
    Whether it be new or old.

I love no roast but a nut-brown toast,
    And a crab laid in the fire;
A little bread shall do me stead;
    Much bread I not desire.
No frost nor snow, no wind, I trow,
    Can hurt me if I wold;
I am so wrapp'd and thoroughly lapp'd
    Of jolly good ale and old.
      Back and side go bare, go bare, &c.

And Tib, my wife, that as her life
    Loveth well good ale to seek,
Full oft drinks she till ye may see
    The tears run down her cheek:
Then doth she trowl to me the bowl
    Even as a maltworm should,
And saith, 'Sweetheart, I took my part
    Of this jolly good ale and old.'
      Back and side go bare, go bare, &c.

Now let them drink till they nod and wink,
    Even as good fellows should do;
They shall not miss to have that bliss
    Good ale doth bring men to;
And all poor souls that have scour'd bowls
    Or have them lustily troll'd,
God save the lives of them and their wives,
    Whether they be young or old.
      Back and side go bare, go bare;
      Both foot and hand go cold;
      But, belly, God send thee good ale enough,
      Whether it be new or old.

WILLIAM SHAKESPEARE

The Phœnix and the Turtle

Let the bird of loudest lay,
On the sole Arabian tree,

Herald sad and trumpet be,
To whose sound chaste wings obey.

But thou shrieking harbinger,
Foul precurrer of the fiend,
Augur of the fever's end,
To this troop come thou not near!

From this session interdict
Every fowl of tyrant wing,
Save the eagle, feather'd king:
Keep the obsequy so strict.

Let the priest in surplice white,
That defunctive music can,
Be the death-divining swan,
Lest the requiem lack his right.

And thou treble-dated crow,
That thy sable gender makest
With the breath thou givest and takest,
'Mongst our mourners shalt thou go.

Here the anthem doth commence:
Love and constancy is dead;
Phœnix and the turtle fled
In a mutual flame from hence.

So they loved, as love in twain
Had the essence but in one;
Two distincts, division none:
Number there in love was slain.

Hearts remote, yet not asunder;
Distance, and no space was seen
'Twixt this turtle and his queen:
But in them it were a wonder.

So between them love did shine,
That the turtle saw his right
Flaming in the phœnix' sight;
Either was the other's mine.

Property was thus appalled,
That the self was not the same;

Single nature's double name
Neither two nor one was called.

Reason, in itself confounded,
Saw division grow together,
To themselves yet either neither,
Simple were so well compounded,

That it cried, How true a twain
Seemeth this concordant one!
Love hath reason, reason none,
If what parts can so remain.

Whereupon it made this threne
To the phœnix and the dove,
Co-supremes and stars of love,
As chorus to their tragic scene.

THRENOS.

Beauty, truth, and rarity,
Grace in all simplicity,
Here enclosed in cinders lie.

Death is now the phœnix' nest;
And the turtle's loyal breast
To eternity doth rest,

Leaving no posterity:
'Twas not their infirmity,
It was married chastity.

Truth may seem, but cannot be:
Beauty brag, but 'tis not she;
Truth and beauty buried be.

To this urn let those repair
That are either true or fair;
For these dead birds sigh a prayer.

The Blossom

On a day—alack the day!—
Love, whose month is ever May,

Spied a blossom passing fair
Playing in the wanton air:
Through the velvet leaves the wind
All unseen 'gan passage find;
That the lover, sick to death,
Wish'd himself the heaven's breath.
Air, quoth he, thy cheeks may blow;
Air, would I might triumph so!
But, alack, my hand is sworn
Ne'er to pluck thee from thy thorn:
Vow, alack, for youth unmeet;
Youth so apt to pluck a sweet!
Do not call it sin in me
That I am forsworn for thee;
Thou for whom e'en Jove would swear
Juno but an Ethiop were;
And deny himself for Jove,
Turning mortal for thy love.

SONNETS

XVIII

Shall I compare thee to a summer's day?
Thou art more lovely and more temperate:
Rough winds do shake the darling buds of May,
And summer's lease hath all too short a date:
Sometime too hot the eye of heaven shines,
And often is his gold complexion dimm'd;
And every fair from fair sometime declines,
By chance or nature's changing course untrimm'd;
But thy eternal summer shall not fade
Nor lose possession of that fair thou owest;
Nor shall Death brag thou wander'st in his shade,
When in eternal lines to time thou growest:
   So long as men can breathe or eyes can see,
   So long lives this and this gives life to thee.

XXX

When to the sessions of sweet silent thought
I summon up remembrance of things past,

I sigh the lack of many a thing I sought,
And with old woes new wail my dear time's waste:
Then can I drown an eye, unused to flow,
For precious friends hid in death's dateless night,
And weep afresh love's long since cancell'd woe,
And moan the expense of many a vanish'd sight:
Then can I grieve at grievances foregone,
And heavily from woe to woe tell o'er
The sad account of fore-bemoanèd moan,
Which I new pay as if not paid before.
  But if the while I think of thee, dear friend,
  All losses are restored and sorrows end.

LV

Not marble, nor the gilded monuments
Of princes, shall outlive this powerful rhyme;
But you shall shine more bright in these contents
Than unswept stone besmear'd with sluttish time.
When wasteful war shall statues overturn,
And broils root out the work of masonry,
Nor Mars his sword nor war's quick fire shall burn
The living record of your memory.
'Gainst death and all-oblivious enmity
Shall you pace forth; your praise shall still find room
Even in the eyes of all posterity
That wear this world out to the ending doom.
  So, till the judgement that yourself arise,
  You live in this, and dwell in lovers' eyes.

SIR HENRY WOTTON

Upon the Death of Sir Albert Morton's Wife

He first deceased; she for a little tried
To live without him, liked it not, and died.

BEN JONSON

Simplex Munditiis

Still to be neat, still to be drest,
As you were going to a feast;

Still to be powder'd, still perfumed:
Lady, it is to be presumed,
Though art's hid causes are not found,
All is not sweet, all is not sound.

Give me a look, give me a face
That makes simplicity a grace;
Robes loosely flowing, hair as free:
Such sweet neglect more taketh me
Than all th' adulteries of art;
They strike mine eyes, but not my heart.

JOHN DONNE

Song

Go, and catch a falling star,
  Get with child a mandrake root,
Tell me, where all past years are,
  Or who cleft the Devil's foot,
Teach me to hear Mermaids singing,
  Or to keep off envy's stinging,
        And find
        What wind
Serves to advance an honest mind.

If thou be'st born to strange sights,
  Things invisible to see,
Ride ten thousand days and nights,
  Till age snow white hairs on thee,
Thou, when thou return'st, wilt tell me
All strange wonders that befell thee,
        And swear
        No where
Lives a woman true, and fair.

If thou find'st one, let me know,
  Such a Pilgrimage were sweet;
Yet do not, I would not go,
  Though at next door we might meet,
Though she were true, when you met her,

And last, till you write your letter,
        Yet she
        Will be
False, ere I come, to two, or three.

The Flea

Mark but this flea, and mark in this,
How little that which thou deny'st me is;
It suck'd me first, and now sucks thee,
And in this flea, our two bloods mingled be;
Thou know'st that this cannot be said
A sin, nor shame, nor loss of maidenhead,
    Yet this enjoys before it woo,
    And pamper'd swells with one blood made of two,
    And this, alas, is more than we would do.

Oh stay, three lives in one flea spare,
Where we almost, yea more than married are.
This flea is you and I, and this
Our marriage bed, and marriage temple is;
Though parents grudge, and you, we're met,
And cloistered in these living walls of jet.
    Though use make you apt to kill me,
    Let not to that, self murder added be,
    And sacrilege, three sins in killing three.

Cruel and sudden, hast thou since
Purpled thy nail, in blood of innocence?
Wherein could this flea guilty be,
Except in that drop which it suck'd from thee?
Yet thou triumph'st, and say'st that thou
Find'st not thyself, nor me the weaker now;
    'Tis true, then learn how false, fears be;
    Just so much honour, when thou yield'st to me,
    Will waste, as this flea's death took life from thee.

A Valediction: Forbidding Mourning

    As virtuous men pass mildly away,
      And whisper to their souls, to go,

Whilst some of their sad friends do say,
    The breath goes now, and some say, no:

So let us melt, and make no noise,
    No tear-floods, nor sigh-tempests move,
'Twere profanation of our joys
    To tell the laity our love.

Moving of th' earth brings harms and fears,
    Men reckon what it did and meant,
But trepidation of the spheres,
    Though greater far, is innocent.

Dull sublunary lovers' love
    (Whose soul is sense) cannot admit
Absence, because it doth remove
    Those things which elemented it.

But we by a love, so much refin'd,
    That ourselves know not what it is,
Inter-assurèd of the mind,
    Care less eyes, lips, and hands to miss.

Our two souls therefore, which are one,
    Though I must go, endure not yet
A breach, but an expansion,
    Like gold to aery thinness beat.

If they be two, they are two so
    As stiff twin compasses are two,
Thy soul the fixed foot, makes no show
    To move, but doth, if th' other do.

And though it in the centre sit,
    Yet when the other far doth roam,
It leans, and hearkens after it,
    And grows erect, as that comes home.

Such wilt thou be to me, who must
    Like th' other foot, obliquely run;
Thy firmness draws my circle just,
    And makes me end, where I begun.

The Ecstasy

Where, like a pillow on a bed,
    A pregnant bank swell'd up, to rest
The violet's reclining head,
    Sat we two, one another's best.
Our hands were firmly cemented
    With a fast balm, which thence did spring,
Our eye-beams twisted, and did thread
    Our eyes, upon one double string;
So t' intergraft our hands, as yet
    Was all the means to make us one,
And pictures in our eyes to get
    Was all our propagation.
As 'twixt two equal Armies, Fate
    Suspends uncertain victory,
Our souls, (which to advance their state,
    Were gone out,) hung 'twixt her, and me.
And whilst our souls negotiate there,
    We like sepulchral statues lay;
All day, the same our postures were,
    And we said nothing, all the day.
If any, so by love refin'd,
    That he soul's language understood,
And by good love were grown all mind,
    Within convenient distance stood,
He (though he knew not which soul spake,
    Because both meant, both spake the same)
Might thence a new concoction take,
    And part far purer than he came.
This Ecstasy doth unperplex
    (We said) and tell us what we love,
We see by this, it was not sex,
    We see, we saw not what did move:
But as all several souls contain
    Mixture of things, they know not what,
Love these mix'd souls doth mix again,
    And makes both one, each this and that.
A single violet transplant,
    The strength, the colour, and the size,
(All which before was poor, and scant,)
    Redoubles still, and multiplies.
When love, with one another so
    Interinanimates two souls,

That abler soul, which thence doth flow,
  Defects of loneliness controls.
We then, who are this new soul, know,
  Of what we are compos'd, and made,
For, th' Atomies of which we grow,
  Are souls, whom no change can invade.
But O alas, so long, so far
  Our bodies why do we forbear?
They are ours, though they are not we, We are
  The intelligences, they the spheres.
We owe them thanks, because they thus,
  Did us, to us, at first convey,
Yielded their forces, sense, to us,
  Nor are dross to us, but allay.
On man heaven's influence works not so,
  But that it first imprints the air,
So soul into the soul may flow,
  Though it to body first repair.
As our blood labours to beget
  Spirits, as like souls as it can,
Because such fingers need to knit
  That subtle knot, which makes us man:
So must pure lovers' souls descend
  T' affections, and to faculties,
Which sense may reach and apprehend,
  Else a great Prince in prison lies.
To our bodies turn we then, that so
  Weak men on love reveal'd may look;
Love's mysteries in souls do grow,
  But yet the body is his book,
And if some lover, such as we,
  Have heard this dialogue of one,
Let him still mark us, he shall see
  Small change, when we're to bodies gone.

At the Round Earth's Imagin'd Corners, Blow

At the round earth's imagin'd corners, blow
Your trumpets, Angels, and arise, arise
From death, you numberless infinities
Of souls, and to your scatter'd bodies go,
All whom the flood did, and fire shall o'erthrow,
All whom war, dearth, age, agues, tyrannies,

Despair, law, chance, hath slain, and you whose eyes,
Shall behold God, and never taste death's woe.
But let them sleep, Lord, and me mourn a space,
For, if above all these, my sins abound,
'Tis late to ask abundance of Thy grace,
When we are there; here on this lowly ground,
Teach me how to repent; for that's as good
As if Thou hadst seal'd my pardon, with Thy blood.

Death Be Not Proud, though Some Have Called Thee

Death be not proud, though some have callèd thee
Mighty and dreadful, for, thou art not so,
For, those, whom thou think'st, thou dost overthrow,
Die not, poor death, nor yet canst thou kill me.
From rest and sleep, which but thy pictures be,
Much pleasure, then from thee, much more must flow,
And soonest our best men with thee do go,
Rest of their bones, and soul's delivery.
Thou art slave to Fate, Chance, kings, and desperate men,
And dost with poison, war, and sickness dwell,
And poppy, or charms can make us sleep as well,
And better than thy stroke; why swell'st thou then?
One short sleep past, we wake eternally,
And death shall be no more; death, thou shalt die.

Batter My Heart, Three-Person'd God; for, You

Batter my heart, three-person'd God; for, you
As yet but knock, breathe, shine, and seek to mend;
That I may rise, and stand, o'erthrow me, and bend
Your force, to break, blow, burn and make me new.
I, like an usurp'd town, to another due,
Labour to admit you, but Oh, to no end,
Reason your viceroy in me, me should defend,
But is captiv'd, and proves weak or untrue.
Yet dearly I love you, and would be loved fain,
But am betroth'd unto your enemy:
Divorce me, untie, or break that knot again,
Take me to you, imprison me, for I

Except you enthral me, never shall be free,
Nor ever chaste, except you ravish me.

A Hymn to God the Father

I

Wilt Thou forgive that sin where I begun,
  Which is my sin, though it were done before?
Wilt Thou forgive that sin, through which I run,
  And do run still: though still I do deplore?
    When Thou hast done, Thou hast not done,
      For, I have more.

II

Wilt Thou forgive that sin by which I have won
  Others to sin? and, made my sin their door?
Wilt Thou forgive that sin which I did shun
  A year, or two: but wallowed in, a score?
    When Thou hast done, Thou hast not done,
      For I have more.

III

I have a sin of fear, that when I have spun
  My last thread, I shall perish on the shore;
Swear by Thyself, that at my death Thy son
  Shall shine as He shines now, and heretofore;
    And, having done that, Thou hast done,
      I fear no more.

Hymn to God My God, in My Sickness

Since I am coming to that Holy room,
  Where, with thy Quire of Saints for evermore,
I shall be made thy Music; as I come
  I tune the Instrument here at the door,
  And what I must do then, think here before.

Whilst my Physicians by their love are grown
  Cosmographers, and I their Map, who lie
Flat on this bed, that by them may be shown
  That this is my South-west discovery
  Per fretum febris, by these straits to die,

I joy, that in these straits, I see my West;
  For, though their currents yield return to none,
What shall my West hurt me? As West and East
  In all flat Maps (and I am one) are one,
  So death doth touch the Resurrection.

Is the Pacific Sea my home? Or are
  The Eastern riches? Is *Jerusalem?*
Anyan, and *Magellan,* and *Gibraltar,*
  All straits, and none but straits, are ways to them,
  Whether where *Japhet* dwelt, or *Cham,* or *Shem.*

We think that *Paradise* and *Calvary,*
  Christ's Cross, and *Adam's* tree, stood in one place;
Look Lord, and find both *Adams* met in me;
  As the first *Adam's* sweat surrounds my face,
  May the last *Adam's* blood my soul embrace.

So, in His purple wrapp'd receive me Lord,
  By these His thorns give me His other Crown;
And as to others' souls I preach'd Thy word,
  Be this my Text, my Sermon to mine own,
  Therefore that He may raise the Lord throws down.

ROBERT HERRICK

Delight in Disorder

A sweet disorder in the dress
Kindles in clothes a wantonness:
A lawn about the shoulders thrown
Into a fine distraction:
An erring lace, which here and there
Enthrals the crimson stomacher:
A cuff neglectful, and thereby
Ribbands to flow confusedly:
A winning wave, deserving note,
In the tempestuous petticoat:
A careless shoe-string, in whose tie
I see a wild civility:
Do more bewitch me than when art
Is too precise in every part.

Upon Julia's Clothes

When as in silks my Julia goes,
Then, then, methinks, how sweetly flows
The liquefaction of her clothes!

Next, when I cast mine eyes and see
That brave vibration each way free,
—O how that glittering taketh me!

FRANCIS QUARLES

A Divine Rapture

E'en like two little bank-dividing brooks,
  That wash the pebbles with their wanton streams,
And having ranged and search'd a thousand nooks,
  Meet both at length in silver-breasted Thames,
    Where in a greater current they conjoin:
So I my Best-belovèd's am; so He is mine.

E'en so we met; and after long pursuit,
  E'en so we joined; we both became entire;
No need for either to renew a suit,
  For I was flax, and He was flames of fire:
    Our firm-united souls did more than twine;
So I my Best-belovèd's am; so He is mine.

If all those glittering Monarchs, that command
  The servile quarters of this earthly ball,
Should tender in exchange their shares of land,
  I would not change my fortunes for them all:
    Their wealth is but a counter to my coin:
The world's but theirs; but my Belovèd's mine.

ANNE BRADSTREET

Upon the Burning of Our House

July 10th, 1666

In silent night when rest I took,
For sorrow near I did not look,

I waken'd was with thund'ring noise
And piteous shrieks of dreadful voice.
That fearful sound of fire and fire,
Let no man know is my desire.

I, starting up, the light did spy,
And to my God my heart did cry
To strengthen me in my distress
And not to leave me succorless.
Then coming out beheld a space,
The flame consume my dwelling place.

And, when I could no longer look,
I blest his Name that gave and took,
That laid my goods now in the dust:
Yea so it was, and so 'twas just.
It was his own: it was not mine;
Far be it that I should repine.

He might of all justly bereft,
But yet sufficient for us left.
When by the ruins oft I past,
My sorrowing eyes aside did cast,
And here and there the places spy
Where oft I sat, and long did lie.

Here stood that trunk, and there that chest;
There lay that store I counted best:
My pleasant things in ashes lie,
And them behold no more shall I.
Under thy roof no guest shall sit,
Nor at thy table eat a bit.

No pleasant tale shall e'er be told,
Nor things recounted done of old.
No candle e'er shall shine in thee,
Nor bridegroom's voice ere heard shall be.
In silence ever shalt thou lie;
Adieu, adieu; all's vanity.

Then straight I gin my heart to chide,
And did thy wealth on earth abide?
Didst fix thy hope on mould'ring dust,
The arm of flesh didst make thy trust?

Raise up thy thoughts above the sky
That dunghill mists away may fly.

Thou hast an house on high erect,
Fram'd by that mighty Architect,
With glory richly furnished,
Stands permanent tho' this be fled.
It's purchased, and paid for too
By him who hath enough to do.

A prize so vast as is unknown,
Yet, by his gift, is made thine own.
There's wealth enough, I need no more;
Farewell my pelf, farewell my store.
The world no longer let me love,
My hope and treasure lies above.

ABRAHAM COWLEY

Drinking

The thirsty earth soaks up the rain,
And drinks and gapes for drink again;
The plants suck in the earth, and are
With constant drinking fresh and fair;
The sea itself (which one would think
Should have but little need of drink)
Drinks twice ten thousand rivers up,
So fill'd that they o'erflow the cup.
The busy Sun (and one would guess
By 's drunken fiery face no less)
Drinks up the sea, and when he's done,
The Moon and Stars drink up the Sun:
They drink and dance by their own light,
They drink and revel all the night:
Nothing in Nature's sober found,
But an eternal health goes round.
Fill up the bowl, then, fill it high,
Fill all the glasses there—for why
Should every creature drink but I?
Why, man of morals, tell me why?

ANDREW MARVELL

To His Coy Mistress

Had we but world enough, and time,
This coyness, Lady, were no crime.
We would sit down and think which way
To walk and pass our long love's day.
Thou by the Indian Ganges' side
Shouldst rubies find: I by the tide
Of Humber would complain. I would
Love you ten years before the Flood,
And you should, if you please, refuse
Till the conversion of the Jews.
My vegetable love should grow
Vaster than empires, and more slow;
An hundred years should go to praise
Thine eyes and on thy forehead gaze;
Two hundred to adore each breast;
But thirty thousand to the rest;
An age at least to every part,
And the last age should show your heart;
For, Lady, you deserve this state,
Nor would I love at lower rate.
    But at my back I always hear
Time's wingèd chariot hurrying near;
And yonder all before us lie
Deserts of vast eternity.
Thy beauty shall no more be found,
Nor, in thy marble vault, shall sound
My echoing song: then worms shall try
That long preserved virginity,
And your quaint honour turn to dust,
And into ashes all my lust:
The grave's a fine and private place,
But none, I think, do there embrace.
    Now therefore, while the youthful hue
Sits on thy skin like morning dew,
And while thy willing soul transpires
At every pore with instant fires,
Now let us sport us while we may,
And now, like amorous birds of prey,
Rather at once our time devour
Than languish in his slow-chapt power.

Let us roll all our strength and all
Our sweetness up into one ball,
And tear our pleasures with rough strife
Thorough the iron gates of life:
Thus, though we cannot make our sun
Stand still, yet we will make him run.

EDWARD TAYLOR

Housewifery

Make me, O Lord, thy spinning wheel complete;
  Thy holy word my distaff make for me.
Make mine affections thy swift flyers neat,
  And make my soul thy holy spool to be.
  My conversation make to be thy reel,
  And reel the yarn thereon spun of thy wheel.

Make me thy loom then, knit therein this twine:
  And make thy holy spirit, Lord, wind quills:
Then weave the web thyself. The yarn is fine.
  Thine ordinances make my fulling mills.
  Then dye the same in heavenly colors choice,
  All pinked with varnished flowers of paradise.

Then clothe therewith mine understanding, will,
  Affections, judgment, conscience, memory;
My words and actions, that their shine may fill
  My ways with glory and thee glorify.
  Then mine apparel shall display before ye
  That I am clothed in holy robes for glory.

WILLIAM OLDYS

On a Fly Drinking out of His Cup

Busy, curious, thirsty fly!
Drink with me and drink as I:
Freely welcome to my cup,
Couldst thou sip and sip it up:

Make the most of life you may,
Life is short and wears away.

Both alike are mine and thine
Hastening quick to their decline:
Thine's a summer, mine's no more,
Though repeated to threescore.
Threescore summers, when they're gone,
Will appear as short as one!

THOMAS GRAY

Elegy Written in a Country Churchyard

The curfew tolls the knell of parting day,
  The lowing herd winds slowly o'er the lea,
The ploughman homeward plods his weary way,
  And leaves the world to darkness and to me.

Now fades the glimmering landscape on the sight,
  And all the air a solemn stillness holds,
Save where the beetle wheels his droning flight,
  And drowsy tinklings lull the distant folds:

Save that from yonder ivy-mantled tow'r,
  The moping owl does to the moon complain
Of such as, wand'ring near her secret bow'r,
  Molest her ancient solitary reign.

Beneath those rugged elms, that yew tree's shade,
  Where heaves the turf in many a mould'ring heap,
Each in his narrow cell for ever laid,
  The rude forefathers of the hamlet sleep.

The breezy call of incense-breathing morn,
  The swallow twitt'ring from the straw-built shed,
The cock's shrill clarion, or the echoing horn,
  No more shall rouse them from their lowly bed.

For them no more the blazing hearth shall burn,
  Or busy housewife ply her evening care;
No children run to lisp their sire's return,
  Or climb his knees the envied kiss to share.

Oft did the harvest to their sickle yield,
    Their furrow oft the stubborn glebe has broke:
How jocund did they drive their team afield!
    How bow'd the woods beneath their sturdy stroke!

Let not ambition mock their useful toil,
    Their homely joys, and destiny obscure;
Nor grandeur hear with a disdainful smile
    The short and simple annals of the poor.

The boast of heraldry, the pomp of pow'r,
    And all that beauty, all that wealth e'er gave,
Await alike th' inevitable hour.
    The paths of glory lead but to the grave.

Nor you, ye proud, impute to these the fault,
    If memory o'er their tomb no trophies raise,
Where through the long-drawn aisle and fretted vault
    The pealing anthem swells the note of praise.

Can storied urn, or animated bust,
    Back to its mansion call the fleeting breath?
Can honour's voice provoke the silent dust,
    Or flatt'ry soothe the dull cold ear of death?

Perhaps in this neglected spot is laid
    Some heart once pregnant with celestial fire;
Hands, that the rod of empire might have sway'd,
    Or waked to ecstasy the living lyre:

But Knowledge to their eyes her ample page
    Rich with the spoils of time did ne'er unroll;
Chill penury repress'd their noble rage,
    And froze the genial current of the soul.

Full many a gem of purest ray serene
    The dark unfathom'd caves of ocean bear:
Full many a flower is born to blush unseen,
    And waste its sweetness on the desert air.

Some village-Hampden, that, with dauntless breast,
    The little tyrant of his fields withstood,
Some mute inglorious Milton here may rest,
    Some Cromwell guiltless of his country's blood.

Th' applause of list'ning senates to command,
    The threats of pain and ruin to despise,
To scatter plenty o'er a smiling land,
    And read their history in a nation's eyes,

Their lot forbade: nor circumscribed alone
    Their growing virtues, but their crimes confined;
Forbade to wade through slaughter to a throne,
    And shut the gates of mercy on mankind,

The struggling pangs of conscious truth to hide,
    To quench the blushes of ingenuous shame,
Or heap the shrine of luxury and pride
    With incense kindled at the Muse's flame.

Far from the madding crowd's ignoble strife,
    Their sober wishes never learn'd to stray;
Along the cool sequester'd vale of life
    They kept the noiseless tenor of their way.

Yet ev'n these bones from insult to protect
    Some frail memorial still erected nigh,
With uncouth rhymes and shapeless sculpture deck'd,
    Implores the passing tribute of a sigh.

Their name, their years, spelt by th' unletter'd Muse,
    The place of fame and elegy supply:
And many a holy text around she strews,
    That teach the rustic moralist to die.

For who, to dumb forgetfulness a prey,
    This pleasing anxious being e'er resign'd,
Left the warm precincts of the cheerful day,
    Nor cast one longing ling'ring look behind?

On some fond breast the parting soul relies,
    Some pious drops the closing eye requires;
E'en from the tomb the voice of nature cries,
    E'en in our ashes live their wonted fires.

For thee, who, mindful of th' unhonour'd dead,
    Dost in these lines their artless tale relate;
If chance, by lonely contemplation led,
    Some kindred spirit shall inquire thy fate,—

Haply some hoary-headed swain may say,
  "Oft have we seen him at the peep of dawn
Brushing with hasty steps the dews away,
  To meet the sun upon the upland lawn:

"There at the foot of yonder nodding beech,
  That wreathes its old fantastic roots so high,
His listless length at noontide would he stretch,
  And pore upon the brook that babbles by.

"Hard by yon wood, now smiling as in scorn,
  Mutt'ring his wayward fancies he would rove;
Now drooping, woful-wan, like one forlorn,
  Or crazed with care, or cross'd in hopeless love.

"One morn I miss'd him on the 'custom'd hill,
  Along the heath, and near his fav'rite tree;
Another came; nor yet beside the rill,
  Nor up the lawn, nor at the wood was he:

"The next, with dirges due in sad array,
  Slow through the church-way path we saw him borne:—
Approach and read (for thou canst read) the lay
  Graved on the stone beneath yon aged thorn."

THE EPITAPH

Here rests his head upon the lap of earth
  A youth to fortune and to fame unknown:
Fair Science frown'd not on his humble birth,
  And Melancholy mark'd him for her own.

Large was his bounty, and his soul sincere,
  Heaven did a recompense as largely send:
He gave to mis'ry (all he had) a tear,
  He gain'd from heav'n ('twas all he wish'd) a friend.

No farther seek his merits to disclose,
  Or draw his frailties from their dread abode,
(There they alike in trembling hope repose,)
  The bosom of his Father and his God.

On the Death of a Favourite Cat,

DROWNED IN A TUB OF GOLD FISHES

'Twas on a lofty vase's side,
Where China's gayest art had dyed

The azure flowers that blow;
Demurest of the tabby kind,
The pensive Selima, reclined,
  Gazed on the lake below.

Her conscious tail her joy declared:
The fair round face, the snowy beard,
  The velvet of her paws,
Her coat, that with the tortoise vies,
Her ears of jet, and emerald eyes,
  She saw; and purr'd applause.

Still had she gazed; but 'midst the tide
Two angel forms were seen to glide,
  The Genii of the stream:
Their scaly armour's Tyrian hue
Through richest purple to the view
  Betray'd a golden gleam.

The hapless nymph with wonder saw:
A whisker first, and then a claw,
  With many an ardent wish,
She stretch'd, in vain, to reach the prize.
What female heart can gold despise?
  What Cat's averse to fish?

Presumptuous maid! with looks intent
Again she stretch'd, again she bent,
  Nor knew the gulf between.
(Malignant Fate sat by, and smiled.)
The slipp'ry verge her feet beguiled,
  She tumbled headlong in.

Eight times emerging from the flood,
She mew'd to ev'ry wat'ry God,
  Some speedy aid to send.
No Dolphin came, no Nereid stirr'd:
Nor cruel Tom, nor Susan heard.
  A fav'rite has no friend!

From hence, ye beauties, undeceived,
Know, one false step is ne'er retrieved,
  And be with caution bold.
Not all that tempts your wand'ring eyes
And heedless hearts is lawful prize,
  Nor all, that glisters, gold.

The Castaway

Obscurest night involved the sky,
   The Atlantic billows roared,
When such a destined wretch as I,
   Washed headlong from on board,
Of friends, of hope, of all bereft,
His floating home for ever left.

No braver chief could Albion boast
   Than he with whom he went,
Nor ever ship left Albion's coast
   With warmer wishes sent.
He loved them both, but both in vain,
Nor him beheld, nor her again.

Not long beneath the whelming brine,
   Expert to swim, he lay;
Nor soon he felt his strength decline,
   Or courage die away:
But waged with Death a lasting strife,
Supported by despair of life.

He shouted; nor his friends had failed
   To check the vessel's course,
But so the furious blast prevailed,
   That, pitiless perforce,
They left their outcast mate behind,
And scudded still before the wind.

Some succour yet they could afford;
   And, such as storms allow,
The cask, the coop, the floated cord,
   Delayed not to bestow:
But he, they knew, nor ship nor shore,
Whate'er they gave, should visit more.

Nor, cruel as it seemed, could he
   Their haste himself condemn,
Aware that flight, in such a sea,
   Alone could rescue them:
Yet bitter felt it still to die
Deserted, and his friends so nigh.

He long survives, who lives an hour
   In ocean, self-upheld:
And so long he, with unspent power,
   His destiny repelled:
And ever, as the minutes flew,
Entreated "Help!" or cried—"Adieu!"

At length, his transient respite past,
   His comrades, who before
Had heard his voice in every blast,
   Could catch the sound no more:
For then, by toil subdued, he drank
The stifling wave, and then he sank.

No poet wept him; but the page
   Of narrative sincere,
That tells his name, his worth, his age,
   Is wet with Anson's tear:
And tears by bards or heroes shed
Alike immortalize the dead.

I therefore purpose not, or dream,
   Descanting on his fate,
To give the melancholy theme
   A more enduring date:
But misery still delights to trace
Its semblance in another's case.

No voice divine the storm allayed,
   No light propitious shone:
When, snatched from all effectual aid,
   We perished, each alone:
But I beneath a rougher sea,
And whelmed in deeper gulfs than he.

PHILIP FRENEAU

On a Honey Bee

DRINKING FROM A GLASS OF WINE AND DROWNED THEREIN

Thou, born to sip the lake or spring,
   Or quaff the waters of the stream,

Why hither come, on vagrant wing?—
   Does Bacchus tempting seem—
      Did he for you this glass prepare?—
      Will I admit you to a share?

Did storms harass or foes perplex,
   Did wasps or king-birds bring dismay—
Did wars distress, or labors vex,
   Or did you miss your way?—
      A better seat you could not take
      Than on the margin of this lake.

Welcome!—I hail you to my glass:
   All welcome, here, you find;
Here, let the cloud of trouble pass,
   Here, be all care resigned.—
      This fluid never fails to please,
      And drown the griefs of men or bees.

What forced you here we cannot know,
   And you will scarcely tell—
But cheery we would have you go
   And bid a glad farewell:
      On lighter wings we bid you fly,
      Your dart will now all foes defy.

Yet take not, oh! too deep a drink,
   And in this ocean die;
Here bigger bees than you might sink,
   Even bees full six feet high.
      Like Pharaoh, then, you would be said
      To perish in a sea of red.

Do as you please, your will is mine;
   Enjoy it without fear—
And your grave will be this glass of wine,
   Your epitaph—a tear;
      Go, take your seat on Charon's boat,
      We'll tell the hive, you died afloat.

WILLIAM BLAKE

The Little Black Boy

My mother bore me in the southern wild,
And I am black, but O! my soul is white;

White as an angel is the English child,
But I am black, as if bereav'd of light.

My mother taught me underneath a tree,
And sitting down before the heat of day,
She took me on her lap and kissèd me,
And pointing to the east, began to say:

"Look on the rising sun: there God does live,
And gives his light, and gives his heat away;
And flowers and trees and beasts and man receive
Comfort in morning, joy in the noonday.

"And we are put on earth a little space,
That we may learn to bear the beams of love;
And these black bodies and this sunburnt face
Is but a cloud, and like a shady grove.

"For when our souls have learn'd that heat to bear,
The cloud will vanish; we shall hear his voice,
Saying: 'Come out from the grove, my love & care,
And round my golden tent like lambs rejoice.'"

Thus did my mother say, and kissèd me;
And thus I say to little English boy:
When I from black and he from white cloud free,
And round the tent of God like lambs we joy,

I'll shade him from the heat, till he can bear
To lean in joy upon our father's knee;
And then I'll stand and stroke his silver hair,
And be like him, and he will then love me.

The Chimney Sweeper

A little black thing among the snow,
Crying ''weep! 'weep!' in notes of woe!
"Where are thy father & mother? say?"
"They are both gone up to the church to pray.

"Because I was happy upon the heath,
And smil'd among the winter's snow,
They clothed me in the clothes of death,
And taught me to sing the notes of woe.

"And because I am happy & dance & sing,
They think they have done me no injury,
And are gone to praise God & his Priest & King,
Who make up a heaven of our misery."

The Little Vagabond

Dear Mother, dear Mother, the Church is cold,
But the Ale-house is healthy & pleasant & warm;
Besides I can tell where I am used well,
Such usage in Heaven will never do well.

But if at the Church they would give us some Ale,
And a pleasant fire our souls to regale,
We'd sing and we'd pray all the live-long day,
Nor ever once wish from the Church to stray.

Then the Parson might preach, & drink, & sing,
And we'd be as happy as birds in the spring;
And modest Dame Lurch, who is always at Church,
Would not have bandy children, nor fasting, nor birch.

And God, like a father rejoicing to see
His children as pleasant and happy as he,
Would have no more quarrel with the Devil or the
    Barrel,
But kiss him, & give him both drink and apparel.

I Saw a Chapel All of Gold

I saw a chapel all of gold
That none did dare to enter in,
And many weeping stood without,
Weeping, mourning, worshipping.

I saw a serpent rise between
The white pillars of the door,
And he forc'd & forc'd & forc'd,
Down the golden hinges tore.

And along the pavement sweet,
Set with pearls & rubies bright,

All his slimy length he drew,
Till upon the altar white

Vomiting his poison out
On the bread & on the wine.
So I turn'd into a sty
And laid me down among the swine.

WILLIAM WORDSWORTH

The Solitary Reaper

Behold her, single in the field,
Yon solitary Highland Lass!
Reaping and singing by herself;
Stop here, or gently pass!
Alone she cuts and binds the grain,
And sings a melancholy strain;
O listen! for the Vale profound
Is overflowing with the sound.

No Nightingale did ever chaunt
More welcome notes to weary bands
Of travellers in some shady haunt,
Among Arabian sands:
A voice so thrilling ne'er was heard
In spring-time from the Cuckoo-bird,
Breaking the silence of the seas
Among the farthest Hebrides.

Will no one tell me what she sings?—
Perhaps the plaintive numbers flow
For old, unhappy, far-off things,
And battles long ago:
Or is it some more humble lay,
Familiar matter of to-day?
Some natural sorrow, loss, or pain,
That has been, and may be again?

Whate'er the theme, the Maiden sang
As if her song could have no ending:
I saw her singing at her work,
And o'er the sickle bending;—

I listened, motionless and still;
And, as I mounted up the hill,
The music in my heart I bore,
Long after it was heard no more.

SAMUEL TAYLOR COLERIDGE

Kubla Khan

OR, A VISION IN A DREAM

A FRAGMENT

In Xanadu did Kubla Khan
A stately pleasure-dome decree:
Where Alph, the sacred river, ran
Through caverns measureless to man
    Down to a sunless sea.
So twice five miles of fertile ground
With walls and towers were girdled round:
And here were gardens bright with sinuous rills,
Where blossomed many an incense-bearing tree;
And here were forests ancient as the hills,
Enfolding sunny spots of greenery.

But oh! that deep romantic chasm which slanted
Down the green hill athwart a cedarn cover!
A savage place! as holy and enchanted
As e'er beneath a waning moon was haunted
By woman wailing for her demon-lover!
And from this chasm, with ceaseless turmoil seething,
As if this earth in fast thick pants were breathing,
A mighty fountain momently was forced:
Amid whose swift half-intermitted burst
Huge fragments vaulted like rebounding hail,
Or chaffy grain beneath the thresher's flail:
And 'mid these dancing rocks at once and ever
It flung up momently the sacred river.
Five miles meandering with a mazy motion
Through wood and dale the sacred river ran,
Then reached the caverns measureless to man,
And sank in tumult to a lifeless ocean:
And 'mid this tumult Kubla heard from far
Ancestral voices prophesying war!

The shadow of the dome of pleasure
Floated midway on the waves;
Where was heard the mingled measure
From the fountain and the caves.
It was a miracle of rare device,
A sunny pleasure-dome with caves of ice!

A damsel with a dulcimer
In a vision once I saw:
It was an Abyssinian maid,
And on her dulcimer she played,
Singing of Mount Abora.
Could I revive with me
Her symphony and song,
To such a deep delight 'twould win me,
That with music loud and long,
I would build that dome in air,
That sunny dome! those caves of ice!
And all who heard should see them there,
And all should cry, Beware! Beware!
His flashing eyes, his floating hair!
Weave a circle round him thrice,
And close your eyes with holy dread,
For he on honey-dew hath fed,
And drunk the milk of Paradise.

PERCY BYSSHE SHELLEY

The Moon

1. THE WANING MOON

And like a dying lady, lean and pale,
Who totters forth, wrapt in a gauzy veil,
From her dim chamber, led by the insane
And feeble wanderings of her fading brain,
The moon arose up on the murky earth,
A white and shapeless mass.

2. TO THE MOON
I

Art thou pale for weariness
Of climbing heaven, and gazing on the earth,

Wandering companionless
Among the stars that have a different birth,—
And ever-changing, like a joyless eye
That finds no object worth its constancy?

II

Thou chosen sister of the Spirit,
That gazes on thee till in thee it pities.

3. THE SONG OF THE MOON

As a violet's gentle eye
Gazes on the azure sky
Until its hue grows like what it beholds;
As a gray and empty mist
Lies like solid amethyst
Over the western mountain it enfolds,
When the sunset sleeps

Upon its snow;
As a strain of sweetest sound
Wraps itself the wind around
Until the voiceless wind be music too;
As aught dark, vain, and dull,
Basking in what is beautiful,
Is full of light and love—

Ozymandias

I met a traveller from an antique land
Who said: Two vast and trunkless legs of stone
Stand in the desert . . . Near them, on the sand,
Half sunk, a shattered visage lies, whose frown,
And wrinkled lip, and sneer of cold command,
Tell that its sculptor well those passions read
Which yet survive, stamped on these lifeless things,
The hand that mocked them, and the heart that fed:
And on the pedestal these words appear:
'My name is Ozymandias, king of kings:
Look on my works, ye Mighty, and despair!'
Nothing beside remains. Round the decay
Of that colossal wreck, boundless and bare
The lone and level sands stretch far away.

Old Nick in Sorel

Old Nick took a fancy, as many men tell,
To come for a winter to live in Sorel.
Yet the snow fell so deep as he came in his sleigh,
That his fingers and toes were frost-nipt on the way.

In truth, saith the demon, who'd ever suppose,
I must go back again with the loss of all those;
In either extreme, sure it matters me not,
If I freeze upon earth or at home I'm too hot;

So he put back his sleigh, for he thought it amiss,
His clime to compare to a climate like this;
And now 'tis resolved that this frightful new-comer
Will winter in hell and be here in the summer.

WILLIAM CULLEN BRYANT

To a Waterfowl

Whither, midst falling dew,
While glow the heavens with the last steps of day,
Far, through their rosy depths, dost thou pursue
Thy solitary way?

Vainly the fowler's eye
Might mark thy distant flight to do thee wrong,
As, darkly painted on the crimson sky,
Thy figure floats along.

Seek'st thou the plashy brink
Of weedy lake, or marge of river wide,
Or where the rocking billows rise and sink
On the chafed ocean-side?

There is a Power whose care
Teaches thy way along that pathless coast,—
The desert and illimitable air,—
Lone wandering, but not lost.

All day thy wings have fanned
At that far height, the cold, thin atmosphere,
Yet stoop not, weary, to the welcome land,
    Though the dark night is near.

And soon that toil shall end;
Soon shalt thou find a summer home, and rest,
And scream among thy fellows; reeds shall bend
    Soon, o'er thy sheltered nest.

Thou'rt gone, the abyss of heaven
Hath swallowed up thy form; yet, on my heart
Deeply hath sunk the lesson thou hast given,
    And shall not soon depart.

He who, from zone to zone,
Guides through the boundless sky thy certain flight,
In the long way that I must tread alone,
    Will lead my steps aright.

JOHN KEATS

To Autumn

1

Season of mists and mellow fruitfulness,
    Close bosom-friend of the maturing sun;
Conspiring with him how to load and bless
    With fruit the vines that round the thatch-eves run;
To bend with apples the moss'd cottage-trees,
    And fill all fruit with ripeness to the core;
      To swell the gourd, and plump the hazel shells
With a sweet kernel; to set budding more,
    And still more, later flowers for the bees,
    Until they think warm days will never cease,
      For Summer has o'er-brimm'd their clammy cells.

2

Who hath not seen thee oft amid thy store?
    Sometimes whoever seeks abroad may find
Thee sitting careless on a granary floor,
    Thy hair soft-lifted by the winnowing wind;
Or on a half-reap'd furrow sound asleep,

Drows'd with the fume of poppies, while thy hook
    Spares the next swath and all its twined flowers:
And sometimes like a gleaner thou dost keep
   Steady thy laden head across a brook;
   Or by a cyder-press, with patient look,
    Thou watchest the last oozings hours by hours.

3

Where are the songs of Spring? Ay, where are they?
   Think not of them, thou hast thy music too,—
While barred clouds bloom the soft-dying day,
   And touch the stubble-plains with rosy hue;
Then in a wailful choir the small gnats mourn
   Among the river shallows, borne aloft
    Or sinking as the light wind lives or dies;
And full-grown lambs loud bleat from hilly bourn;
   Hedge-crickets sing; and now with treble soft
The red-breast whistles from a garden-croft;
   And gathering swallows twitter in the skies.

To Sleep

O soft embalmer of the still midnight,
   Shutting, with careful fingers and benign,
Our gloom-pleas'd eyes, embower'd from the light,
   Enshaded in forgetfulness divine;
O soothest Sleep! if so it please thee, close,
   In midst of this thine hymn, my willing eyes,
Or wait the amen, ere thy poppy throws
   Around my bed its lulling charities;
   Then save me, or the passed day will shine
Upon my pillow, breeding many woes;
   Save me from curious conscience, that still lords
Its strength for darkness, burrowing like a mole;
   Turn the key deftly in the oiled wards,
And seal the hushed casket of my soul.

THOMAS HOOD

Silence

There is a silence where hath been no sound,
There is a silence where no sound may be,

In the cold grave—under the deep, deep sea,
Or in wide desert where no life is found,
Which hath been mute, and still must sleep profound;
No voice is hushed—no life treads silently,
But clouds and cloudy shadows wander free,
That never spoke, over the idle ground:
But in green ruins, in the desolate walls
Of antique palaces, where Man hath been,
Though the dun fox, or wild hyena calls,
And owls, that flit continually between,
Shriek to the echo, and the low winds moan,
There the true Silence is, self-conscious and alone.

RALPH WALDO EMERSON

The Snow-Storm

Announced by all the trumpets of the sky,
Arrives the snow, and, driving o'er the fields,
Seems nowhere to alight: the whited air
Hides hills and woods, the river, and the heaven,
And veils the farm-house at the garden's end.
The sled and traveller stopped, the courier's feet
Delayed, all friends shut out, the housemates sit
Around the radiant fireplace, enclosed
In a tumultuous privacy of storm.

Come see the north wind's masonry.
Out of an unseen quarry evermore
Furnished with tile, the fierce artificer
Curves his white bastions with projected roof
Round every windward stake, or tree, or door.
Speeding, the myriad-handed, his wild work
So fanciful, so savage, nought cares he
For number or proportion. Mockingly,
On coop or kennel he hangs Parian wreaths;
A swan-like form invests the hidden thorn;
Fills up the farmer's lane from wall to wall,
Maugre the farmer's sighs; and at the gate
A tapering turret overtops the work.
And when his hours are numbered, and the world
Is all his own, retiring, as he were not,
Leaves, when the sun appears, astonished Art

To mimic in slow structures, stone by stone,
Built in an age, the mad wind's night-work,
The frolic architecture of the snow.

HENRY WADSWORTH LONGFELLOW

Curfew

I

Solemnly, mournfully,
  Dealing its dole,
The Curfew Bell
  Is beginning to toll.

Cover the embers,
  And put out the light;
Toil comes with the morning
  And rest with the night.

Dark grow the windows,
  And quenched is the fire;
Sound fades into silence,—
  All footsteps retire.

No voice in the chambers,
  No sound in the hall!
Sleep and oblivion
  Reign over all!

II

The book is completed,
  And closed, like the day;
And the hand that has written it
  Lays it away.

Dim grow its fancies;
  Forgotten they lie;
Like coals in the ashes,
  They darken and die.

Song sinks into silence,
  The story is told,

The windows are darkened,
  The hearth-stone is cold.

Dark and darker
  The black shadows fall;
Sleep and oblivion
  Reign over all.

EDGAR ALLAN POE

A Dream Within a Dream

Take this kiss upon the brow!
And, in parting from you now,
Thus much let me avow—
You are not wrong, who deem
That my days have been a dream;
Yet if Hope has flown away
In a night, or in a day,
In a vision, or in none,
Is it therefore the less *gone?*
All that we see or seem
Is but a dream within a dream.

I stand amid the roar
Of a surf-tormented shore,
And I hold within my hand
Grains of the golden sand—
How few! yet how they creep
Through my fingers to the deep,
While I weep—while I weep!
O God! can I not grasp
Them with a tighter clasp?
O God! can I not save
One from the pitiless wave?
Is *all* that we see or seem
But a dream within a dream?

Israfel

And the angel Israfel, whose heart-strings are a lute, and who has the
sweetest voice of all God's creatures.—KORAN.

In Heaven a spirit doth dwell
   "Whose heart-strings are a lute;"
None sing so wildly well
As the angel Israfel,
And the giddy stars (so legends tell)
Ceasing their hymns, attend the spell
   Of his voice, all mute.

Tottering above
   In her highest noon,
   The enamoured moon
Blushes with love,
   While, to listen, the red levin
   (With the rapid Pleiads, even,
   Which were seven,)
   Pauses in Heaven.

And they say (the starry choir
   And the other listening things)
That Israfeli's fire
Is owing to that lyre
   By which he sits and sings—
The trembling living wire
   Of those unusual strings.

But the skies that angel trod,
   Where deep thoughts are a duty—
Where Love's a grown-up God—
   Where the Houri glances are
   Imbued with all the beauty
   Which we worship in a star.

Therefore, thou art not wrong,
   Israfeli, who despisest
An unimpassioned song;
To thee the laurels belong,
   Best bard, because the wisest!
Merrily live, and long!

The ecstasies above
   With thy burning measures suit—
Thy grief, thy joy, thy hate, thy love,
   With the fervour of thy lute—
   Well may the stars be mute!

Yes, Heaven is thine; but this
   Is a world of sweets and sours;
   Our flowers are merely—flowers,
And the shadow of thy perfect bliss
   Is the sunshine of ours.

If I could dwell
Where Israfel
   Hath dwelt, and he where I,
He might not sing so wildly well
   A mortal melody,
While a bolder note than this might swell
   From my lyre within the sky.

The City in the Sea

Lo! Death has reared himself a throne
In a strange city lying alone
Far down within the dim West,
Where the good and the bad and the worst and the best
Have gone to their eternal rest.
There shrines and palaces and towers
(Time-eaten towers that tremble not!)
Resemble nothing that is ours.
Around, by lifting winds forgot,
Resignedly beneath the sky
The melancholy waters lie.

No rays from the holy heaven come down
On the long night-time of that town;
But light from out the lurid sea
Streams up the turrets silently—
Gleams up the pinnacles far and free—
Up domes—up spires—up kingly halls—
Up fanes—up Babylon-like walls—
Up shadowy long-forgotten bowers
Of sculptured ivy and stone flowers—
Up many and many a marvellous shrine
Whose wreathéd friezes intertwine
The viol, the violet, and the vine.

Resignedly beneath the sky
The melancholy waters lie.

So blend the turrets and shadows there
That all seem pendulous in air,
While from a proud tower in the town
Death looks gigantically down.

There open fanes and gaping graves
Yawn level with the luminous waves;
But not the riches there that lie
In each idol's diamond eye—
Not the gaily-jewelled dead
Tempt the waters from their bed;
For no ripples curl, alas!
Along that wilderness of glass—
No swellings tell that winds may be
Upon some far-off happier sea—
No heavings hint that winds have been
On seas less hideously serene.

But lo, a stir is in the air!
The wave—there is a movement there!
As if the towers had thrust aside,
In slightly sinking, the dull tide—
As if their tops had feebly given
A void within the filmy Heaven.
The waves have now a redder glow—
The hours are breathing faint and low—
And when, amid no earthly moans,
Down, down that town shall settle hence,
Hell, rising from a thousand thrones,
Shall do it reverence.

The Valley of Unrest

Once it smiled a silent dell
Where the people did not dwell;
They had gone unto the wars,
Trusting to the mild-eyed stars,
Nightly, from their azure towers,
To keep watch above the flowers,
In the midst of which all day
The red sun-light lazily lay.
Now each visiter shall confess
The sad valley's restlessness.

Nothing there is motionless—
Nothing save the airs that brood
Over the magic solitude.
Ah, by no wind are stirred those trees
That palpitate like the chill seas
Around the misty Hebrides!
Ah, by no wind those clouds are driven
That rustle through the unquiet Heaven
Uneasily, from morn till even,
Over the violets there that lie
In myriad types of the human eye—
Over the lilies there that wave
And weep above a nameless grave!
They wave:—from out their fragrant tops
Eternal dews come down in drops.
They weep:—from off their delicate stems
Perennial tears descend in gems.

The Sleeper

At midnight, in the month of June,
I stand beneath the mystic moon.
An opiate vapour, dewy, dim,
Exhales from out her golden rim,
And, softly dripping, drop by drop,
Upon the quiet mountain top,
Steals drowsily and musically
Into the universal valley.
The rosemary nods upon the grave;
The lily lolls upon the wave;
Wrapping the fog about its breast,
The ruin moulders into rest;
Looking like Lethe, see! the lake
A conscious slumber seems to take,
And would not, for the world, awake.
All Beauty sleeps!—and lo! where lies
Irene, with her Destinies!

Oh, lady bright! can it be right—
This window open to the night?
The wanton airs, from the tree-top,
Laughingly through the lattice drop—
The bodiless airs, a wizard rout,
Flit through thy chamber in and out,

And wave the curtain canopy
So fitfully—so fearfully—
Above the closed and fringéd lid
'Neath which thy slumb'ring soul lies hid,
That, o'er the floor and down the wall,
Like ghosts the shadows rise and fall!
Oh, lady dear, hast thou no fear?
Why and what art thou dreaming here?
Sure thou art come o'er far-off seas,
A wonder to these garden trees!
Strange is thy pallor! strange thy dress!
Strange, above all, thy length of tress,
And this all solemn silentness!

The lady sleeps! Oh, may her sleep,
Which is enduring, so be deep!
Heaven have her in its sacred keep!
This chamber changed for one more holy,
This bed for one more melancholy,
I pray to God that she may lie
Forever with unopened eye,
While the pale sheeted ghosts go by!

My love, she sleeps! Oh, may her sleep,
As it is lasting, so be deep!
Soft may the worms about her creep!
Far in the forest, dim and old,
For her may some tall vault unfold—
Some vault that oft hath flung its black
And wingéd pannels fluttering back,
Triumphant, o'er the crested palls,
Of her grand family funerals—
Some sepulchre, remote, alone,
Against whose portal she hath thrown,
In childhood, many an idle stone—
Some tomb from out whose sounding door
She ne'er shall force an echo more,
Thrilling to think, poor child of sin!
It was the dead who groaned within.

The Haunted Palace

In the greenest of our valleys
  By good angels tenanted,

Once a fair and stately palace—
    Radiant palace—reared its head.
In the monarch Thought's dominion—
    It stood there!
Never seraph spread a pinion
    Over fabric half so fair!

Banners yellow, glorious, golden,
    On its roof did float and flow,
(This—all this—was in the olden
    Time long ago,)
And every gentle air that dallied,
    In that sweet day,
Along the ramparts plumed and pallid,
    A wingéd odor went away.

Wanderers in that happy valley,
    Through two luminous windows, saw
Spirits moving musically,
    To a lute's well-tuned law,
Round about a throne where, sitting,
    Porphyrogene,
In state his glory well befitting,
    The ruler of the realm was seen.

And all with pearl and ruby glowing
    Was the fair palace door,
Through which came flowing, flowing, flowing,
    And sparkling evermore,
A troop of Echoes, whose sweet duty
    Was but to sing,
In voices of surpassing beauty,
    The wit and wisdom of their king.

But evil things, in robes of sorrow,
    Assailed the monarch's high estate.
(Ah, let us mourn!—for never morrow
    Shall dawn upon him desolate!)
And round about his home the glory
    That blushed and bloomed,
Is but a dim-remembered story
    Of the old time entombed.

And travellers, now, within that valley,
    Through the red-litten windows see

Vast forms, that move fantastically
    To a discordant melody,
While, like a ghastly rapid river,
    Through the pale door
A hideous throng rush out forever
    And laugh—but smile no more.

The Conqueror Worm

Lo! 'tis a gala night
    Within the lonesome latter years!
An angel throng, bewinged, bedight
    In veils, and drowned in tears,
Sit in a theatre, to see
    A play of hopes and fears,
While the orchestra breathes fitfully
    The music of the spheres.

Mimes, in the form of God on high,
    Mutter and mumble low,
And hither and thither fly—
    Mere puppets they, who come and go
At bidding of vast formless things
    That shift the scenery to and fro,
Flapping from out their Condor wings
    Invisible Wo!

That motley drama—oh, be sure
    It shall not be forgot!
With its Phantom chased for evermore,
    By a crowd that seize it not,
Through a circle that ever returneth in
    To the self-same spot,
And much of Madness, and more of Sin,
    And Horror the soul of the plot.

But see, amid the mimic rout
    A crawling shape intrude!
A blood-red thing that writhes from out
    The scenic solitude!
It writhes!—it writhes!—with mortal pangs
    The mimes become its food,

And seraphs sob at vermin fangs
  In human gore imbued.

Out—out are the lights—out all!
  And, over each quivering form,
The curtain, a funeral pall,
  Comes down with the rush of a storm,
While the angels, all pallid and wan,
  Uprising, unveiling, affirm
That the play is the tragedy, "Man,"
  And its hero the Conqueror Worm.

The Raven

Once upon a midnight dreary, while I pondered, weak and weary,
Over many a quaint and curious volume of forgotten lore—
While I nodded, nearly napping, suddenly there came a tapping,
As of some one gently rapping, rapping at my chamber door.
"'Tis some visiter," I muttered, "tapping at my chamber door—
    Only this and nothing more."

Ah, distinctly I remember it was in the bleak December;
And each separate dying ember wrought its ghost upon the floor.
Eagerly I wished the morrow;—vainly I had sought to borrow
From my books surcease of sorrow—sorrow for the lost Lenore—
For the rare and radiant maiden whom the angels name Lenore—
    Nameless *here* for evermore.

And the silken, sad, uncertain rustling of each purple curtain
Thrilled me—filled me with fantastic terrors never felt before;
So that now, to still the beating of my heart, I stood repeating
"'Tis some visiter entreating entrance at my chamber door—
Some late visiter entreating entrance at my chamber door;—
    This it is and nothing more."

Presently my soul grew stronger; hesitating then no longer,
"Sir," said I, "or Madam, truly your forgiveness I implore;
But the fact is I was napping, and so gently you came rapping,
And so faintly you came tapping, tapping at my chamber door,
That I scarce was sure I heard you"—here I opened wide
    the door;—
        Darkness there and nothing more.

Deep into that darkness peering, long I stood there wondering, fearing,
Doubting, dreaming dreams no mortal ever dared to dream before;
But the silence was unbroken, and the stillness gave no token,
And the only word there spoken was the whispered word, "Lenore?"
This I whispered, and an echo murmured back the word, "Lenore!"
　　　　　Merely this and nothing more.

Back into the chamber turning, all my soul within me burning,
Soon again I heard a tapping somewhat louder than before.
"Surely," said I, "surely that is something at my window lattice;
Let me see, then, what thereat is, and this mystery explore—
Let my heart be still a moment and this mystery explore;—
　　　　　'Tis the wind and nothing more!"

Open here I flung the shutter, when, with many a flirt and flutter,
In there stepped a stately Raven of the saintly days of yore;
Not the least obeisance made he; not a minute stopped or stayed he;
But, with mien of lord or lady, perched above my chamber door—
Perched upon a bust of Pallas just above my chamber door—
　　　　　Perched, and sat, and nothing more.

Then this ebony bird beguiling my sad fancy into smiling,
By the grave and stern decorum of the countenance it wore,
"Though thy crest be shorn and shaven, thou," I said, "art sure
　　　no craven,
Ghastly grim and ancient Raven wandering from the Nightly shore—
Tell me what thy lordly name is on the Night's Plutonian shore!"
　　　　　Quoth the Raven "Nevermore."

Much I marvelled this ungainly fowl to hear discourse so plainly,
Though its answer little meaning—little relevancy bore;
For we cannot help agreeing that no living human being
Ever yet was blessed with seeing bird above his chamber door—
Bird or beast upon the sculptured bust above his chamber door,
　　　　　With such name as "Nevermore."

But the Raven, sitting lonely on the placid bust, spoke only
That one word, as if his soul in that one word he did outpour.
Nothing farther then he uttered—not a feather then he fluttered—
Till I scarcely more than muttered "Other friends have flown before—
On the morrow *he* will leave me, as my Hopes have flown before."
　　　　　Then the bird said "Nevermore."

Startled at the stillness broken by reply so aptly spoken,
"Doubtless," said I, "what it utters is its only stock and store

Caught from some unhappy master whom unmerciful Disaster
Followed fast and followed faster till his songs one burden bore—
Till the dirges of his Hope that melancholy burden bore
        Of 'Never—nevermore.' "

But the Raven still beguiling all my fancy into smiling,
Straight I wheeled a cushioned seat in front of bird, and bust and door;
Then, upon the velvet sinking, I betook myself to linking
Fancy unto fancy, thinking what this ominous bird of yore—
What this grim, ungainly, ghastly, gaunt, and ominous bird of yore
        Meant in croaking "Nevermore."

This I sat engaged in guessing, but no syllable expressing
To the fowl whose fiery eyes now burned into my bosom's core;
This and more I sat divining, with my head at ease reclining
On the cushion's velvet lining that the lamp-light gloated o'er,
But whose velvet-violet lining with the lamp-light gloating o'er,
        She shall press, ah, nevermore!

Then, methought, the air grew denser, perfumed from an unseen censer
Swung by Seraphim whose foot-falls tinkled on the tufted floor.
"Wretch," I cried, "thy God hath lent thee—by these angels he hath
    sent thee
Respite—respite and nepenthe from thy memories of Lenore;
Quaff, oh quaff this kind nepenthe and forget this lost Lenore!"
        Quoth the Raven "Nevermore."

"Prophet!" said I, "thing of evil!—prophet still, if bird or devil!—
Whether Tempter sent, or whether tempest tossed thee here ashore,
Desolate yet all undaunted, on this desert land enchanted—
On this home by Horror haunted—tell me truly, I implore—
Is there—*is* there balm in Gilead?—tell me—tell me, I implore!"
        Quoth the Raven "Nevermore."

"Prophet!" said I, "thing of evil!—prophet still, if bird or devil!
By that Heaven that bends above us—by that God we both adore—
Tell this soul with sorrow laden if, within the distant Aidenn,
It shall clasp a sainted maiden whom the angels name Lenore—
Clasp a rare and radiant maiden whom the angels name Lenore."
        Quoth the Raven "Nevermore."

"Be that word our sign of parting, bird or fiend!" I shrieked,
    upstarting—
"Get thee back into the tempest and the Night's Plutonian shore!
Leave no black plume as a token of that lie thy soul hath spoken!

Leave my loneliness unbroken!—quit the bust above my door!
Take thy beak from out my heart, and take thy form from off my door!"
                Quoth the Raven "Nevermore."

And the Raven, never flitting, still is sitting, *still* is sitting
On the pallid bust of Pallas just above my chamber door;
And his eyes have all the seeming of a demon's that is dreaming,
And the lamp-light o'er him streaming throws his shadow on the floor;
And my soul from out that shadow that lies floating on the floor
                Shall be lifted—nevermore!

Ulalume—a Ballad

The skies they were ashen and sober;
        The leaves they were crispéd and sere—
        The leaves they were withering and sere:
It was night, in the lonesome October
        Of my most immemorial year:
It was hard by the dim lake of Auber,
        In the misty mid region of Weir:—
It was down by the dank tarn of Auber,
        In the ghoul-haunted woodland of Weir.

Here once, through an alley Titanic,
        Of cypress, I roamed with my Soul—
        Of cypress, with Psyche, my Soul.
These were days when my heart was volcanic
        As the scoriac rivers that roll—
        As the lavas that restlessly roll
Their sulphurous currents down Yaanek,
        In the ultimate climes of the Pole—
That groan as they roll down Mount Yaanek,
        In the realms of the Boreal Pole.

Our talk had been serious and sober,
        But our thoughts they were palsied and sere—
        Our memories were treacherous and sere;
For we knew not the month was October,
        And we marked not the night of the year—
        (Ah, night of all nights in the year!)
We noted not the dim lake of Auber,
        (Though once we had journeyed down here)

We remembered not the dank tarn of Auber,
    Nor the ghoul-haunted woodland of Weir.

And now, as the night was senescent,
    And star-dials pointed to morn—
    As the star-dials hinted of morn—
At the end of our path a liquescent
    And nebulous lustre was born
Out of which a miraculous crescent
    Arose with a duplicate horn—
Astarte's bediamonded crescent,
    Distinct with its duplicate horn.

And I said—"She is warmer than Dian;
    She rolls through an ether of sighs—
    She revels in a region of sighs.
She has seen that the tears are not dry on
    These cheeks where the worm never dies,
And has come past the stars of the Lion,
    To point us the path to the skies—
    To the Lethean peace of the skies—
Come up, in despite of the Lion,
    To shine on us with her bright eyes—
Come up, through the lair of the Lion,
    With Love in her luminous eyes."

But Psyche, uplifting her finger,
    Said—"Sadly this star I mistrust—
    Her pallor I strangely mistrust—
Ah, hasten!—ah, let us not linger!
    Ah, fly!—let us fly!—for we must."
In terror she spoke; letting sink her
    Wings till they trailed in the dust—
In agony sobbed; letting sink her
    Plumes till they trailed in the dust—
    Till they sorrowfully trailed in the dust.

I replied—"This is nothing but dreaming.
    Let us on, by this tremulous light!
    Let us bathe in this crystalline light!
Its Sybillic splendor is beaming
    With Hope and in Beauty to-night—
    See!—it flickers up the sky through the night!
Ah, we safely may trust to its gleaming
    And be sure it will lead us aright—

We surely may trust to a gleaming
     That cannot but guide us aright
     Since it flickers up to Heaven through the night."

Thus I pacified Psyche and kissed her,
     And tempted her out of her gloom—
     And conquered her scruples and gloom;
And we passed to the end of the vista—
     But were stopped by the door of a tomb—
     By the door of a legended tomb:—
And I said—"What is written, sweet sister,
     On the door of this legended tomb?"
     She replied—"Ulalume—Ulalume!—
     'Tis the vault of thy lost Ulalume!"

Then my heart it grew ashen and sober
     As the leaves that were crispéd and sere—
     As the leaves that were withering and sere—
And I cried—"It was surely October,
     On *this* very night of last year,
     That I journeyed—I journeyed down here!—
     That I brought a dread burden down here—
     On this night, of all nights in the year,
     Ah, what demon hath tempted me here?
Well I know, now, this dim lake of Auber—
     This misty mid region of Weir:—
Well I know, now, this dank tarn of Auber—
     This ghoul-haunted woodland of Weir."

Said we, then—the two, then—"Ah, can it
     Have been that the woodlandish ghouls—
     The pitiful, the merciful ghouls,
To bar up our way and to ban it
     From the secret that lies in these wolds—
     From the thing that lies hidden in these wolds—
Have drawn up the spectre of a planet
     From the limbo of lunary souls—
This sinfully scintillant planet
     From the Hell of the planetary souls?"

Eldorado

     Gaily bedight,
     A gallant knight,

In sunshine and in shadow,
     Had journeyed long,
     Singing a song,
In search of Eldorado.

     But he grew old—
     This knight so bold—
And o'er his heart a shadow
     Fell as he found
     No spot of ground
That looked like Eldorado.

     And, as his strength
     Failed him at length,
He met a pilgrim shadow—
     "Shadow," said he,
     "Where can it be—
This land of Eldorado?"

     "Over the Mountains
     Of the Moon,
Down the Valley of the Shadow,
     Ride, boldly ride,"
     The shade replied,—
"If you seek for Eldorado!"

ALFRED, LORD TENNYSON

The Eagle

He clasps the crag with crooked hands;
Close to the sun in lonely lands,
Ring'd with the azure world, he stands.

The wrinkled sea beneath him crawls;
He watches from his mountain walls,
And like a thunderbolt he falls.

ROBERT BROWNING

Soliloquy of the Spanish Cloister

I

Gr-r-r—there go, my heart's abhorrence!
  Water your damned flower-pots, do!
If hate killed men, Brother Lawrence,
  God's blood, would not mine kill you!
What? your myrtle-bush wants trimming?
  Oh, that rose has prior claims—
Needs its leaden vase filled brimming?
  Hell dry you up with its flames!

II

At the meal we sit together:
  Salve tibi! I must hear
Wise talk of the kind of weather,
  Sort of season, time of year:
Not a plenteous cork-crop: scarcely
  Dare we hope oak-galls, I doubt:
What's the Latin name for "parsely"?
  What's the Greek name for Swine's Snout?

III

Whew! We'll have our platter burnished,
  Laid with care on our own shelf!
With a fire-new spoon we're furnished,
  And a goblet for ourself,
Rinsed like something sacrificial
  Ere 't is fit to touch our chaps—
Marked with L. for our initial!
  (He-he! There his lily snaps!)

IV

Saint, forsooth! While brown Dolores
  Squats outside the Convent bank
With Sanchicha, telling stories,
  Steeping tresses in the tank,
Blue-black, lustrous, thick like horsehairs,
  —Can't I see his dead eye glow,
Bright as 't were a Barbary corsair's?
  (That is, if he'd let it show!)

When he finishes refection,
  Knife and fork he never lays
Cross-wise, to my recollection,
  As do I, in Jesu's praise.
I the Trinity illustrate,
  Drinking watered orange-pulp—
In three sips the Arian frustrate;
  While he drains his at one gulp.

Oh, those melons? If he's able
  We're to have a feast! so nice!
One goes to the Abbot's table,
  All of us get each a slice.
How go on your flowers? None double?
  Not one fruit-sort can you spy?
Strange!—And I, too, at such trouble,
  Keep them close-nipped on the sly!

There's a great text in Galatians,
  Once you trip on it, entails
Twenty-nine distinct damnations,
  One sure, if another fails:
If I trip him just a-dying,
  Sure of heaven as sure can be,
Spin him round and send him flying
  Off to hell, a Manichee?

Or, my scrofulous French novel
  On grey paper with blunt type!
Simply glance at it, you grovel
  Hand and foot in Belial's gripe:
If I double down its pages
  At the woeful sixteenth print,
When he gathers his greengages,
  Ope a sieve and slip it in 't?

Or there's Satan!—one might venture
  Pledge one's soul to him, yet leave
Such a flaw in the indenture
  As he'd miss till, past retrieve,

Blasted lay that rose-acacia
    We're so proud of! *Hy, Zy, Hine* . . .
'St, there's Vespers! *Plena gratiâ*
    Ave, Virgo! Gr-r-r—you swine!

WALT WHITMAN

Once I Pass'd through a Populous City

Once I pass'd through a populous city imprinting my brain for future use
    with its shows, architecture, customs, traditions,
Yet now of all that city I remember only a woman I casually met there
    who detain'd me for love of me,
Day by day and night by night we were together—all else has long been
    forgotten by me,
I remember I say only that woman who passionately clung to me,
Again we wander, we love, we separate again,
Again she holds me by the hand, I must not go,
I see her close beside me with silent lips sad and tremulous.

When I Heard at the Close of the Day

When I heard at the close of the day how my name had been receiv'd
    with plaudits in the capitol, still it was not a happy night for me
    that follow'd,
And else when I carous'd, or when my plans were accomplish'd, still I
    was not happy,
But the day when I rose at dawn from the bed of perfect health,
    refresh'd, singing, inhaling the ripe breath of autumn,
When I saw the full moon in the west grow pale and disappear in the
    morning light,
When I wander'd alone over the beach, and undressing bathed, laughing
    with the cool waters, and saw the sun rise,
And when I thought how my dear friend my lover was on his way
    coming, O then I was happy,
O then each breath tasted sweeter, and all that day my food nourish'd
    me more, and the beautiful day pass'd well,
And the next came with equal joy, and with the next at evening came
    my friend,
And that night while all was still I heard the waters roll slowly
    continually up the shores,

I heard the hissing rustle of the liquid and sands as directed to me
     whispering to congratulate me,
For the one I love most lay sleeping by me under the same cover in the
     cool night,
In the stillness in the autumn moonbeams his face was inclined toward
     me,
And his arm lay lightly around my breast—and that night I was happy.

A Hand-Mirror

Hold it up sternly—see this it sends back, (who is it? is it you?)
Outside fair costume, within ashes and filth,
No more a flashing eye, no more a sonorous voice or springy step,
Now some slave's eye, voice, hands, step,
A drunkard's breath, unwholesome eater's face, venerealee's flesh,
Lungs rotting away piecemeal, stomach sour and cankerous,
Joints rheumatic, bowels clogged with abomination,
Blood circulating dark and poisonous streams,
Words babble, hearing and touch callous,
No brain, no heart left, no magnetism of sex;
Such from one look in this looking-glass ere you go hence,
Such a result so soon—and from such a beginning!

The Dalliance of the Eagles

Skirting the river road, (my forenoon walk, my rest,)
Skyward in air a sudden muffled sound, the dalliance of the eagles,
The rushing amorous contact high in space together,
The clinching interlocking claws, a living, fierce, gyrating wheel,
Four beating wings, two beaks, a swirling mass tight grappling,
In tumbling turning clustering loops, straight downward falling,
Till o'er the river pois'd, the twain yet one, a moment's lull,
A motionless still balance in the air, then parting, talons loosing,
Upward again on slow-firm pinions slanting, their separate diverse flight,
She hers, he his, pursuing.

Cavalry Crossing a Ford

A line in long array where they wind betwixt green islands,
They take a serpentine course, their arms flash in the sun—hark to the
     musical clank,

Behold the silvery river, in it the splashing horses loitering stop to drink,
Behold the brown-faced men, each group, each person a picture, the
negligent rest on the saddles,
Some emerge on the opposite bank, others are just entering the ford—
while,
Scarlet and blue and snowy white,
The guidon flags flutter gayly in the wind.

By the Bivouac's Fitful Flame

By the bivouac's fitful flame,
A procession winding around me, solemn and sweet and slow—but first I
note,
The tents of the sleeping army, the fields' and woods' dim outline,
The darkness lit by spots of kindled fire, the silence,
Like a phantom far or near an occasional figure moving,
The shrubs and trees, (as I lift my eyes they seem to be stealthily watching
me,)
While wind in procession thoughts, O tender and wondrous thoughts,
Of life and death, of home and the past and loved, and of those that are
far away;
A solemn and slow procession there as I sit on the ground,
By the bivouac's fitful flame.

A Sight in Camp in the Daybreak Gray and Dim

A sight in camp in the daybreak gray and dim,
As from my tent I emerge so early sleepless,
As slow I walk in the cool fresh air the path near by the hospital tent,
Three forms I see on stretchers lying, brought out there untended lying,
Over each the blanket spread, ample brownish woolen blanket,
Gray and heavy blanket, folding, covering all.

Curious I halt and silent stand,
Then with light fingers I from the face of the nearest the first just lift the
blanket;
Who are you elderly man so gaunt and grim, with well-gray'd hair, and
flesh all sunken about the eyes?
Who are you my dear comrade?
Then to the second I step—and who are you my child and darling?
Who are you sweet boy with cheeks yet blooming?

Then to the third—a face nor child nor old, very calm, as of beautiful
    yellow-white ivory;
Young man I think I know you—I think this face is the face of the Christ
    himself,
Dead and divine and brother of all, and here again he lies.

When Lilacs Last in the Dooryard Bloom'd

1

When lilacs last in the dooryard bloom'd,
And the great star early droop'd in the western sky in the night,
I mourn'd, and yet shall mourn with ever-returning spring.

Ever-returning spring, trinity sure to me you bring,
Lilac blooming perennial and drooping star in the west,
And thought of him I love.

2

O powerful western fallen star!
O shades of night—O moody, tearful night!
O great star disappear'd—O the black murk that hides the star!
O cruel hands that hold me powerless—O helpless soul of me!
O harsh surrounding cloud that will not free my soul.

3

In the dooryard fronting an old farm-house near the white-wash'd
    palings,
Stands the lilac-bush tall-growing with heart-shaped leaves of rich green,
With many a pointed blossom rising delicate, with the perfume strong I
    love,
With every leaf a miracle—and from this bush in the dooryard,
With delicate-color'd blossoms and heart-shaped leaves of rich green,
A sprig with its flower I break.

4

In the swamp in secluded recesses,
A shy and hidden bird is warbling a song.

Solitary the thrush,
The hermit withdrawn to himself, avoiding the settlements,
Sings by himself a song.

Song of the bleeding throat,
Death's outlet song of life, (for well dear brother I know,
If thou wast not granted to sing thou would'st surely die.)

5

Over the breast of the spring, the land, amid cities,
Amid lanes and through old woods, where lately the violets peep'd from
     the ground, spotting the gray debris,
Amid the grass in the fields each side of the lanes, passing the endless
     grass,
Passing the yellow-spear'd wheat, every grain from its shroud in the dark-
     brown fields uprisen,
Passing the apple-tree blows of white and pink in the orchards,
Carrying a corpse to where it shall rest in the grave,
Night and day journeys a coffin.

6

Coffin that passes through lanes and streets,
Through day and night with the great cloud darkening the land,
With the pomp of the inloop'd flags with the cities draped in black,
With the show of the States themselves as of crape-veil'd women
     standing,
With processions long and winding and the flambeaus of the night,
With the countless torches lit, with the silent sea of faces and the
     unbared heads,
With the waiting depot, the arriving coffin, and the sombre faces,
With dirges through the night, with the thousand voices rising strong
     and solemn,
With all the mournful voices of the dirges pour'd around the coffin,
The dim-lit churches and the shuddering organs—where amid these you
     journey,
With the tolling tolling bells' perpetual clang,
Here, coffin that slowly passes,
I give you my sprig of lilac.

7

(Nor for you, for one alone,
Blossoms and branches green to coffins all I bring,
For fresh as the morning, thus would I chant a song for you O sane and
     sacred death.

All over bouquets of roses,
O death, I cover you over with roses and early lilies,
But mostly and now the lilac that blooms the first,

Copious I break, I break the sprigs from the bushes,
With loaded arms I come, pouring for you,
For you and the coffins all of you O death.)

8

O western orb sailing the heaven,
Now I know what you must have meant as a month since I walk'd,
As I walk'd in silence the transparent shadowy night,
As I saw you had something to tell as you bent to me night after night,
As you droop'd from the sky low down as if to my side, (while the other
    stars all look'd on,)
As we wander'd together the solemn night, (for something I know not
    what kept me from sleep,)
As the night advanced, and I saw on the rim of the west how full you
    were of woe,
As I stood on the rising ground in the breeze in the cool transparent
    night,
As I watch'd where you pass'd and was lost in the netherward black of
    the night,
As my soul in its trouble dissatisfied sank, as where you sad orb,
Concluded, dropt in the night, and was gone.

9

Sing on there in the swamp,
O singer bashful and tender, I hear your notes, I hear your call,
I hear, I come presently, I understand you,
But a moment I linger, for the lustrous star has detain'd me,
The star my departing comrade holds and detains me.

10

O how shall I warble myself for the dead one there I loved?
And how shall I deck my song for the large sweet soul that has gone?
And what shall my perfume be for the grave of him I love?

Sea-winds blown from east and west,
Blown from the Eastern sea and blown from the Western sea, till there
    on the prairies meeting,
These and with these and the breath of my chant,
I'll perfume the grave of him I love.

11

O what shall I hang on the chamber walls?
And what shall the pictures be that I hang on the walls,
To adorn the burial-house of him I love?

Pictures of growing spring and farms and homes,
With the Fourth-month eve at sundown, and the gray smoke lucid and
    bright,
With floods of the yellow gold of the gorgeous, indolent, sinking sun,
    burning, expanding the air,
With the fresh sweet herbage under foot, and the pale green leaves
    of the trees prolific,
In the distance the flowing glaze, the breast of the river, with a wind-
    dapple here and there,
With ranging hills on the banks, with many a line against the sky, and
    shadows,
And the city at hand with dwellings so dense, and stacks of chimneys,
And all the scenes of life and the workshops, and the workmen
    homeward returning.

12

Lo, body and soul—this land,
My own Manhattan with spires, and the sparkling and hurrying tides,
    and the ships,
The varied and ample land, the South and the North in the light, Ohio's
    shores and flashing Missouri,
And ever the far-spreading prairies cover'd with grass and corn.

Lo, the most excellent sun so calm and haughty,
The violet and purple morn with just-felt breezes,
The gentle soft-born measureless light,
The miracle spreading bathing all, the fulfill'd noon,
The coming eve delicious, the welcome night and the stars,
Over my cities shining all, enveloping man and land.

13

Sing on, sing on you gray-brown bird,
Sing from the swamps, the recesses, pour your chant from the bushes,
Limitless out of the dusk, out of the cedars and pines.

Sing on dearest brother, warble your reedy song,
Loud human song, with voice of uttermost woe.

O liquid and free and tender!
O wild and loose to my soul—O wondrous singer!
You only I hear—yet the star holds me, (but will soon depart,)
Yet the lilac with mastering odor holds me.

14

Now while I sat in the day and look'd forth,

In the close of the day with its light and the fields of spring, and the
  farmers preparing their crops,
In the large unconscious scenery of my land with its lakes and forests,
In the heavenly aerial beauty, (after the perturb'd winds and the storms,)
Under the arching heavens of the afternoon swift passing, and the voices
  of children and women,
The many-moving sea-tides, and I saw the ships how they sail'd,
And the summer approaching with richness, and the fields all busy with
  labor,
And the infinite separate houses, how they all went on, each with its
  meals and minutia of daily usages,
And the streets how their throbbings throbb'd, and the cities pent—lo,
  then and there,
Falling upon them all and among them all, enveloping me with the rest,
Appear'd the cloud, appear'd the long black trail,
And I knew death, its thought, and the sacred knowledge of death.
Then with the knowledge of death as walking one side of me,
And the thought of death close-walking the other side of me,
And I in the middle as with companions, and as holding the hands of
  companions,
I fled forth to the hiding receiving night that talks not,
Down to the shores of the water, the path by the swamp in the dimness,
To the solemn shadowy cedars and ghostly pines so still.

And the singer so shy to the rest receiv'd me,
The gray-brown bird I know receiv'd us comrades three,
And he sang the carol of death, and a verse for him I love.

From deep secluded recesses,
From the fragrant cedars and the ghostly pines so still,
Came the carol of the bird.

And the charm of the carol rapt me,
As I held as if by their hands my comrades in the night,
And the voice of my spirit tallied the song of the bird.

Come lovely and soothing death,
Undulate round the world, serenely arriving, arriving,
In the day, in the night, to all, to each,
Sooner or later delicate death.

Prais'd be the fathomless universe,
For life and joy, and for objects and knowledge curious,
And for love, sweet love—but praise! praise! praise!
For the sure-enwinding arms of cool-enfolding death.

Dark mother always gliding near with soft feet,
Have none chanted for thee a chant of fullest welcome?
Then I chant it for thee, I glorify thee above all,
I bring thee a song that when thou must indeed come, come
      unfalteringly.

Approach strong deliveress,
When it is so, when thou hast taken them I joyously sing the dead,
Lost in the loving floating ocean of thee,
Laved in the flood of thy bliss O death.

From me to thee glad serenades,
Dances for thee I propose saluting thee, adornments and feastings for
      thee,
And the sights of the open landscape and the high-spread sky are fitting,
And life and the fields, and the huge and thoughtful night.

The night in silence under many a star,
The ocean shore and the husky whispering wave whose voice I know,
And the soul turning to thee O vast and well-veil'd death,
And the body gratefully nestling close to thee.

Over the tree-tops I float thee a song,
Over the rising and sinking waves, over the myriad fields and the prairies
      wide,
Over the dense-pack'd cities all and the teeming wharves and ways,
I float this carol with joy, with joy to thee O death.

15

To the tally of my soul,
Loud and strong kept up the gray-brown bird,
With pure deliberate notes spreading filling the night.

Loud in the pines and cedars dim,
Clear in the freshness moist and the swamp-perfume,
And I with my comrades there in the night.

While my sight that was bound in my eyes unclosed,
As to long panoramas of visions.

And I saw askant the armies,
I saw as in noiseless dreams hundreds of battle-flags,
Borne through the smoke of the battles and pierc'd with missiles I saw
      them,

And carried hither and yon through the smoke, and torn and bloody,
And at last but a few shreds left on the staffs, (and all in silence,)
And the staffs all splinter'd and broken.

I saw battle-corpses, myriads of them,
And the white skeletons of young men, I saw them,
I saw the debris and debris of all the slain soldiers of the war,
But I saw they were not as was thought,
They themselves were fully at rest, they suffer'd not,
The living remain'd and suffer'd, the mother suffer'd,
And the wife and the child and the musing comrade suffer'd,
And the armies that remain'd suffer'd.

16

Passing the visions, passing the night,
Passing, unloosing the hold of my comrades' hands,
Passing the song of the hermit bird and the tallying song of my soul,
Victorious song, death's outlet song, yet varying ever-altering song,
As low and wailing, yet clear the notes, rising and falling, flooding the
     night,
Sadly sinking and fainting, as warning and warning, and yet again
     bursting with joy,
Covering the earth and filling the spread of the heaven,
As that powerful psalm in the night I heard from recesses,
Passing, I leave thee lilac with heart-shaped leaves,
I leave thee there in the door-yard, blooming, returning with spring.
I cease from my song for thee,
From my gaze on thee in the west, fronting the west, communing with
     thee,
O comrade lustrous with silver face in the night.

Yet each to keep and all, retrievements out of the night,
The song, the wondrous chant of the gray-brown bird,
And the tallying chant, the echo arous'd in my soul,
With the lustrous and drooping star with the countenance full of woe,
With the holders holding my hand nearing the call of the bird,
Comrades mine and I in the midst, and their memory ever to keep, for
     the dead I loved so well,
For the sweetest, wisest soul of all my days and lands—and this for his
     dear sake,
Lilac and star and bird twined with the chant of my soul,
There in the fragrant pines and the cedars dusk and dim.

A Noiseless Patient Spider

A noiseless patient spider,
I mark'd where on a little promontory it stood isolated,
Mark'd how to explore the vacant vast surrounding,
It launch'd forth filament, filament, filament, out of itself,
Ever unreeling them, ever tirelessly speeding them.

And you O my soul where you stand,
Surrounded, detached, in measureless oceans of space,
Ceaselessly musing, venturing, throwing, seeking the spheres to connect
    them,
Till the bridge you will need be form'd, till the ductile anchor hold,
Till the gossamer thread you fling catch somewhere, O my soul.

HERMAN MELVILLE

The Portent

(1859)

Hanging from the beam,
  Slowly swaying (such the law),
Gaunt the shadow on your green,
  Shenandoah!
The cut is on the crown
  (Lo, John Brown),
And the stabs shall heal no more.

Hidden in the cap
  Is the anguish none can draw;
So your future veils its face,
  Shenandoah!
But the streaming beard is shown
  (Weird John Brown),
The meteor of the war.

Shiloh

A REQUIEM

(April, 1862)

Skimming lightly, wheeling still,
  The swallows fly low

Over the field in clouded days,
    The forest-field of Shiloh—
Over the field where April rain
Solaced the parched ones stretched in pain
Through the pause of night
That followed the Sunday fight
    Around the church of Shiloh—
The church so lone, the log-built one,
That echoed to many a parting groan
        And natural prayer
    Of dying foemen mingled there—
Foemen at morn, but friends at eve—
    Fame or country least their care:
(What like a bullet can undeceive!)
    But now they lie low,
While over them the swallows skim,
    And all is hushed at Shiloh.

Malvern Hill

(July, 1862)

Ye elms that wave on Malvern Hill
    In prime of morn and May,
Recall ye how McClellan's men
        Here stood at bay?
While deep within yon forest dim
    Our rigid comrades lay—
Some with the cartridge in their mouth,
Others with fixed arms lifted South—
        Invoking so
The cypress glades? Ah wilds of woe!

The spires of Richmond, late beheld
    Through rifts in musket-haze,
Were closed from view in clouds of dust
        On leaf-walled ways,
Where streamed our wagons in caravan;
    And the Seven Nights and Days
Of march and fast, retreat and fight,
Pinched our grimed faces to ghastly plight—
        Does the elm wood
Recall the haggard beards of blood?

The battle-smoked flag, with stars eclipsed,
    We followed (it never fell!)—
In silence husbanded our strength—
    Received their yell;
Till on this slope we patient turned
    With cannon ordered well;
Reverse we proved was not defeat;
But ah, the sod what thousands meet!—
        Does Malvern Wood
Bethink itself, and muse and brood?

    We elms of Malvern Hill
      Remember every thing;
    But sap the twig will fill:
    Wag the world how it will,
      Leaves must be green in Spring.

The House-Top

A NIGHT PIECE

(July, 1863)

No sleep. The sultriness pervades the air
And binds the brain—a dense oppression, such
As tawny tigers feel in matted shades,
Vexing their blood and making apt for ravage.
Beneath the stars the roofy desert spreads
Vacant as Libya. All is hushed near by.
Yet fitfully from far breaks a mixed surf
Of muffled sound, the Atheist roar of riot.
Yonder, where parching Sirius set in drought,
Balefully glares red Arson—there—and there.
The Town is taken by its rats—ship-rats
And rats of the wharves. All civil charms
And priestly spells which late held hearts in awe—
Fear-bound, subjected to a better sway
Than sway of self; these like a dream dissolve,
And man rebounds whole æons back in nature.
Hail to the low dull rumble, dull and dead,
And ponderous drag that jars the wall.
Wise Draco comes, deep in the midnight roll
Of black artillery; he comes, though late;

In code corroborating Calvin's creed
And cynic tyrannies of honest kings;
He comes, nor parlies; and the Town, redeemed,
Gives thanks devout; nor, being thankful, heeds
The grimy slur on the Republic's faith implied,
Which holds that Man is naturally good,
And—more—is Nature's Roman, never to be scourged.

The Maldive Shark

About the Shark, phlegmatical one,
Pale sot of the Maldive sea,
The sleek little pilot-fish, azure and slim,
How alert in attendance be.
From his saw-pit of mouth, from his charnel of maw
They have nothing of harm to dread,
But liquidly glide on his ghastly flank
Or before his Gorgonian head;
Or lurk in the port of serrated teeth
In white triple tiers of glittering gates,
And there find a haven when peril's abroad,
An asylum in jaws of the Fates!
They are friends; and friendly they guide him to prey,
Yet never partake of the treat—
Eyes and brains to the dotard lethargic and dull,
Pale ravener of horrible meat.

MATTHEW ARNOLD

Dover Beach

The sea is calm to-night.
The tide is full, the moon lies fair
Upon the straits;—on the French coast the light
Gleams and is gone; the cliffs of England stand,
Glimmering and vast, out in the tranquil bay.
Come to the window, sweet is the night-air!
Only, from the long line of spray
Where the sea meets the moon-blanch'd land,
Listen! you hear the grating roar

Of pebbles which the waves draw back, and fling,
At their return, up the high strand,
Begin, and cease, and then again begin,
With tremulous cadence slow, and bring
The eternal note of sadness in.

Sophocles long ago
Heard it on the Ægæan, and it brought
Into his mind the turbid ebb and flow
Of human misery; we
Find also in the sound a thought,
Hearing it by this distant northern sea.

The Sea of Faith
Was once, too, at the full, and round earth's shore
Lay like the folds of a bright girdle furl'd.
But now I only hear
Its melancholy, long, withdrawing roar,
Retreating, to the breath
Of the night-wind, down the vast edges drear
And naked shingles of the world.

Ah, love, let us be true
To one another! for the world, which seems
To lie before us like a land of dreams,
So various, so beautiful, so new,
Hath really neither joy, nor love, nor light,
Nor certitude, nor peace, nor help for pain;
And we are here as on a darkling plain
Swept with confused alarms of struggle and flight,
Where ignorant armies clash by night.

GEORGE MEREDITH

Dirge in Woods

A wind sways the pines,
        And below
Not a breath of wild air;
Still as the mosses that glow
On the flooring and over the lines
Of the roots here and there.

The pine-tree drops its dead;
They are quiet, as under the sea.
Overhead, overhead
Rushes life in a race,
As the clouds the clouds chase;
    And we go,
And we drop like the fruits of the tree,
    Even we,
    Even so.

EMILY DICKINSON

These Are the Days when Birds Come Back—

These are the days when Birds come back—
A very few—a Bird or two—
To take a backward look.

These are the days when skies resume
The old—old sophistries of June—
A blue and gold mistake.

Oh fraud that cannot cheat the Bee—
Almost thy plausibility
Induces my belief.

Till ranks of seeds their witness bear—
And softly thro' the altered air
Hurries a timid leaf.

Oh Sacrament of summer days,
Oh Last Communion in the Haze—
Permit a child to join.

Thy sacred emblems to partake—
Thy consecrated bread to take
And thine immortal wine!

I Bring an Unaccustomed Wine

I bring an unaccustomed wine
To lips long parching

Next to mine,
And summon them to drink;

Crackling with fever, they Essay,
I turn my brimming eyes away,
And come next hour to look.

The hands still hug the tardy glass—
The lips I would have cooled, alas—
Are so superfluous Cold—

I would as soon attempt to warm
The bosoms where the frost has lain
Ages beneath the mould—

Some other thirsty there may be
To whom this would have pointed me
Had it remained to speak—

And so I always bear the cup
If, haply, mine may be the drop
Some pilgrim thirst to slake—

If, haply, any say to me
"Unto the little, unto me,"
When I at last awake.

I Know Some Lonely Houses off the Road

I know some lonely Houses off the Road
A Robber'd like the look of—
Wooden barred,
And Windows hanging low,
Inviting to—
A Portico,
Where two could creep—
One—hand the Tools—
The other peep—
To make sure All's Asleep—
Old fashioned eyes—
Not easy to surprise!

How orderly the Kitchen'd look, by night,
With just a Clock—

But they could gag the Tick—
And Mice won't bark—
And so the Walls—don't tell—
None—will—

A pair of Spectacles ajar just stir—
An Almanac's aware—
Was it the Mat—winked,
Or a Nervous Star?
The Moon—slides down the stair,
To see who's there!

There's plunder—where—
Tankard, or Spoon—
Earring—or Stone—
A Watch—Some Ancient Brooch
To match the Grandmama—
Staid sleeping—there—

Day—rattles—too
Stealth's—slow—
The Sun has got as far
As the third Sycamore—
Screams Chanticleer
"Who's there"?

And Echoes—Trains away,
Sneer—"Where"!
While the old Couple, just astir,
Fancy the Sunrise—left the door ajar!

A Bird Came Down the Walk—

A Bird came down the Walk—
He did not know I saw—
He bit an Angleworm in halves
And ate the fellow, raw,

And then he drank a Dew
From a convenient Grass—
And then hopped sidewise to the Wall
To let a Beetle pass—

He glanced with rapid eyes
That hurried all around—
They looked like frightened Beads, I thought—
He stirred his Velvet Head

Like one in danger, Cautious,
I offered him a Crumb
And he unrolled his feathers
And rowed him softer home—

Than Oars divide the Ocean,
Too silver for a seam—
Or Butterflies, off Banks of Noon
Leap, plashless as they swim.

I Heard a Fly Buzz—when I Died—

I heard a Fly buzz—when I died—
The Stillness in the Room
Was like the Stillness in the Air—
Between the Heaves of Storm—

The Eyes around—had wrung them dry—
And Breaths were gathering firm
For that last Onset—when the King
Be witnessed—in the Room—

I willed my Keepsakes—Signed away
What portion of me be
Assignable—and then it was
There interposed a Fly—

With Blue—uncertain stumbling Buzz—
Between the light—and me—
And then the Windows failed—and then
I could not see to see—

Because I Could Not Stop for Death—

Because I could not stop for Death—
He kindly stopped for me—

The Carriage held but just Ourselves—
And Immortality.

We slowly drove—He knew no haste
And I had put away
My labor and my leisure too,
For His Civility—

We passed the School, where Children strove
At Recess—in the Ring—
We passed the Fields of Gazing Grain—
We passed the Setting Sun—

Or rather—He passed Us—
The Dews drew quivering and chill—
For only Gossamer, my Gown—
My Tippet—only Tulle—

We paused before a House that seemed
A Swelling of the Ground—
The Roof was scarcely visible—
The Cornice—in the Ground—

Since then—'tis Centuries—and yet
Feels shorter than the Day
I first surmised the Horses' Heads
Were toward Eternity—

A Narrow Fellow in the Grass

A narrow Fellow in the Grass
Occasionally rides—
You may have met Him—did you not
His notice sudden is—

The Grass divides as with a Comb—
A spotted shaft is seen—
And then it closes at your feet
And opens further on—

He likes a Boggy Acre
A Floor too cool for Corn—
Yet when a Boy, and Barefoot—

I more than once at Noon
Have passed, I thought, a Whip lash
Unbraiding in the Sun
When stooping to secure it
It wrinkled, and was gone—

Several of Nature's People
I know, and they know me—
I feel for them a transport
Of cordiality—

But never met this Fellow
Attended, or alone
Without a tighter breathing
And Zero at the Bone—

At Half Past Three, a Single Bird

At Half past Three, a single Bird
Unto a silent Sky
Propounded but a single term
Of cautious melody.

At Half past Four, Experiment
Had subjugated test
And lo, Her silver Principle
Supplanted all the rest.

At Half past Seven, Element
Nor Implement, be seen—
And Place was where the Presence was
Circumference between.

The Last Night that She Lived

The last Night that She lived
It was a Common Night
Except the Dying—this to Us
Made Nature different

We noticed smallest things—
Things overlooked before

By this great light upon our Minds
Italicized—as 'twere.

As We went out and in
Between Her final Room
And Rooms where Those to be alive
Tomorrow were, a Blame

That Others could exist
While She must finish quite
A Jealousy for Her arose
So nearly infinite—

We waited while She passed—
It was a narrow time—
Too jostled were Our Souls to speak
At length the notice came.

She mentioned, and forgot—
Then lightly as a Reed
Bent to the Water, struggled scarce—
Consented, and was dead—

And We—We placed the Hair—
And drew the Head erect—
And then an awful leisure was
Belief to regulate—

A Bee His Burnished Carriage

A Bee his burnished Carriage
Drove boldly to a Rose—
Combinedly alighting—
Himself—his Carriage was—
The Rose received his visit
With frank tranquillity
Withholding not a Crescent
To his Cupidity—
Their Moment consummated—
Remained for him—to flee—
Remained for her—of rapture
But the humility.

THOMAS HARDY

The Subalterns

I

"Poor wanderer," said the leaden sky,
    "I fain would lighten thee,
But there are laws in force on high
    Which say it must not be."

II

—"I would not freeze thee, shorn one," cried
    The North, "knew I but how
To warm my breath, to slack my stride;
    But I am ruled as thou."

III

—"To-morrow I attack thee, wight,"
    Said Sickness. "Yet I swear
I bear thy little ark no spite,
    But am bid enter there."

IV

—"Come hither, Son," I heard Death say;
    "I did not will a grave
Should end thy pilgrimage to-day,
    But I, too, am a slave!"

V

We smiled upon each other then,
    And life to me had less
Of that fell look it wore ere when
    They owned their passiveness.

Channel Firing

That night your great guns, unawares,
Shook all our coffins as we lay,
And broke the chancel window-squares,
We thought it was the Judgment-day

And sat upright. While drearisome
Arose the howl of wakened hounds:

The mouse let fall the altar-crumb,
The worms drew back into the mounds,

The glebe cow drooled. Till God called, "No;
It's gunnery practice out at sea
Just as before you went below;
The world is as it used to be:

"All nations striving strong to make
Red war yet redder. Mad as hatters
They do no more for Christés sake
Than you who are helpless in such matters.

"That this is not the judgment-hour
For some of them's a blessed thing,
For if it were they'd have to scour
Hell's floor for so much threatening. . . .

"Ha, ha. It will be warmer when
I blow the trumpet (if indeed
I ever do; for you are men,
And rest eternal sorely need)."

So down we lay again. "I wonder,
Will the world ever saner be,"
Said one, "than when He sent us under
In our indifferent century!"

And many a skeleton shook his head.
"Instead of preaching forty year,"
My neighbour Parson Thirdly said,
"I wish I had stuck to pipes and beer."

Again the guns disturbed the hour,
Roaring their readiness to avenge,
As far inland as Stourton Tower,
And Camelot, and starlit Stonehenge.

April 1914.

In Time of "The Breaking of Nations"[1]

I

Only a man harrowing clods
In a slow silent walk

[1] Jer. li, 20.

With an old horse that stumbles and nods
    Half asleep as they stalk.

II

Only thin smoke without flame
    From the heaps of couch-grass;
Yet this will go onward the same
    Though Dynasties pass.

III

Yonder a maid and her wight
    Come whispering by:
War's annals will fade into night
    Ere their story die.

"And There Was a Great Calm"

(ON THE SIGNING OF THE ARMISTICE, NOV. 11, 1918)

I

There had been years of Passion—scorching, cold,
And much Despair, and Anger heaving high,
Care whitely watching, Sorrows manifold,
Among the young, among the weak and old,
And the pensive Spirit of Pity whispered, "Why?"

II

Men had not paused to answer. Foes distraught
Pierced the thinned peoples in a brute-like blindness,
Philosophies that sages long had taught,
And Selflessness, were as an unknown thought,
And "Hell!" and "Shell!" were yapped at Lovingkindness.

III

The feeble folk at home had grown full-used
To "dug-outs," "snipers," "Huns," from the war-adept
In the mornings heard, and at evetides perused;
To day-dreamt men in millions, when they mused—
To nightmare-men in millions when they slept.

IV

Waking to wish existence timeless, null,
Sirius they watched above where armies fell;
He seemed to check his flapping when, in the lull

Of night a boom came thencewise, like the dull
Plunge of a stone dropped into some deep well.

v

So, when old hopes that earth was bettering slowly
Were dead and damned, there sounded "War is done!"
One morrow. Said the bereft, and meek, and lowly,
"Will men some day be given to grace? yea, wholly,
And in good sooth, as our dreams used to run?"

VI

Breathless they paused. Out there men raised their glance
To where had stood those poplars lank and lopped,
As they had raised it through the four years' dance
Of Death in the now familiar flats of France;
And murmured, "Strange, this! How? All firing stopped?"

VII

Aye; all was hushed. The about-to-fire fired not,
The aimed-at moved away in trance-lipped song.
One checkless regiment slung a clinching shot
And turned. The Spirit of Irony smirked out, "What?
Spoil peradventures woven of Rage and Wrong?"

VIII

Thenceforth no flying fires inflamed the gray,
No hurtlings shook the dewdrop from the thorn,
No moan perplexed the mute bird on the spray;
Worn horses mused: "We are not whipped to-day";
No weft-winged engines blurred the moon's thin horn.

IX

Calm fell. From Heaven distilled a clemency;
There was peace on earth, and silence in the sky;
Some could, some could not, shake off misery:
The Sinister Spirit sneered: "It had to be!"
And again the Spirit of Pity whispered, "Why?"

The Harbour Bridge

From here, the quay, one looks above to mark
The bridge across the harbour, hanging dark
Against the day's-end sky, fair-green in glow

Over and under the middle archway's bow:
It draws its skeleton where the sun has set,
Yea, clear from cutwater to parapet;
On which mild glow, too, lines of rope and spar
    Trace themselves black as char.

Down here in shade we hear the painters shift
Against the bollards with a drowsy lift,
As moved by the incoming stealthy tide.
High up across the bridge the burghers glide
As cut black-paper portraits hastening on
In conversation none knows what upon:
Their sharp-edged lips move quickly word by word
    To speech that is not heard.

There trails the dreamful girl, who leans and stops,
There presses the practical woman to the shops,
There is a sailor, meeting his wife with a start,
And we, drawn nearer, judge they are keeping apart.
Both pause. She says: "I've looked for you. I thought
We'd make it up." Then no words can be caught.
At last: "Won't you come home?" She moves still nigher:
    "'Tis comfortable, with a fire."

"No," he says gloomily. "And, anyhow,
I can't give up the other woman now:
You should have talked like that in former days,
When I was last home." They go different ways.
And the west dims, and yellow lamplights shine:
And soon above, like lamps more opaline,
White stars ghost forth, that care not for men's wives,
    Or any other lives.

GERARD MANLEY HOPKINS

God's Grandeur

The world is charged with the grandeur of God.
  It will flame out, like shining from shook foil;
  It gathers to a greatness, like the ooze of oil
Crushed. Why do men then now not reck his rod?
Generations have trod, have trod, have trod;
  And all is seared with trade; bleared, smeared with toil;

And wears man's smudge and shares man's smell: the soil
Is bare now, nor can foot feel, being shod.

And for all this, nature is never spent;
    There lives the dearest freshness deep down things;
And though the last lights off the black West went
    Oh, morning, at the brown brink eastward, springs—
Because the Holy Ghost over the bent
    World broods with warm breast and with ah! bright wings.

The Windhover:

TO CHRIST OUR LORD

I caught this morning morning's minion, king-
    Dom of daylight's dauphin, dapple-dawn-drawn Falcon, in his riding
    Of the rolling level underneath him steady air, and striding
High there, how he rung upon the rein of a wimpling wing
In his ecstasy! then off, off forth on swing,
    As a skate's heel sweeps smooth on a bow-bend: the hurl and gliding
    Rebuffed the big wind. My heart in hiding
Stirred for a bird,—the achieve of, the mastery of the thing!

Brute beauty and valour and act, oh, air, pride, plume, here
    Buckle! AND the fire that breaks from thee then, a billion
Times told lovelier, more dangerous, O my chevalier!

    No wonder of it: shéer plód makes plough down sillion
Shine, and blue-bleak embers, ah my dear,
    Fall, gall themselves, and gash gold-vermilion.

The Caged Skylark

As a dare-gale skylark scanted in a dull cage
    Man's mounting spirit in his bone-house, mean house, dwells—
    That bird beyond the remembering his free fells;
This in drudgery, day-labouring-out life's age.

Though aloft on turf or perch or poor low stage,
    Both sing sometímes the sweetest, sweetest spells,
    Yet both droop deadly sómetimes in their cells
Or wring their barriers in bursts of fear or rage.

Not that the sweet-fowl, song-fowl, needs no rest—
Why, hear him, hear him babble and drop down to his nest,
  But his own nest, wild nest, no prison.

Man's spirit will be flesh-bound when found at best,
But uncumberèd: meadow-down is not distressed
  For a rainbow footing it nor he for his bónes rísen.

Spring and Fall:

TO A YOUNG CHILD

Márgarét, áre you gríeving
Over Goldengrove unleaving?
Leáves, líke the things of man, you
With your fresh thoughts care for, can you?
Áh! ás the heart grows older
It will come to such sights colder
By and by, nor spare a sigh
Though worlds of wanwood leafmeal lie;
And yet you *will* weep and know why.
Now no matter, child, the name:
Sórrow's spríngs áre the same.
Nor mouth had, no nor mind, expressed
What heart heard of, ghost guessed:
It ís the blight man was born for,
It is Margaret you mourn for.

Inversnaid

This darksome burn, horseback brown,
His rollrock highroad roaring down,
In coop and in comb the fleece of his foam
Flutes and low to the lake falls home.

A windpuff-bonnet of fáwn-fróth
Turns and twindles over the broth
Of a pool so pitchblack, féll-frówning,
It rounds and rounds Despair to drowning.

Degged with dew, dappled with dew
Are the groins of the braes that the brook treads through,

Wiry heathpacks, flitches of fern,
And the beadbonny ash that sits over the burn.

What would the world be, once bereft
Of wet and of wildness? Let them be left,
O let them be left, wildness and wet;
Long live the weeds and the wilderness yet.

WILLIAM ERNEST HENLEY

Margaritæ Sorori

A late lark twitters from the quiet skies;
And from the west,
Where the sun, his day's work ended,
Lingers as in content,
There falls on the old, grey city
An influence luminous and serene,
A shining peace.

The smoke ascends
In a rosy-and-golden haze. The spires
Shine, and are changed. In the valley
Shadows rise. The lark sings on. The sun,
Closing his benediction,
Sinks, and the darkening air
Thrills with a sense of the triumphing night—
Night with her train of stars
And her great gift of sleep.

So be my passing!
My task accomplished and the long day done,
My wages taken, and in my heart
Some late lark singing,
Let me be gathered to the quiet west,
The sundown splendid and serene,
Death.

A. E. HOUSMAN

Loveliest of Trees, the Cherry Now

Loveliest of trees, the cherry now
Is hung with bloom along the bough,

And stands about the woodland ride
Wearing white for Eastertide.

Now, of my threescore years and ten,
Twenty will not come again,
And take from seventy springs a score,
It only leaves me fifty more.

And since to look at things in bloom
Fifty springs are little room,
About the woodlands I will go
To see the cherry hung with snow.

Reveille

Wake: the silver dusk returning
    Up the beach of darkness brims,
And the ship of sunrise burning
    Strands upon the eastern rims.

Wake: the vaulted shadow shatters,
    Trampled to the floor it spanned,
And the tent of night in tatters
    Straws the sky-pavilioned land.

Up, lad, up, 'tis late for lying:
    Hear the drums of morning play;
Hark, the empty highways crying
    'Who'll beyond the hills away?'

Towns and countries woo together,
    Forelands beacon, belfries call;
Never lad that trod on leather
    Lived to feast his heart with all.

Up, lad: thews that lie and cumber
    Sunlit pallets never thrive;
Morns abed and daylight slumber
    Were not meant for man alive.

Clay lies still, but blood's a rover;
    Breath's a ware that will not keep.
Up, lad: when the journey's over
    There'll be time enough to sleep.

To an Athlete Dying Young

The time you won your town the race
We chaired you through the market-place;
Man and boy stood cheering by,
And home we brought you shoulder-high.

To-day, the road all runners come,
Shoulder-high we bring you home,
And set you at your threshold down,
Townsman of a stiller town.

Smart lad, to slip betimes away
From fields where glory does not stay
And early though the laurel grows
It withers quicker than the rose.

Eyes the shady night has shut
Cannot see the record cut,
And silence sounds no worse than cheers
After earth has stopped the ears:

Now you will not swell the rout
Of lads that wore their honours out,
Runners whom renown outran
And the name died before the man.

So set, before its echoes fade,
The fleet foot on the sill of shade,
And hold to the low lintel up
The still-defended challenge-cup.

And round that early-laurelled head
Will flock to gaze the strengthless dead
And find unwithered on its curls
The garland briefer than a girl's.

On the Idle Hill of Summer

On the idle hill of summer,
  Sleepy with the flow of streams,
Far I hear the steady drummer
  Drumming like a noise in dreams.

Far and near and low and louder
   On the roads of earth go by,
Dear to friends and food for powder,
   Soldiers marching, all to die.

East and west on fields forgotten
   Bleach the bones of comrades slain
Lovely lads and dead and rotten;
   None that go return again.

Far the calling bugles hollo,
   High the screaming fife replies,
Gay the files of scarlet follow:
   Woman bore me, I will rise.

The Chestnut Casts His Flambeaux, and the Flowers

The chestnut casts his flambeaux, and the flowers
   Stream from the hawthorn on the wind away,
The doors clap to, the pane is blind with showers.
   Pass me the can, lad; there's an end of May.

There's one spoilt spring to scant our mortal lot,
   One season ruined of our little store.
May will be fine next year as like as not:
   Oh ay, but then we shall be twenty-four.

We for a certainty are not the first
   Have sat in taverns while the tempest hurled
Their hopeful plans to emptiness, and cursed
   Whatever brute and blackguard made the world.

It is in truth iniquity on high
   To cheat our sentenced souls of aught they crave,
And mar the merriment as you and I
   Fare on our long fool's-errand to the grave.

Iniquity it is; but pass the can.
   My lad, no pair of kings our mothers bore;
Our only portion is the estate of man:
   We want the moon, but we shall get no more.

If here to-day the cloud of thunder lours
    To-morrow it will hie on far behests;
The flesh will grieve on other bones than ours
    Soon, and the soul will mourn in other breasts.

The troubles of our proud and angry dust
    Are from eternity, and shall not fail.
Bear them we can, and if we can we must.
    Shoulder the sky, my lad, and drink your ale.

SIR CHARLES G. D. ROBERTS

Ice

When Winter scourged the meadow and the hill
And in the withered leafage worked his will,
The water shrank, and shuddered, and stood still,—
Then built himself a magic house of glass,
Irised with memories of flowers and grass,
Wherein to sit and watch the fury pass.

WILFRED CAMPBELL

How One Winter Came in the Lake Region

For weeks and weeks the autumn world stood still,
    Clothed in the shadow of a smoky haze;
The fields were dead, the wind had lost its will,
And all the lands were hushed by wood and hill,
    In those grey, withered days.

Behind a mist the blear sun rose and set,
    At night the moon would nestle in a cloud;
The fisherman, a ghost, did cast his net;
The lake its shores forgot to chafe and fret,
    And hushed its caverns loud.

Far in the smoky woods the birds were mute,
    Save that from blackened tree a jay would scream,
Or far in swamps the lizard's lonesome lute
Would pipe in thirst, or by some gnarled root
    The tree-toad trilled his dream.

From day to day still hushed the season's mood,
   The streams stayed in their runnels shrunk and dry;
Suns rose aghast by wave and shore and wood,
And all the world, with ominous silence, stood
   In weird expectancy.

When one strange night the sun like blood went down,
   Flooding the heavens in a ruddy hue;
Red grew the lake, the sere fields parched and brown,
Red grew the marshes where the creeks stole down,
   But never a wind-breath blew.

That night I felt the winter in my veins,
   A joyous tremor of the icy glow;
And woke to hear the North's wild vibrant strains,
While far and wide, by withered woods and plains,
   Fast fell the driving snow.

RUDYARD KIPLING

The Way through the Woods

They shut the road through the woods
Seventy years ago.
Weather and rain have undone it again,
And now you would never know
There was once a road through the woods
Before they planted the trees.
It is underneath the coppice and heath
And the thin anemones.
Only the keeper sees
That, where the ring-dove broods,
And the badgers roll at ease,
There was once a road through the woods.
Yet, if you enter the woods
Of a summer evening late,
When the night-air cools on the trout-ringed pools
Where the otter whistles his mate,
(They fear not men in the woods,
Because they see so few.)
You will hear the beat of a horse's feet,
And the swish of a skirt in the dew,
Steadily cantering through

The misty solitudes,
As though they perfectly knew
The old lost road through the woods. . . .
But there is no road through the woods.

WILLIAM BUTLER YEATS

The Lake Isle of Innisfree

I will arise and go now, and go to Innisfree,
And a small cabin build there, of clay and wattles made:
Nine bean-rows will I have there, a hive for the honey-bee,
And live alone in the bee-loud glade.

And I shall have some peace there, for peace comes dropping slow,
Dropping from the veils of the morning to where the cricket sings;
There midnight's all a glimmer, and noon a purple glow,
And evening full of the linnet's wings.

I will arise and go now, for always night and day
I hear lake water lapping with low sounds by the shore;
While I stand on the roadway, or on the pavements grey,
I hear it in the deep heart's core.

The Song of Wandering Aengus

I went out to the hazel wood,
Because a fire was in my head,
And cut and peeled a hazel wand,
And hooked a berry to a thread;
And when white moths were on the wing,
And moth-like stars were flickering out,
I dropped the berry in a stream
And caught a little silver trout.

When I had laid it on the floor
I went to blow the fire aflame,
But something rustled on the floor,
And some one called me by my name:
It had become a glimmering girl
With apple blossom in her hair

Who called me by my name and ran
And faded through the brightening air.

Though I am old with wandering
Through hollow lands and hilly lands,
I will find out where she has gone,
And kiss her lips and take her hands;
And walk among long dappled grass,
And pluck till time and times are done
The silver apples of the moon,
The golden apples of the sun.

The Three Hermits

Three old hermits took the air
By a cold and desolate sea,
First was muttering a prayer,
Second rummaged for a flea;
On a windy stone, the third,
Giddy with his hundredth year,
Sang unnoticed like a bird:
'Though the Door of Death is near
And what waits behind the door,
Three times in a single day
I, though upright on the shore,
Fall asleep when I should pray.'
So the first, but now the second:
'We're but given what we have earned
When all thoughts and deeds are reckoned,
So it's plain to be discerned
That the shades of holy men
Who have failed, being weak of will,
Pass the Door of Birth again,
And are plagued by crowds, until
They've the passion to escape.'
Moaned the other, 'They are thrown
Into some most fearful shape.'
But the second mocked his moan:
'They are not changed to anything,
Having loved God once, but maybe
To a poet or a king
Or a witty lovely lady.'
While he'd rummaged rags and hair,

Caught and cracked his flea, the third,
Giddy with his hundredth year,
Sang unnoticed like a bird.

The Wild Swans at Coole

The trees are in their autumn beauty,
The woodland paths are dry,
Under the October twilight the water
Mirrors a still sky;
Upon the brimming water among the stones
Are nine-and-fifty swans.

The nineteenth autumn has come upon me
Since I first made my count;
I saw, before I had well finished,
All suddenly mount
And scatter wheeling in great broken rings
Upon their clamorous wings.

I have looked upon those brilliant creatures,
And now my heart is sore.
All's changed since I, hearing at twilight,
The first time on this shore,
The bell-beat of their wings above my head,
Trod with a lighter tread.

Unwearied still, lover by lover,
They paddle in the cold
Companionable streams or climb the air;
Their hearts have not grown old;
Passion or conquest, wander where they will,
Attend upon them still.

But now they drift on the still water,
Mysterious, beautiful;
Among what rushes will they build,
By what lake's edge or pool
Delight men's eyes when I awake some day
To find they have flown away?

The Scholars

Bald heads forgetful of their sins,
Old, learned, respectable bald heads
Edit and annotate the lines
That young men, tossing on their beds,
Rhymed out in love's despair
To flatter beauty's ignorant ear.

All shuffle there; all cough in ink;
All wear the carpet with their shoes;
All think what other people think;
All know the man their neighbour knows.
Lord, what would they say
Did their Catullus walk that way?

The Second Coming

Turning and turning in the widening gyre
The falcon cannot hear the falconer;
Things fall apart; the centre cannot hold;
Mere anarchy is loosed upon the world,
The blood-dimmed tide is loosed, and everywhere
The ceremony of innocence is drowned;
The best lack all conviction, while the worst
Are full of passionate intensity.

Surely some revelation is at hand;
Surely the Second Coming is at hand.
The Second Coming! Hardly are those words out
When a vast image out of *Spiritus Mundi*
Troubles my sight: somewhere in sands of the desert
A shape with lion body and the head of a man,
A gaze blank and pitiless as the sun,
Is moving its slow thighs, while all about it
Reel shadows of the indignant desert birds.
The darkness drops again; but now I know
That twenty centuries of stony sleep
Were vexed to nightmare by a rocking cradle,
And what rough beast, its hour come round at last,
Slouches towards Bethlehem to be born?

Leda and the Swan

A sudden blow: the great wings beating still
Above the staggering girl, her thighs caressed
By the dark webs, her nape caught in his bill,
He holds her helpless breast upon his breast.

How can those terrified vague fingers push
The feathered glory from her loosening thighs?
And how can body, laid in that white rush,
But feel the strange heart beating where it lies?

A shudder in the loins engenders there
The broken wall, the burning roof and tower
And Agamemnon dead.
               Being so caught up,
So mastered by the brute blood of the air,
Did she put on his knowledge with his power
Before the indifferent beak could let her drop?

Among School Children

I

I walk through the long schoolroom questioning;
A kind old nun in a white hood replies;
The children learn to cipher and to sing,
To study reading-books and history,
To cut and sew, be neat in everything
In the best modern way—the children's eyes
In momentary wonder stare upon
A sixty-year-old smiling public man.

II

I dream of a Ledaean body, bent
Above a sinking fire, a tale that she
Told of a harsh reproof, or trivial event
That changed some childish day to tragedy—
Told, and it seemed that our two natures blent
Into a sphere from youthful sympathy,
Or else, to alter Plato's parable,
Into the yolk and white of the one shell.

And thinking of that fit of grief or rage
I look upon one child or t'other there
And wonder if she stood so at that age—
For even daughters of the swan can share
Something of every paddler's heritage—
And had that colour upon cheek or hair,
And thereupon my heart is driven wild:
She stands before me as a living child.

IV

Her present image floats into the mind—
Did Quattrocento finger fashion it
Hollow of cheek as though it drank the wind
And took a mess of shadows for its meat?
And I though never of Ledaean kind
Had pretty plumage once—enough of that,
Better to smile on all that smile, and show
There is a comfortable kind of old scarecrow.

What youthful mother, a shape upon her lap
Honey of generation had betrayed,
And that must sleep, shriek, struggle to escape
As recollection or the drug decide,
Would think her son, did she but see that shape
With sixty or more winters on its head,
A compensation for the pang of his birth,
Or the uncertainty of his setting forth?

VI

Plato thought nature but a spume that plays
Upon a ghostly paradigm of things;
Solider Aristotle played the taws
Upon the bottom of a king of kings;
World-famous golden-thighed Pythagoras
Fingered upon a fiddle-stick or strings
What a star sang and careless Muses heard:
Old clothes upon old sticks to scare a bird.

Both nuns and mothers worship images,
But those the candles light are not as those
That animate a mother's reveries,

But keep a marble or a bronze repose.
And yet they too break hearts—O Presences
That passion, piety or affection knows,
And that all heavenly glory symbolise—
O self-born mockers of man's enterprise;

VIII

Labour is blossoming or dancing where
The body is not bruised to pleasure soul,
Nor beauty born out of its own despair,
Nor blear-eyed wisdom out of midnight oil.
O chestnut-tree, great-rooted blossomer,
Are you the leaf, the blossom or the bole?
O body swayed to music, O brightening glance,
How can we know the dancer from the dance?

Coole Park and Ballylee, 1931

Under my window-ledge the waters race,
Otters below and moor-hens on the top,
Run for a mile undimmed in Heaven's face
Then darkening through 'dark' Raftery's 'cellar' drop,
Run underground, rise in a rocky place
In Coole demesne, and there to finish up
Spread to a lake and drop into a hole.
What's water but the generated soul?

Upon the border of that lake's a wood
Now all dry sticks under a wintry sun,
And in a copse of beeches there I stood,
For Nature's pulled her tragic buskin on
And all the rant's a mirror of my mood:
At sudden thunder of the mounting swan
I turned about and looked where branches break
The glittering reaches of the flooded lake.

Another emblem there! That stormy white
But seems a concentration of the sky;
And, like the soul, it sails into the sight
And in the morning's gone, no man knows why;
And is so lovely that it sets to right
What knowledge or its lack had set awry,

So arrogantly pure, a child might think
It can be murdered with a spot of ink.

Sound of a stick upon the floor, a sound
From somebody that toils from chair to chair;
Beloved books that famous hands have bound,
Old marble heads, old pictures everywhere;
Great rooms where travelled men and children found
Content or joy; a last inheritor
Where none has reigned that lacked a name and fame
Or out of folly into folly came.

A spot whereon the founders lived and died
Seemed once more dear than life; ancestral trees,
Or gardens rich in memory glorified
Marriages, alliances and families,
And every bride's ambition satisfied.
Where fashion or mere fantasy decrees
We shift about—all that great glory spent—
Like some poor Arab tribesman and his tent.

We were the last romantics—chose for theme
Traditional sanctity and loveliness;
Whatever's written in what poets name
The book of the people; whatever most can bless
The mind of man or elevate a rhyme;
But all is changed, that high horse riderless,
Though mounted in that saddle Homer rode
Where the swan drifts upon a darkening flood.

For Anne Gregory

'Never shall a young man,
Thrown into despair
By those great honey-coloured
Ramparts at your ear,
Love you for yourself alone
And not your yellow hair.'

'But I can get a hair-dye
And set such colour there,
Brown, or black, or carrot,

That young men in despair
May love me for myself alone
And not my yellow hair.'

'I heard an old religious man
But yesternight declare
That he had found a text to prove
That only God, my dear,
Could love you for yourself alone
And not your yellow hair.'

EDWIN ARLINGTON ROBINSON

The House on the Hill

They are all gone away,
    The House is shut and still,
There is nothing more to say.

Through broken walls and gray
    The winds blow bleak and shrill:
They are all gone away.

Nor is there one to-day
    To speak them good or ill:
There is nothing more to say.

Why is it then we stray
    Around the sunken sill?
They are all gone away,

And our poor fancy-play
    For them is wasted skill:
There is nothing more to say.

There is ruin and decay
    In the House on the Hill:
They are all gone away,
There is nothing more to say.

Richard Cory

Whenever Richard Cory went down town,
We people on the pavement looked at him:
He was a gentleman from sole to crown,
Clean favored, and imperially slim.

And he was always quietly arrayed,
And he was always human when he talked;
But still he fluttered pulses when he said,
"Good-morning," and he glittered when he walked.

And he was rich—yes, richer than a king—
And admirably schooled in every grace:
In fine, we thought that he was everything
To make us wish that we were in his place.

So on we worked, and waited for the light,
And went without the meat, and cursed the bread;
And Richard Cory, one calm summer night,
Went home and put a bullet through his head.

Miniver Cheevy

Miniver Cheevy, child of scorn,
    Grew lean while he assailed the seasons;
He wept that he was ever born,
    And he had reasons.

Miniver loved the days of old
    When swords were bright and steeds were prancing;
The vision of a warrior bold
    Would set him dancing.

Miniver sighed for what was not,
    And dreamed, and rested from his labors;
He dreamed of Thebes and Camelot,
    And Priam's neighbors.

Miniver mourned the ripe renown
    That made so many a name so fragrant;

He mourned Romance, now on the town,
  And Art, a vagrant.

Miniver loved the Medici,
  Albeit he had never seen one;
He would have sinned incessantly
  Could he have been one.

Miniver cursed the commonplace
  And eyed a khaki suit with loathing;
He missed the mediæval grace
  Of iron clothing.

Miniver scorned the gold he sought,
  But sore annoyed was he without it;
Miniver thought, and thought, and thought,
  And thought about it.

Miniver Cheevy, born too late,
  Scratched his head and kept on thinking;
Miniver coughed, and called it fate,
  And kept on drinking.

Eros Turannos

She fears him, and will always ask
  What fated her to choose him;
She meets in his engaging mask
  All reasons to refuse him;
But what she meets and what she fears
Are less than are the downward years,
Drawn slowly to the foamless weirs
  Of age, were she to lose him.

Between a blurred sagacity
  That once had power to sound him,
And Love, that will not let him be
  The Judas that she found him,
Her pride assuages her almost,
As if it were alone the cost.—
He sees that he will not be lost,
  And waits and looks around him.

A sense of ocean and old trees
   Envelops and allures him;
Tradition, touching all he sees,
   Beguiles and reassures him;
And all her doubts of what he says
Are dimmed with what she knows of days—
Till even prejudice delays
   And fades, and she secures him.

The falling leaf inaugurates
   The reign of her confusion;
The pounding wave reverberates
   The dirge of her illusion;
And home, where passion lived and died,
Becomes a place where she can hide,
While all the town and harbor side
   Vibrate with her seclusion.

We tell you, tapping on our brows,
   The story as it should be,—
As if the story of a house
   Were told, or ever could be;
We'll have no kindly veil between
Her visions and those we have seen,—
As if we guessed what hers have been,
   Or what they are or would be.

Meanwhile we do no harm; for they
   That with a god have striven,
Not hearing much of what we say,
   Take what the god has given;
Though like waves breaking it may be,
Or like a changed familiar tree,
Or like a stairway to the sea
   Where down the blind are driven.

Mr. Flood's Party

Old Eben Flood, climbing alone one night
Over the hill between the town below
And the forsaken upland hermitage
That held as much as he should ever know
On earth again of home, paused warily.

The road was his with not a native near;
And Eben, having leisure, said aloud,
For no man else in Tilbury Town to hear:

"Well, Mr. Flood, we have the harvest moon
Again, and we may not have many more;
The bird is on the wing, the poet says,
And you and I have said it here before.
Drink to the bird." He raised up to the light
The jug that he had gone so far to fill,
And answered huskily: "Well, Mr. Flood,
Since you propose it, I believe I will."

Alone, as if enduring to the end
A valiant armor of scarred hopes outworn,
He stood there in the middle of the road
Like Roland's ghost winding a silent horn.
Below him, in the town among the trees,
Where friends of other days had honored him,
A phantom salutation of the dead
Rang thinly till old Eben's eyes were dim.

Then, as a mother lays her sleeping child
Down tenderly, fearing it may awake,
He set the jug down slowly at his feet
With trembling care, knowing that most things break;
And only when assured that on firm earth
It stood, as the uncertain lives of men
Assuredly did not, he paced away,
And with his hand extended paused again:

"Well, Mr. Flood, we have not met like this
In a long time; and many a change has come
To both of us, I fear, since last it was
We had a drop together. Welcome home!"
Convivially returning with himself,
Again he raised the jug up to the light;
And with an acquiescent quaver said:
"Well, Mr. Flood, if you insist, I might.

"Only a very little, Mr. Flood—
For auld lang syne. No more, sir; that will do."
So, for the time, apparently it did,
And Eben evidently thought so too;

For soon amid the silver loneliness
Of night he lifted up his voice and sang,
Secure, with only two moons listening,
Until the whole harmonious landscape rang—

"For auld lang syne." The weary throat gave out,
The last word wavered, and the song was done.
He raised again the jug regretfully
And shook his head, and was again alone.
There was not much that was ahead of him,
And there was nothing in the town below—
Where strangers would have shut the many doors
That many friends had opened long ago.

EDGAR LEE MASTERS

Fiddler Jones

The earth keeps some vibration going
There in your heart, and that is you.
And if the people find you can fiddle,
Why, fiddle you must, for all your life.
What do you see, a harvest of clover?
Or a meadow to walk through to the river;
The wind's in the corn; you rub your hands
For beeves hereafter ready for market;
Or else you hear the rustle of skirts
Like the girls when dancing at Little Grove.
To Cooney Potter a pillar of dust
Or whirling leaves meant ruinous drouth;
They looked to me like Red-Head Sammy
Stepping it off, to "Toor-a-Loor."
How could I till my forty acres
Not to speak of getting more,
With a medley of horns, bassoons and piccolos
Stirred in my brain by crows and robins
And the creak of a wind-mill—only these?
And I never started to plow in my life
That some one did not stop in the road
And take me away to a dance or picnic.
I ended up with forty acres;
I ended up with a broken fiddle—

And a broken laugh, and a thousand memories,
And not a single regret.

Jonathan Houghton

There is the caw of a crow,
And the hesitant song of a thrush.
There is the tinkle of a cowbell far away,
And the voice of a plowman on Shipley's hill.
The forest beyond the orchard is still
With midsummer stillness;
And along the road a wagon chuckles,
Loaded with corn, going to Atterbury.
And an old man sits under a tree asleep,
And an old woman crosses the road,
Coming from the orchard with a bucket of blackberries.
And a boy lies in the grass
Near the feet of the old man,
And looks up at the sailing clouds,
And longs, and longs, and longs
For what, he knows not:
For manhood, for life, for the unknown world!
Then thirty years passed,
And the boy returned worn out by life
And found the orchard vanished,
And the forest gone,
And the house made over,
And the roadway filled with dust from automobiles—
And himself desiring The Hill!

TRUMBULL STICKNEY

Mnemosyne

It's autumn in the country I remember.

How warm a wind blew here about the ways!
And shadows on the hillside lay to slumber
During the long sun-sweetened summer-days.

It's cold abroad the country I remember.

The swallows veering skimmed the golden grain
At midday with a wing aslant and limber;
And yellow cattle browsed upon the plain.

It's empty down the country I remember.

I had a sister lovely in my sight:
Her hair was dark, her eyes were very sombre;
We sang together in the woods at night.

It's lonely in the country I remember.

The babble of our children fills my ears,
And on our hearth I stare the perished ember
To flames that show all starry thro' my tears.

It's dark about the country I remember.

There are the mountains where I lived. The path
Is slushed with cattle-tracks and fallen timber,
The stumps are twisted by the tempests' wrath.

But that I knew these places are my own,
I'd ask how came such wretchedness to cumber
The earth, and I to people it alone.

It rains across the country I remember.

ROBERT FROST

After Apple-Picking

My long two-pointed ladder's sticking through a tree
Toward heaven still,
And there's a barrel that I didn't fill
Beside it, and there may be two or three
Apples I didn't pick upon some bough.
But I am done with apple-picking now.
Essence of winter sleep is on the night,
The scent of apples: I am drowsing off.
I cannot rub the strangeness from my sight
I got from looking through a pane of glass
I skimmed this morning from the drinking trough

And held against the world of hoary grass.
It melted, and I let it fall and break.
But I was well
Upon my way to sleep before it fell,
And I could tell
What form my dreaming was about to take.
Magnified apples appear and disappear,
Stem end and blossom end,
And every fleck of russet showing clear.
My instep arch not only keeps the ache,
It keeps the pressure of a ladder-round.
I feel the ladder sway as the boughs bend.
And I keep hearing from the cellar bin
The rumbling sound
Of load on load of apples coming in.
For I have had too much
Of apple-picking: I am overtired
Of the great harvest I myself desired.
There were ten thousand thousand fruit to touch,
Cherish in hand, lift down, and not let fall.
For all
That struck the earth,
No matter if not bruised or spiked with stubble,
Went surely to the cider-apple heap
As of no worth.
One can see what will trouble
This sleep of mine, whatever sleep it is.
Were he not gone,
The woodchuck could say whether it's like his
Long sleep, as I describe its coming on,
Or just some human sleep.

'Out, Out—'

The buzz saw snarled and rattled in the yard
And made dust and dropped stove-length sticks of wood,
Sweet-scented stuff when the breeze drew across it.
And from there those that lifted eyes could count
Five mountain ranges one behind the other
Under the sunset far into Vermont.
And the saw snarled and rattled, snarled and rattled,
As it ran light, or had to bear a load.
And nothing happened: day was all but done.

Call it a day, I wish they might have said
To please the boy by giving him the half hour
That a boy counts so much when saved from work.
His sister stood beside them in her apron
To tell them 'Supper.' At the word, the saw,
As if to prove saws knew what supper meant,
Leaped out at the boy's hand, or seemed to leap—
He must have given the hand. However it was,
Neither refused the meeting. But the hand!
The boy's first outcry was a rueful laugh,
As he swung toward them holding up the hand
Half in appeal, but half as if to keep
The life from spilling. Then the boy saw all—
Since he was old enough to know, big boy
Doing a man's work, though a child at heart—
He saw all spoiled. 'Don't let him cut my hand off—
The doctor, when he comes. Don't let him, sister!'
So. But the hand was gone already.
The doctor put him in the dark of ether.
He lay and puffed his lips out with his breath.
And then—the watcher at his pulse took fright.
No one believed. They listened at his heart.
Little—less—nothing!—and that ended it.
No more to build on there. And they, since they
Were not the one dead, turned to their affairs.

Fire and Ice

Some say the world will end in fire,
Some say in ice.
From what I've tasted of desire
I hold with those who favor fire.
But if it had to perish twice,
I think I know enough of hate
To say that for destruction ice
Is also great
And would suffice.

Stopping by Woods on a Snowy Evening

Whose woods these are I think I know.
His house is in the village though;

He will not see me stopping here
To watch his woods fill up with snow.

My little horse must think it queer
To stop without a farmhouse near
Between the woods and frozen lake
The darkest evening of the year.

He gives his harness bells a shake
To ask if there is some mistake.
The only other sound's the sweep
Of easy wind and downy flake.

The woods are lovely, dark and deep,
But I have promises to keep,
And miles to go before I sleep,
And miles to go before I sleep.

Provide, Provide

The witch that came (the withered hag)
To wash the steps with pail and rag,
Was once the beauty Abishag,

The picture pride of Hollywood.
Too many fall from great and good
For you to doubt the likelihood.

Die early and avoid the fate.
Or if predestined to die late,
Make up your mind to die in state.

Make the whole stock exchange your own!
If need be occupy a throne,
Where nobody can call *you* crone.

Some have relied on what they knew;
Others on being simply true.
What worked for them might work for you.

No memory of having starred
Atones for later disregard,
Or keeps the end from being hard.

Better to go down dignified
With boughten friendship at your side
Than none at all. Provide, provide!

In Divés' Dive

It is late at night and still I am losing,
But still I am steady and unaccusing.

As long as the Declaration guards
My right to be equal in number of cards,

It is nothing to me who runs the Dive.
Let's have a look at another five.

A Cabin in the Clearing

FOR ALFRED EDWARDS

MIST

I don't believe the sleepers in this house
Know where they are.

SMOKE

They've been here long enough
To push the woods back from around the house
And part them in the middle with a path.

MIST

And still I doubt if they know where they are.
And I begin to fear they never will.
All they maintain the path for is the comfort
Of visiting with the equally bewildered.
Nearer in plight their neighbors are than distance.

SMOKE

I am the guardian wraith of starlit smoke
That leans out this and that way from their chimney.
I will not have their happiness despaired of.

MIST

No one—not I—would give them up for lost
Simply because they don't know where they are.

I am the damper counterpart of smoke
That gives off from a garden ground at night
But lifts no higher than a garden grows.
I cotton to their landscape. That's who I am.
I am no further from their fate than you are.

SMOKE

They must by now have learned the native tongue.
Why don't they ask the Red Man where they are?

MIST

They often do, and none the wiser for it.
So do they also ask philosophers
Who come to look in on them from the pulpit.
They will ask anyone there is to ask—
In the fond faith accumulated fact
Will of itself take fire and light the world up.
Learning has been a part of their religion.

SMOKE

If the day ever comes when they know who
They are, they may know better where they are.
But who they are is too much to believe—
Either for them or the onlooking world.
They are too sudden to be credible.

MIST

Listen, they murmur talking in the dark
On what should be their daylong theme continued.
Putting the lamp out has not put their thought out.
Let us pretend the dewdrops from the eaves
Are you and I eavesdropping on their unrest—
A mist and smoke eavesdropping on a haze—
And see if we can tell the bass from the soprano.

Than smoke and mist who better could appraise
The kindred spirit of an inner haze.

Questioning Faces

The winter owl banked just in time to pass
And save herself from breaking window glass.
And her wings straining suddenly aspread

Caught color from the last of evening red
In a display of underdown and quill
To glassed-in children at the window sill.

F. C. SLATER

Milking Kraal

When stars begin softly to spatter
Milky drops in the bowl overhead;
And the wings of brown bats shear obliquely
The fleece of the dusk;
In the kraal squatting milkers are stitching
Each cow to a pail
With silvery thread.

Full-bellied cows chew serenely
The cud, and they gulp and they sigh
With contentment; while milkers chant slowly
Songs wordless and strange:
In the distance a veld-ranging jackal
Screws into the silence
His agonized cry.

Now the kindly harvest is gathered,
The milk-pails are carried away;
And sly little herdboys gleefully
Tickle their teeth
With gleanings of milk from reaped udders,
Wisely squeezing last drops
Of delight from spent day.

Lament for a Dead Cow

Siyalila, siyalila, inkomo yetu ifile! [1]
    Beautiful was Wetu as a blue shadow,
That nests on the grey rocks
About a sunbaked hilltop:
Her coat was black and shiny
Like an isipingo-berry;

[1] We weep, we weep, our cow is dead!

Her horns were as sharp as the horns of the new moon
That tosses aloft the evening star;
Her round eyes were as clear and soft
As a mountain-pool,
Where shadows dive from the high rocks.
No more will Wetu banish teasing flies
With her whistling tail;
No more will she face yapping curs
With lowered horns and bewildered eyes;
No more will her slow shadow
Comfort the sunburnt veld, and her sweet lowing
Delight the hills in the evening.
The fountain that filled our calabashes
Has been drained by a thirsty sun;
The black cloud that brought us white rain
Has vanished—the sky is empty;
Our kraal is desolate;
Our calabashes are dry:
And we weep.

THEODORE GOODRIDGE ROBERTS

The Blue Heron

In a green place lanced through
With amber and gold and blue;
A place of water and weeds
And roses pinker than dawn,
And ranks of lush young reeds,
And grasses straightly withdrawn
From graven ripples of sands,
The still blue heron stands.

Smoke-blue he is, and grey
As embers of yesterday.
Still he is, as death;
Like stone, or shadow of stone,
Without a pulse or breath,
Motionless and alone
There in the lily stems:
But his eyes are alive like gems.

Still as a shadow; still
Grey feather and yellow bill:

Still as an image made
Of mist and smoke half hid
By windless sunshine and shade,
Save when a yellow lid
Slides and is gone like a breath:
Death-still—and sudden as death.

WALLACE STEVENS

Domination of Black

At night, by the fire,
The colors of the bushes
And of the fallen leaves,
Repeating themselves,
Turned in the room,
Like the leaves themselves
Turning in the wind.
Yes: but the color of the heavy hemlocks
Came striding.
And I remembered the cry of the peacocks.

The colors of their tails
Were like the leaves themselves
Turning in the wind,
In the twilight wind.
They swept over the room,
Just as they flew from the boughs of the hemlocks
Down to the ground.
I heard them cry—the peacocks.
Was it a cry against the twilight
Or against the leaves themselves
Turning in the wind,
Turning as the flames
Turned in the fire,
Turning as the tails of the peacocks
Turned in the loud fire,
Loud as the hemlocks
Full of the cry of the peacocks?
Or was it a cry against the hemlocks?

Out of the window,
I saw how the planets gathered
Like the leaves themselves
Turning in the wind.

I saw how the night came,
Came striding like the color of the heavy hemlocks
I felt afraid.
And I remembered the cry of the peacocks.

The Snow Man

One must have a mind of winter
To regard the frost and the boughs
Of the pine-trees crusted with snow;

And have been cold a long time
To behold the junipers shagged with ice,
The spruces rough in the distant glitter

Of the January sun; and not to think
Of any misery in the sound of the wind,
In the sound of a few leaves,

Which is the sound of the land
Full of the same wind
That is blowing in the same bare place

For the listener, who listens in the snow,
And, nothing himself, beholds
Nothing that is not there and the nothing that is.

The Emperor of Ice-Cream

Call the roller of big cigars,
The muscular one, and bid him whip
In kitchen cups concupiscent curds.
Let the wenches dawdle in such dress
As they are used to wear, and let the boys
Bring flowers in last month's newspapers.
Let be be finale of seem.
The only emperor is the emperor of ice-cream.

Take from the dresser of deal
Lacking the three glass knobs, that sheet
On which she embroidered fantails once
And spread it so as to cover her face.

If her horny feet protrude, they come
To show how cold she is, and dumb.
Let the lamp affix its beam.
The only emperor is the emperor of ice-cream.

Sunday Morning

I

Complacencies of the peignoir, and late
Coffee and oranges in a sunny chair,
And the green freedom of a cockatoo
Upon a rug mingle to dissipate
The holy hush of ancient sacrifice.
She dreams a little, and she feels the dark
Encroachment of that old catastrophe,
As a calm darkens among water-lights.
The pungent oranges and bright, green wings
Seem things in some procession of the dead,
Winding across wide water, without sound.
The day is like wide water, without sound,
Stilled for the passing of her dreaming feet
Over the seas, to silent Palestine,
Dominion of the blood and sepulchre.

II

Why should she give her bounty to the dead?
What is divinity if it can come
Only in silent shadows and in dreams?
Shall she not find in comforts of the sun,
In pungent fruit and bright, green wings, or else
In any balm or beauty of the earth,
Things to be cherished like the thought of heaven?
Divinity must live within herself:
Passions of rain, or moods in falling snow;
Grievings in loneliness, or unsubdued
Elations when the forest blooms; gusty
Emotions on wet roads on autumn nights;
All pleasures and all pains, remembering
The bough of summer and the winter branch.
There are the measures destined for her soul.

III

Jove in the clouds had his inhuman birth.
No mother suckled him, no sweet land gave

Large-mannered motions to his mythy mind
He moved among us, as a muttering king,
Magnificent, would move among his hinds,
Until our blood, commingling, virginal,
With heaven, brought such requital to desire
The very hinds discerned it, in a star.
Shall our blood fail? Or shall it come to be
The blood of paradise? And shall the earth
Seem all of paradise that we shall know?
The sky will be much friendlier then than now,
A part of labor and a part of pain,
And next in glory to enduring love,
Not this dividing and indifferent blue.

IV

She says, "I am content when wakened birds,
Before they fly, test the reality
Of misty fields, by their sweet questionings;
But when the birds are gone, and their warm fields
Return no more, where, then, is paradise?"
There is not any haunt of prophecy,
Nor any old chimera of the grave,
Neither the golden underground, nor isle
Melodious, where spirits gat them home,
Nor visionary south, nor cloudy palm
Remote on heaven's hill, that has endured
As April's green endures; or will endure
Like her remembrance of awakened birds,
Or her desire for June and evening, tipped
By the consummation of the swallow's wings.

V

She says, "But in contentment I still feel
The need of some imperishable bliss."
Death is the mother of beauty; hence from her,
Alone, shall come fulfilment to our dreams
And our desires. Although she strews the leaves
Of sure obliteration on our paths,
The path sick sorrow took, the many paths
Where triumph rang its brassy phrase, or love
Whispered a little out of tenderness,
She makes the willow shiver in the sun
For maidens who were wont to sit and gaze
Upon the grass, relinquished to their feet.

She causes boys to pile new plums and pears
On disregarded plate. The maidens taste
And stray impassioned in the littering leaves.

VI

Is there no change of death in paradise?
Does ripe fruit never fall? Or do the boughs
Hang always heavy in that perfect sky,
Unchanging, yet so like our perishing earth,
With rivers like our own that seek for seas
They never find, the same receding shores
That never touch with inarticulate pang?
Why set the pear upon those river-banks
Or spice the shores with odors of the plum?
Alas, that they should wear our colors there,
The silken weavings of our afternoons,
And pick the strings of our insipid lutes!
Death is the mother of beauty, mystical,
Within whose burning bosom we devise
Our earthly mothers waiting, sleeplessly.

VII

Supple and turbulent, a ring of men
Shall chant in orgy on a summer morn
Their boisterous devotion to the sun,
Not as a god, but as a god might be,
Naked among them, like a savage source.
Their chant shall be a chant of paradise,
Out of their blood, returning to the sky;
And in their chant shall enter, voice by voice,
The windy lake wherein their lord delights,
The trees, like serafin, and echoing hills,
That choir among themselves long afterward.
They shall know well the heavenly fellowship
Of men that perish and of summer morn.
And whence they came and whither they shall go
The dew upon their feet shall manifest.

VIII

She hears, upon that water without sound,
A voice that cries, "The tomb in Palestine
Is not the porch of spirits lingering.
It is the grave of Jesus, where he lay."
We live in an old chaos of the sun,

Or old dependency of day and night,
Or island solitude, unsponsored, free,
Of that wide water, inescapable.
Deer walk upon our mountains, and the quail
Whistle about us their spontaneous cries;
Sweet berries ripen in the wilderness;
And, in the isolation of the sky,
At evening, casual flocks of pigeons make
Ambiguous undulations as they sink,
Downward to darkness, on extended wings.

Life Is Motion

In Oklahoma,
Bonnie and Josie,
Dressed in calico,
Danced around a stump.
They cried,
"Ohoyaho,
Ohoo" . . .
Celebrating the marriage
Of flesh and air.

Peter Quince at the Clavier

I

Just as my fingers on these keys
Make music, so the selfsame sounds
On my spirit make a music, too.

Music is feeling, then, not sound;
And thus it is that what I feel,
Here in this room, desiring you,

Thinking of your blue-shadowed silk,
Is music. It is like the strain
Waked in the elders by Susanna.

Of a green evening, clear and warm,
She bathed in her still garden, while
The red-eyed elders watching, felt

The basses of their beings throb
In witching chords, and their thin blood
Pulse pizzicati of Hosanna.

II

In the green water, clear and warm,
Susanna lay.
She searched
The touch of springs,
And found
Concealed imaginings.
She sighed,
For so much melody.

Upon the bank, she stood
In the cool
Of spent emotions.
She felt, among the leaves,
The dew
Of old devotions.

She walked upon the grass,
Still quavering.
The winds were like her maids,
On timid feet,
Fetching her woven scarves,
Yet wavering.

A breath upon her hand
Muted the night.
She turned—
A cymbal crashed,
And roaring horns.

III

Soon, with a noise like tambourines,
Came her attendant Byzantines.

They wondered why Susanna cried
Against the elders by her side;

And as they whispered, the refrain
Was like a willow swept by rain.

Anon, their lamps' uplifted flame
Revealed Susanna and her shame.

And then, the simpering Byzantines
Fled, with a noise like tambourines.

IV

Beauty is momentary in the mind—
The fitful tracing of a portal;
But in the flesh it is immortal.
The body dies; the body's beauty lives.
So evenings die, in their green going,
A wave, interminably flowing.
So gardens die, their meek breath scenting
The cowl of winter, done repenting.
So maidens die, to the auroral
Celebration of a maiden's choral.
Susanna's music touched the bawdy strings
Of those white elders; but, escaping,
Left only Death's ironic scraping.
Now, in its immortality, it plays
On the clear viol of her memory,
And makes a constant sacrament of praise.

Autumn Refrain

The skreak and skritter of evening gone
And grackles gone and sorrows of the sun,
The sorrows of sun, too, gone . . . the moon and moon,
The yellow moon of words about the nightingale
In measureless measures, not a bird for me
But the name of a bird and the name of a nameless air
I have never—shall never hear. And yet beneath
The stillness of everything gone, and being still,
Being and sitting still, something resides,
Some skreaking and skrittering residuum,
And grates these evasions of the nightingale
Though I have never—shall never hear that bird.
And the stillness is in the key, all of it is,
The stillness is all in the key of that desolate sound.

Study of Two Pears

I

Opusculum paedagogum.
The pears are not viols,
Nudes or bottles.
They resemble nothing else.

II

They are yellow forms
Composed of curves
Bulging toward the base.
They are touched red.

III

They are not flat surfaces
Having curved outlines.
They are round
Tapering toward the top.

IV

In the way they are modelled
There are bits of blue.
A hard dry leaf hangs
From the stem.

V

The yellow glistens.
It glistens with various yellows,
Citrons, oranges and greens
Flowering over the skin.

VI

The shadows of the pears
Are blobs on the green cloth.
The pears are not seen
As the observer wills.

Woman Looking at a Vase of Flowers

It was as if thunder took form upon
The piano, that time: the time when the crude

And jealous grandeurs of sun and sky
Scattered themselves in the garden, like
The wind dissolving into birds,
The clouds becoming braided girls.
It was like the sea poured out again
In east wind beating the shutters at night.

Hoot, little owl within her, how
High blue became particular
In the leaf and bud and how the red,
Flicked into pieces, points of air,
Became—how the central, essential red
Escaped its large abstraction, became,
First, summer, then a lesser time,
Then the sides of peaches, of dusky pears.

Hoot how the inhuman colors fell
Into place beside her, where she was,
Like human conciliations, more like
A profounder reconciling, an act,
An affirmation free from doubt.
The crude and jealous formlessness
Became the form and the fragrance of things
Without clairvoyance, close to her.

WILLIAM CARLOS WILLIAMS

Tract

I will teach you my townspeople
how to perform a funeral
for you have it over a troop
of artists—
unless one should scour the world—
you have the ground sense necessary.

See! the hearse leads.
I begin with a design for a hearse.
For Christ's sake not black—
nor white either—and not polished!
Let it be weathered—like a farm wagon—
with gilt wheels (this could be

applied fresh at small expense)
or no wheels at all:
a rough dray to drag over the ground.

Knock the glass out!
My God—glass, my townspeople!
For what purpose? Is it for the dead
to look out or for us to see
how well he is housed or to see
the flowers or the lack of them—
or what?
To keep the rain and snow from him?
He will have a heavier rain soon:
pebbles and dirt and what not.
Let there be no glass—
and no upholstery, phew!
and no little brass rollers
and small easy wheels on the bottom—
my townspeople what are you thinking of?
A rough plain hearse then
with gilt wheels and no top at all.
On this the coffin lies
by its own weight.

                      No wreaths please—
especially no hot house flowers.
Some common memento is better,
something he prized and is known by:
his old clothes—a few books perhaps—
God knows what! You realize
how we are about these things
my townspeople—
something will be found—anything
even flowers if he had come to that.
So much for the hearse.

For heaven's sake though see to the driver!
Take off the silk hat! In fact
that's no place at all for him—
up there unceremoniously
dragging our friend out to his own dignity!
Bring him down—bring him down!
Low and inconspicuous! I'd not have him ride
on the wagon at all—damn him—

the undertaker's understrapper!
Let him hold the reins
and walk at the side
and inconspicuously too!

Then briefly as to yourselves:
Walk behind—as they do in France,
seventh class, or if you ride
Hell take curtains! Go with some show
of inconvenience; sit openly—
to the weather as to grief.
Or do you think you can shut grief in?
What—from us? We who have perhaps
nothing to lose? Share with us
share with us—it will be money
in your pockets.
                              Go now
I think you are ready.

Queen-Ann's-Lace

Her body is not so white as
anemone petals nor so smooth—nor
so remote a thing. It is a field
of the wild carrot taking
the field by force; the grass
does not raise above it.
Here is no question of whiteness,
white as can be, with a purple mole
at the center of each flower.
Each flower is a hand's span
of her whiteness. Wherever
his hand has lain there is
a tiny purple blemish. Each part
is a blossom under his touch
to which the fibres of her being
stem one by one, each to its end,
until the whole field is a
white desire, empty, a single stem,
a cluster, flower by flower,
a pious wish to whiteness gone over—
or nothing.

The Lonely Street

School is over. It is too hot
to walk at ease. At ease
in light frocks they walk the streets
to while the time away.
They have grown tall. They hold
pink flames in their right hands.
In white from head to foot,
with sidelong, idle look—
in yellow, floating stuff,
black sash and stockings—
touching their avid mouths
with pink sugar on a stick—
like a carnation each holds in her hand—
they mount the lonely street.

The Bull

It is in captivity—
ringed, haltered, chained
to a drag
the bull is godlike

Unlike the cows
he lives alone, nozzles
the sweet grass gingerly
to pass the time away

He kneels, lies down
and stretching out
a foreleg licks himself
about the hoof

then stays
with half-closed eyes,
Olympian commentary on
the bright passage of days.

—The round sun
smooth his lacquer
through
the glossy pinetrees

his substance hard
as ivory or glass—
through which the wind
yet plays—
            milkless

he nods
the hair between his horns
and eyes matted
with hyacinthine curls

The Lily

The branching head of
tiger-lilies through the window
in the air—

A humming bird
is still on whirring wings
above the flowers—

By spotted petals curling back
and tongues that hang
the air is seen—

It's raining—
water's caught
among the curled-back petals

Caught and held
and there's a fly—
are blossoming

Nantucket

Flowers through the window
lavender and yellow

changed by white curtains—
Smell of cleanliness—

Sunshine of late afternoon—
On the glass tray

a glass pitcher, the tumbler
turned down, by which

a key is lying—And the
immaculate white bed

To a Poor Old Woman

munching a plum on
the street a paper bag
of them in her hand

They taste good to her
They taste good
to her. They taste
good to her

You can see it by
the way she gives herself
to the one half
sucked out in her hand

Comforted
a solace of ripe plums
seeming to fill the air
They taste good to her

Franklin Square

Instead of
the flower of the hawthorn
the spine:

The tree is in bloom
the flowers
and the leaves together

sheltering
the noisy sparrows
that give

by their intimate
indifference,
the squirrels and pigeons

on the sharp-
edged lawns—the figure
of a park:

A city, a decadence
of bounty—
a tall negress approaching

the bench
pursing her old mouth
for what coin?

The Dance

In Breughel's great picture, The Kermess,
the dancers go round, they go round and
around, the squeal and the blare and the
tweedle of bagpipes, a bugle and fiddles
tipping their bellies (round as the thick-
sided glasses whose wash they impound)
their hips and their bellies off balance
to turn them. Kicking and rolling about
the Fair Grounds, swinging their butts, those
shanks must be sound to bear up under such
rollicking measures, prance as they dance
in Breughel's great picture, The Kermess.

Landscape with the Fall of Icarus

According to Brueghel
when Icarus fell
it was spring

a farmer was ploughing
his field
the whole pageantry

of the year was
awake tingling
near

the edge of the sea
concerned
with itself

sweating in the sun
that melted
the wings' wax

unsignificantly
off the coast
there was

a splash quite unnoticed
this was
Icarus drowning

MARIANNE MOORE

To a Giraffe

If it is unpermissible, in fact fatal
to be personal and undesirable

to be literal—detrimental as well
if the eye is not innocent—does it mean that

one can live only on top leaves that are small
reachable only by a beast that is tall?—

of which the giraffe is the best example—
the unconversational animal.

When plagued by the psychological
a creature can be unbearable

that could have been irresistible;
or to be exact, exceptional

since less conversational
than some emotionally-tied-in-knots animal.

    After all
consolations of the metaphysical
can be profound. In Homer, existence

is flawed; transcendence, conditional;
"the journey from sin to redemption, perpetual."

JOHN CROWE RANSOM

Miriam Tazewell

When Miriam Tazewell heard the tempest bursting
And his wrathy whips across the sky drawn crackling
She stuffed her ears for fright like a young thing
And with heart full of the flowers took to weeping.

But the earth shook dry his old back in good season,
He had weathered storms that drenched him deep as this one,
And the sun, Miriam, ascended to his dominion,
The storm was withered against his empyrean.

After the storm she went forth with skirts kilted
To see in the strong sun her lawn deflowered,
Her tulip, iris, peony strung and pelted,
Pots of geranium spilled and the stalks naked.

The spring transpired in that year with no flowers
But the regular stars went busily on their courses,
Suppers and cards were calendared, and some bridals,
And the birds demurely sang in the bitten poplars.

To Miriam Tazewell the whole world was villain
To prosper when the fragile babes were fallen,
And not to unstop her own storm and be maudlin,
For weeks she went untidy, she went sullen.

The Tall Girl

The Queens of Hell had lissome necks to crane
At the tall girl approaching with long tread
And, when she was caught up even with them, nodded:
"If the young miss with gold hair might not disdain,
We would esteem her company over the plain,
To profit us all where the dogs will be out barking,
And we'll go by the windows where the young men are working
And tomorrow we will all come home again."

But the Queen of Heaven on the other side of the road
In the likeness, I hear, of a plain motherly woman
Made a wry face, despite it was so common
To be worsted by the smooth ladies of Hell,
And crisped her sweet tongue: "This never will come to good!
Just an old woman, my pet, that wishes you well."

Bells for John Whiteside's Daughter

There was such speed in her little body,
And such lightness in her footfall,
It is no wonder her brown study
Astonishes us all.

Her wars were bruited in our high window.
We looked among orchard trees and beyond
Where she took arms against her shadow,
Or harried unto the pond

The lazy geese, like a snow cloud
Dripping their snow on the green grass,
Tricking and stopping, sleepy and proud,
Who cried in goose, Alas,

For the tireless heart within the little
Lady with rod that made them rise
From their noon apple-dreams and scuttle
Goose-fashion under the skies!

But now go the bells, and we are ready,
In one house we are sternly stopped
To say we are vexed at her brown study,
Lying so primly propped.

ARCHIBALD MacLEISH

You, Andrew Marvell

And here face down beneath the sun
And here upon earth's noonward height
To feel the always coming on
The always rising of the night

To feel creep up the curving east
The earthy chill of dusk and slow
Upon those under lands the vast
And ever climbing shadow grow

And strange at Ecbatan the trees
Take leaf by leaf the evening strange
The flooding dark about their knees
The mountains over Persia change

And now at Kermanshah the gate
Dark empty and the withered grass
And through the twilight now the late
Few travelers in the westward pass

And Baghdad darken and the bridge
Across the silent river gone
And through Arabia the edge
Of evening widen and steal on

And deepen on Palmyra's street
The wheel rut in the ruined stone
And Lebanon fade out and Crete
High through the clouds and overblown

And over Sicily the air
Still flashing with the landward gulls
And loom and slowly disappear
The sails above the shadowy hulls

And Spain go under and the shore
Of Africa the gilded sand
And evening vanish and no more
The low pale light across that land

Nor now the long light on the sea

And here face downward in the sun
To feel how swift how secretly
The shadow of the night comes on . . .

because you take life in your stride(instead

because you take life in your stride(instead
of scheming how to beat the noblest game
a man can proudly lose,or playing dead
and hoping death himself will do the same

because you aren't afraid to kiss the dirt
(and consequently dare to climb the sky)
because a mind no other mind should try
to fool has always failed to fool your heart

but most(without the smallest doubt)because
no best is quite so good you don't conceive
a better;and because no evil is
so worse than worst you fall in hate with love

—human one mortally immortal i
can turn immense all time's because to why

mr u will not be missed

mr u will not be missed
who as an anthologist
sold the many on the few
not excluding mr u

HART CRANE

To Brooklyn Bridge

How many dawns, chill from his rippling rest
The seagull's wings shall dip and pivot him,
Shedding white rings of tumult, building high
Over the chained bay waters Liberty—

Then, with inviolate curve, forsake our eyes
As apparitional as sails that cross

Some page of figures to be filed away;
—Till elevators drop us from our day . . .

I think of cinemas, panoramic sleights
With multitudes bent toward some flashing scene
Never disclosed, but hastened to again,
Foretold to other eyes on the same screen;

And Thee, across the harbor, silver-paced
As though the sun took step of thee, yet left
Some motion ever unspent in thy stride,—
Implicitly thy freedom staying thee!

Out of some subway scuttle, cell or loft
A bedlamite speeds to thy parapets,
Tilting there momently, shrill shirt ballooning,
A jest falls from the speechless caravan.

Down Wall, from girder into street noon leaks,
A rip-tooth of the sky's acetylene;
All afternoon the cloud-flown derricks turn . . .
Thy cables breathe the North Atlantic still.

And obscure as that heaven of the Jews,
Thy guerdon . . . Accolade thou dost bestow
Of anonymity time cannot raise:
Vibrant reprieve and pardon thou dost show.

O harp and altar, of the fury fused,
(How could mere toil align thy choiring strings!)
Terrific threshold of the prophet's pledge,
Prayer of pariah, and the lover's cry,—

Again the traffic lights that skim thy swift
Unfractioned idiom, immaculate sigh of stars,
Beading thy path—condense eternity:
And we have seen night lifted in thine arms.

Under thy shadow by the piers I waited;
Only in darkness is thy shadow clear.
The City's fiery parcels all undone,
Already snow submerges an iron year . . .

O Sleepless as the river under thee,
Vaulting the sea, the prairies' dreaming sod,

Unto us lowliest sometime sweep, descend
And of the curveship lend a myth to God.

National Winter Garden

Outspoken buttocks in pink beads
Invite the necessary cloudy clinch
Of bandy eyes. . . . No extra mufflings here:
The world's one flagrant, sweating cinch.

And while legs waken salads in the brain
You pick your blonde out neatly through the smoke.
Always you wait for someone else though, always—
(Then rush the nearest exit through the smoke).

Always and last, before the final ring
When all the fireworks blare, begins
A tom-tom scrimmage with a somewhere violin,
Some cheapest echo of them all—begins.

And shall we call her whiter than the snow?
Sprayed first with ruby, then with emerald sheen—
Least tearful and least glad (who knows her smile?)
A caught slide shows her sandstone grey between.

Her eyes exist in swivellings of her teats,
Pearls whip her hips, a drench of whirling strands.
Her silly snake rings begin to mount, surmount
Each other—turquoise fakes on tinselled hands.

We wait that writhing pool, her pearls collapsed,
—All but her belly buried in the floor;
And the lewd trounce of a final muted beat!
We flee her spasm through a fleshless door. . . .

Yet, to the empty trapeze of your flesh,
O Magdalene, each comes back to die alone.
Then you, the burlesque of our lust—and faith,
Lug us back lifeward—bone by infant bone.

Repose of Rivers

The willows carried a slow sound,
A sarabande the wind mowed on the mead.
I could never remember
That seething, steady leveling of the marshes
Till age had brought me to the sea.

Flags, weeds. And remembrance of steep alcoves
Where cypresses shared the noon's
Tyranny; they drew me into hades almost.
And mammoth turtles climbing sulphur dreams
Yielded, while sun-silt rippled them
Asunder. . .

How much I would have bartered! the black gorge
And all the singular nestings in the hills
Where beavers learn stitch and tooth.
The pond I entered once and quickly fled—
I remember now its singing willow rim.

And finally, in that memory all things nurse;
After the city that I finally passed
With scalding unguents spread and smoking darts
The monsoon cut across the delta
At gulf gates . . . There, beyond the dykes

I heard wind flaking sapphire, like this summer,
And willows could not hold more steady sound.

Voyages: I

Above the fresh ruffles of the surf
Bright striped urchins flay each other with sand.
They have contrived a conquest for shell shucks,
And their fingers crumble fragments of baked weed
Gaily digging and scattering.

And in answer to their treble interjections
The sun beats lightning on the waves,
The waves fold thunder on the sand;
And could they hear me I would tell them:

O brilliant kids, frisk with your dog,
Fondle your shells and sticks, bleached
By time and the elements; but there is a line
You must not cross nor ever trust beyond it
Spry cordage of your bodies to caresses
Too lichen-faithful from too wide a breast.
The bottom of the sea is cruel.

Royal Palm

FOR GRACE HART CRANE

Green rustlings, more than regal charities
Drift coolly from that tower of whispered light.
Amid the noontide's blazed asperities
I watched the sun's most gracious anchorite

Climb up as by communings, year on year
Uneaten of the earth or aught earth holds,
And the grey trunk, that's elephantine, rear
Its frondings sighing in æthereal folds.

Forever fruitless, and beyond that yield
Of sweat the jungle presses with hot love
And tendril till our deathward breath is sealed—
It grazes the horizons, launched above

Mortality—ascending emerald-bright,
A fountain at salute, a crown in view—
Unshackled, casual of its azured height
As though it soared suchwise through heaven too.

EARLE BIRNEY

Slug in Woods

For eyes he waves greentipped
taut horns of slime. They dipped,
hours back, across a reef,
a salmonberry leaf.
Then strained to grope past fin
of spruce. Now eyes suck in

as through the hemlock butts
of his day's ledge there cuts
a vixen chipmunk. Stilled
is he—green mucus chilled,
or blotched and soapy stone,
pinguid in moss, alone.
Hours on, he will resume
his silver scrawl, illume
his palimpsest, emboss
his diver's line across
that waving green illim-
itable seafloor. Slim
young jay his sudden shark;
the wrecks he skirts are dark
and fungussed firlogs, whom
spirea sprays emplume,
encoral. Dew his shell,
while mounting boles foretell
of isles in dappled air
fathoms above his care.
Azygous muted life,
himself his viscid wife,
foodward he noses cold beneath his sea.
So spends a summer's jasper century.

RICHARD EBERHART

For a Lamb

I saw on the slant hill a putrid lamb,
Propped with daisies. The sleep looked deep,
The face nudged in the green pillow
But the guts were out for crows to eat.

Where's the lamb? whose tender plaint
Said all for the mute breezes.
Say he's in the wind somewhere,
Say, there's a lamb in the daisies.

'Where Are Those High and Haunting Skies'

Where are those high and haunting skies,
Higher than the see-through wind? Where are

The rocky springs beyond desire? And where
The sudden source of purity?

Now they are gone again. Though world
Decrease the wraith-like eye so holy,
And bring a summer in, and with it folly,
Though the senses bless and quell,

I would not with such blessings be beguiled.
But seek an image far more dear. Oh where
Has gone that madness wild? Where stays
The abrupt essence and the final shield?

Sestina

I die, no matter what I do I die.
Is this the sum of what man has to do?
There is no use to fly to be at ease.
Man flies, but knows not what he does.
It is in war you want to be in peace.
In Heaven, in Heaven I want to be in Hell.

The mortal span to find out Heaven and Hell!
No matter what I have to do I die,
The gods comply to cancel you to peace.
Before this then what is it man should do?
And after, does it matter what he does?
Will Christ-like Christ then put him at his ease?

Will will will him his own, a fabled ease?
Will, some say, is the whole road to Hell.
But man is bound to Hell whatever he does.
No matter what he does he has to die.
It is the dying that you have to do
Defies the hyaline lustre of the peace.

Despair has not the end in view of peace
Nor has desire the purposes of ease,
But action, while you live, is what's to do.
Thought is three crossed roads that lead to Hell,
Your thought is fatal and will make you die,
For thinking kills as much as action does.

It is not what he thinks, nor what he does
Nor what cold mystery of the Prince of Peace

Avails—no matter what I do I die,
May nothing, nothing put me at my ease
Except the reality of Heaven and Hell.
No one told me what I ought to do.

The scriptures told you what you ought to do.
They are unreasonable truth, and what man does
Believe when most he believes in Heaven and Hell.
That passes understanding, that is peace.
But sky-fallen man will not be put at ease.
I die, no matter what I do I die.

No matter what I do I have no peace.
No matter what man does he has no ease.
Heaven and Hell are changeless when I die.

STANLEY KUNITZ

The Science of the Night

I touch you in the night, whose gift was you,
My careless sprawler,
And I touch you cold, unstirring, star-bemused,
That are become the land of your self-strangeness.
What long seduction of the bone has led you
Down the imploring roads I cannot take
Into the arms of ghosts I never knew,
Leaving my manhood on a rumpled field
To guard you where you lie so deep
In absent-mindedness,
Caught in the calcium snows of sleep?

And even should I track you to your birth
Through all the cities of your mortal trial,
As in my jealous thought I try to do,
You would escape me—from the brink of earth
Take off to where the lawless auroras run,
You with your wild and metaphysic heart.
My touch is on you, who are light-years gone.
We are not souls but systems, and we move
In clouds of our unknowing
                              like great nebulae.

Our very motives swirl and have their start
With father lion and with mother crab.

Dreamer, my own lost rib,
Whose planetary dust is blowing
Past archipelagoes of myth and light,
What far Magellans are you mistress of
To whom you speed the pleasure of your art?
As through a glass that magnifies my loss
I see the lines of your spectrum shifting red,
The universe expanding, thinning out,
Our worlds flying, oh flying, fast apart.

From hooded powers and from abstract flight
I summon you, your person and your pride.
Fall to me now from outer space,
Still fastened desperately to my side;
Through gulfs of streaming air
Bring me the mornings of the milky ways
Down to my threshold in your drowsy eyes;
And by the virtue of your honeyed word
Restore the liquid language of the moon,
That in gold mines of secrecy you delve.
Awake!
       My whirling hands stay at the noon,
Each cell within my body holds a heart
And all my hearts in unison strike twelve.

ROBERT PENN WARREN

Eidolon

All night, in May, dogs barked in the hollow woods;
Hoarse, from secret huddles of no light,
By moonlit bole, hoarse, the dogs gave tongue.
In May, by moon, no moon, thus: I remember
Of their far clamor the throaty, infatuate timbre.

The boy, all night, lay in the black room,
Tick-straw, all night, harsh to the bare side.
Staring, he heard; the clotted dark swam slow.
Far off, by wind, no wind, unappeasable riot
Provoked, resurgent, the bosom's nocturnal disquiet.

What hungers kept the house? under the rooftree
The boy; the man, clod-heavy, hard hand uncurled;
The old man, eyes wide, spittle on his beard.
In dark was crushed the may-apple: plunging, the rangers
Of dark remotelier belled their unhoused angers.

Dogs quartered the black woods: blood black on
May-apple at dawn, old beech-husk. And trails are lost
By rock, in ferns lost, by pools unlit.
I heard the hunt. Who saw, in darkness, how fled
The white eidolon from the fanged commotion rude?

Bearded Oaks

The oaks, how subtle and marine,
Bearded, and all the layered light
Above them swims; and thus the scene,
Recessed, awaits the positive night.

So, waiting, we in the grass now lie
Beneath the languorous tread of light:
The grasses, kelp-like, satisfy
The nameless motions of the air.

Upon the floor of light, and time,
Unmurmuring, of polyp made,
We rest; we are, as light withdraws,
Twin atolls on a shelf of shade.

Ages to our construction went,
Dim architecture, hour by hour:
And violence, forgot now, lent
The present stillness all its power.

The storm of noon above us rolled,
Of light the fury, furious gold,
The long drag troubling us, the depth:
Dark is unrocking, unrippling, still.

Passion and slaughter, ruth, decay
Descend, minutely whispering down,
Silted down swaying steams, to lay
Foundation for our voicelessness.

All our debate is voiceless here,
As all our rage, the rage of stone;
If hope is hopeless, then fearless is fear,
And history is thus undone.

Our feet once wrought the hollow street
With echo when the lamps were dead
At windows, once our headlight glare
Disturbed the doe that, leaping, fled.

I do not love you less that now
The caged heart makes iron stroke,
Or less that all that light once gave
The graduate dark should now revoke.

We live in time so little time
And we learn all so painfully,
That we may spare this hour's term
To practice for eternity.

W. H. AUDEN

The Three Companions

'O where are you going?' said reader to rider,
'That valley is fatal when furnaces burn,
Yonder's the midden whose odours will madden,
That gap is the grave where the tall return.'

'O do you imagine,' said fearer to farer,
'That dusk will delay on your path to the pass,
Your diligent looking discover the lacking
Your footsteps feel from granite to grass?'

'O what was that bird,' said horror to hearer,
'Did you see that shape in the twisted trees?
Behind you swiftly the figure comes softly,
The spot on your skin is a shocking disease.'

'Out of this house'—said rider to reader,
'Yours never will'—said farer to fearer,
'They're looking for you'—said hearer to horror,
As he left them there, as he left them there.

As I Walked out One Evening

As I walked out one evening,
  Walking down Bristol Street,
The crowds upon the pavement
  Were fields of harvest wheat.

And down by the brimming river
  I heard a lover sing
Under an arch of the railway:
  'Love has no ending.

'I'll love you, dear, I'll love you
  Till China and Africa meet,
And the river jumps over the mountain
  And the salmon sing in the street,

'I'll love you till the ocean
  Is folded and hung up to dry
And the seven stars go squawking
  Like geese about the sky.

The years shall run like rabbits,
  For in my arms I hold
The Flower of the Ages,
  And the first love of the world.'

But all the clocks in the city
  Began to whirr and chime:
'O let not Time deceive you,
  You cannot conquer Time.

'In the burrows of the Nightmare
  Where Justice naked is,
Time watches from the shadow
  And coughs when you would kiss.

'In headaches and in worry
  Vaguely life leaks away,
And Time will have his fancy
  To-morrow or to-day.

'Into many a green valley
  Drifts the appalling snow;

Time breaks the threaded dances
    And the diver's brilliant bow.

'O plunge your hands in water,
    Plunge them in up to the wrist;
Stare, stare in the basin
    And wonder what you've missed.

'The glacier knocks in the cupboard,
    The desert sighs in the bed,
And the crack in the tea-cup opens
    A lane to the land of the dead.

'Where the beggars raffle the banknotes
    And the Giant is enchanting to Jack,
And the Lily-white Boy is a Roarer,
    And Jill goes down on her back.

'O look, look in the mirror,
    O look in your distress;
Life remains a blessing
    Although you cannot bless.

'O stand, stand at the window
    As the tears scald and start;
You shall love your crooked neighbour
    With your crooked heart.'

It was late, late in the evening,
    The lovers they were gone;
The clocks had ceased their chiming,
    And the deep river ran on.

Fish in the Unruffled Lakes

Fish in the unruffled lakes
Their swarming colours wear,
Swans in the winter air
A white perfection have,
And the great lion walks
Through his innocent grove;
Lion, fish and swan
Act, and are gone
Upon Time's toppling wave.

We, till shadowed days are done,
We must weep and sing
Duty's conscious wrong,
The Devil in the clock,
The goodness carefully worn
For atonement or for luck;
We must lose our loves,
On each beast and bird that moves
Turn an envious look.

Sighs for folly done and said
Twist our narrow days,
But I must bless, I must praise
That you, my swan, who have
All gifts that to the swan
Impulsive Nature gave,
The majesty and pride,
Last night should add
Your voluntary love.

In Memory of W. B. Yeats

(d. Jan. 1939)

I

He disappeared in the dead of winter:
The brooks were frozen, the airports almost deserted,
And snow disfigured the public statues;
The mercury sank in the mouth of the dying day.
What instruments we have agree
The day of his death was a dark cold day.

Far from his illness
The wolves ran on through the evergreen forests,
The peasant river was untempted by the fashionable quays;
By mourning tongues
The death of the poet was kept from his poems.

But for him it was his last afternoon as himself,
An afternoon of nurses and rumours;
The provinces of his body revolted,
The squares of his mind were empty,
Silence invaded the suburbs,
The current of his feeling failed; he became his admirers.

Now he is scattered among a hundred cities
And wholly given over to unfamiliar affections,
To find his happiness in another kind of wood
And be punished under a foreign code of conscience.
The words of a dead man
Are modified in the guts of the living.

But in the importance and noise of to-morrow
When the brokers are roaring like beasts on the floor of the Bourse,
And the poor have the sufferings to which they are fairly accustomed,
And each in the cell of himself is almost convinced of his freedom,
A few thousand will think of this day
As one thinks of a day when one did something slightly unusual.
What instruments we have agree
The day of his death was a dark cold day.

II

You were silly like us; your gift survived it all:
The parish of rich women, physical decay,
Yourself. Mad Ireland hurt you into poetry.
Now Ireland has her madness and her weather still,
For poetry makes nothing happen: it survives
In the valley of its making where executives
Would never want to tamper, flows on south
From ranches of isolation and the busy griefs,
Raw towns that we believe and die in; it survives,
A way of happening, a mouth.

III

Earth, receive an honoured guest:
William Yeats is laid to rest.
Let the Irish vessel lie
Emptied of its poetry.

In the nightmare of the dark
All the dogs of Europe bark,
And the living nations wait,
Each sequestered in its hate;

Intellectual disgrace
Stares from every human face,
And the seas of pity lie
Locked and frozen in each eye.

Follow, poet, follow right
To the bottom of the night,
With your unconstraining voice
Still persuade us to rejoice;

With the farming of a verse
Make a vineyard of the curse,
Sing of human unsuccess
In a rapture of distress;

In the deserts of the heart
Let the healing fountain start,
In the prison of his days
Teach the free man how to praise.

If I Could Tell You

Time will say nothing but I told you so,
Time only knows the price we have to pay;
If I could tell you I would let you know.

If we should weep when clowns put on their show,
If we should stumble when musicians play,
Time will say nothing but I told you so.

There are no fortunes to be told, although,
Because I love you more than I can say,
If I could tell you I would let you know.

The winds must come from somewhere when they blow,
There must be reasons why the leaves decay;
Time will say nothing but I told you so.

Perhaps the roses really want to grow,
The vision seriously intends to stay;
If I could tell you I would let you know.

Suppose the lions all get up and go,
And all the brooks and soldiers run away;
Will Time say nothing but I told you so?
If I could tell you I would let you know.

Order to View

It was a big house, bleak;
Grass on the drive;
We had been there before
But memory, weak in front of
A blistered door, could find
Nothing alive now;
The shrubbery dripped, a crypt
Of leafmould dreams; a tarnished
Arrow over an empty stable
Shifted a little in the almost wind,

And wishes were unable
To rise; on the garden wall
The pear trees had come loose
From rotten loops; one wish,
A rainbow bubble, rose,
Faltered, broke in the dull
Air—What was the use?
The bell-pull would not pull
And the whole place, one might
Have supposed, was deadly ill:
The world was closed,

And remained closed until
A sudden angry tree
Shook itself like a setter
Flouncing out of a pond
And beyond the sombre line
Of limes a cavalcade
Of clouds rose like a shout of
Defiance. Near at hand
Somewhere in a loose-box
A horse neighed
And all the curtains flew out of
The windows; the world was open.

Coda

Maybe we knew each other better
When the night was young and unrepeated
And the moon stood still over Jericho.

So much for the past; in the present
There are moments caught between heart-beats
When maybe we know each other better.

But what is that clinking in the darkness?
Maybe we shall know each other better
When the tunnels meet beneath the mountain.

THEODORE ROETHKE

Highway: Michigan

Here from the field's edge we survey
The progress of the jaded. Mile
On mile of traffic from the town
Rides by, for at the end of day
The time of workers is their own.

They jockey for position on
The strip reserved for passing only.
The drivers from production lines
Hold to advantage dearly won.
They toy with death and traffic fines.

Acceleration is their need:
A mania keeps them on the move
Until the toughest nerves are frayed.
They are the prisoners of speed
Who flee in what their hands have made.

The pavement smokes when two cars meet
And steel rips through conflicting steel.
We shiver at the siren's blast.
One driver, pinned beneath the seat,
Escapes from the machine at last.

My Papa's Waltz

The whiskey on your breath
Could make a small boy dizzy;
But I hung on like death:
Such waltzing was not easy.

We romped until the pans
Slid from the kitchen shelf;
My mother's countenance
Could not unfrown itself.

The hand that held my wrist
Was battered on one knuckle;
At every step you missed
My right ear scraped a buckle.

You beat time on my head
With a palm caked hard by dirt,
Then waltzed me off to bed
Still clinging to your shirt.

Elegy for Jane

MY STUDENT, THROWN BY A HORSE

I remember the neckcurls, limp and damp as tendrils;
And her quick look, a sidelong pickerel smile;
And how, once startled into talk, the light syllables leaped for her,
And she balanced in the delight of her thought,
A wren, happy, tail into the wind,
Her song trembling the twigs and small branches.
The shade sang with her;
The leaves, their whispers turned to kissing;
And the mold sang in the bleached valleys under the rose.

Oh, when she was sad, she cast herself down into such a pure depth,
Even a father could not find her:
Scraping her cheek against straw;
Stirring the clearest water.

My sparrow, you are not here,
Waiting like a fern, making a spiny shadow.
The sides of wet stones cannot console me,
Nor the moss, wound with the last light.

If only I could nudge you from this sleep,
My maimed darling, my skittery pigeon.
Over this damp grave I speak the words of my love:
I, with no rights in this matter,
Neither father nor lover.

The Waking

I wake to sleep, and take my waking slow.
I feel my fate in what I cannot fear.
I learn by going where I have to go.

We think by feeling. What is there to know?
I hear my being dance from ear to ear.
I wake to sleep, and take my waking slow.

Of those so close beside me, which are you?
God bless the Ground! I shall walk softly there,
And learn by going where I have to go.

Light takes the Tree; but who can tell us how?
The lowly worm climbs up a winding stair;
I wake to sleep, and take my waking slow.

Great Nature has another thing to do
To you and me; so take the lively air,
And, lovely, learn by going where to go.

This shaking keeps me steady. I should know.
What falls away is always. And is near.
I wake to sleep, and take my waking slow.
I learn by going where I have to go.

Reply to a Lady Editor

If the Poem (beginning "I knew a woman, lovely in her bones") in *The London Times Literary Supplement* has not appeared here, we offer you $75 for it. Could you wire us collect your answer?

Sincerely yours,
Alice S. Morris
Literary Editor, *Harper's Bazaar*

Sweet Alice S. Morris, I *am* pleased, of course,
You take the *Times Supplement,* and read its verse,
And know that True Love is more than a Life-Force
—And so like my poem called *Poem.*

Dan Cupid, I tell you's a braw laddie-buck;
A visit from him is a piece of pure luck,

And should he arrive, why just lean yourself back
—And recite him my poem called *Poem*.

O print it, my dear, do publish it, yes,
That ladies their true natures never suppress,
When they come, dazedly, to the pretty pass
—Of acting my poem called *Poem*.

My darling, my dearest, most-honest-alive,
Just send me along that sweet seventy-five;
I'll continue to think on the nature of love,
—As I dance to my poem called *Poem*.

Snake

I saw a young snake glide
Out of the mottled shade
And hang, limp on a stone:
A thin mouth, and a tongue
Stayed, in the still air.

It turned; it drew away;
Its shadow bent in half;
It quickened, and was gone.

I felt my slow blood warm.
I longed to be that thing,
The pure, sensuous form.

And I may be, some time.

The Yak

There was a most odious Yak
Who took only toads on his Back:
If you asked for a Ride,
He would act very Snide,
And go humping off, yicketty-yak.

The Thing

Suddenly they came flying, like a long scarf of smoke,
Trailing a thing—what was it?—small as a lark
Above the blue air, in the slight haze beyond,
A thing in and out of sight,
Flashing between gold levels of the late sun,
Then throwing itself up and away from the implacable swift pursuers,
Confusing them once flying straight into the sun
So they circled aimlessly for almost a minute,
Only to find, with their long terrible eyes
The small thing diving down toward a hill,
Where they dropped again
In one streak of pursuit.

Then the first bird
Struck;
Then another, another,
Until there was nothing left,
Not even feathers from so far away.

And we turned to our picnic
Of veal soaked in marsala and little larks arranged on a long platter,
And we drank the dry harsh wine
While I poked with a stick at a stone near a four-pronged flower,
And a black bull nudged at a wall in the valley below,
And the blue air darkened.

In a Dark Time

In a dark time, the eye begins to see,
I meet my shadow in the deepening shade;
I hear my echo in the echoing wood—
A lord of nature weeping to a tree.
I live between the heron and the wren,
Beasts of the hill and serpents of the den.

What's madness but nobility of soul
At odds with circumstance? The day's on fire!
I know the purity of pure despair,
My shadow pinned against a sweating wall.
That place among the rocks—is it a cave,
Or winding path? The edge is what I have.

A steady storm of correspondences!
A night flowing with birds, a ragged moon,
And in broad day the midnight come again!
A man goes far to find out what he is—
Death of the self in a long, tearless night,
All natural shapes blazing unnatural light.

Dark, dark my light, and darker my desire.
My soul, like some heat-maddened summer fly,
Keeps buzzing at the sill. Which I is *I*?
A fallen man, I climb out of my fear.
The mind enters itself, and God the mind,
And one is One, free in the tearing wind.

The Harsh Country

There was a hardness of stone,
An uncertain glory,
Glitter of basalt and mica,
And the sheen of ravens.

Between cliffs of light
We strayed like children,
Not feeling the coarse shale
That cut like razors,

For a blond hill beckoned
Like an enormous beacon,
Shifting in sea change,
Not ever farther.

Yet for this we travelled
With hope, and not alone,
In the country of ourselves,
In a country of bright stone.

MALCOLM LOWRY

Sestina in a Cantina

Scene: A waterfront tavern in Vera Cruz at daybreak.

LEGION

Watching this dawn's mnemonic of old dawning:
Jonquil-colored, delicate, some in prison,

Green dawns of drinking tenderer than sunset,
But clean and delicate like dawns of ocean
Flooding the heart with pale light in which horrors
Stampede like plump wolves in distorting mirrors.

Oh, we have seen ourselves in many mirrors;
Confusing all our sunsets with the dawning,
Investing every tongue and leaf with horrors,
And every stranger overtones for prison,
And seeing mainly in the nauseous ocean
The last shot of our life before the sunset.

ST. LUKE (a ship's doctor)

How long since you have really seen a sunset?
The mind has many slanting lying mirrors,
The mind is like that sparkling greenhouse ocean
Glass-deceptive in the Bengal dawning;
The mind has ways of keeping us in prison,
The better there to supervise its horrors.

SIR PHILIP SIDNEY

Why do you not, sir, organize your horrors
And shoot them one day, preferably at sunset,
That we may wake up next day not in prison,
No more deceived by lies and many mirrors,
And go down to the cold beach at dawning
To lave away the past in colder ocean?

ST. LUKE

No longer is there freedom on the ocean.
And even if there were, he likes his horrors,
And if he shot them would do so at dawning
That he might have acquired some more by sunset,
Breaking them in by that time before mirrors
To thoughts of spending many nights in prison.

LEGION

The fungus-colored sky of dawns in prison,
The fate that broods on every pictured ocean,
The fatal conversations before mirrors,
The fiends and all the spindly breeds of horrors,
Have shattered by their beauty every sunset
And rendered quite intolerable old dawning.

The oxen standing motionless at dawning—
Outside our tavern now, outside our prison—
Red through the wagon wheels, jalousies like sunset,
Swinging now in a sky as calm as ocean,
Where Venus hangs her obscene horn of horrors
For us now swaying in a hall of mirrors—

Such horrid beauty maddened all my mirrors,
Has burst in heart's eye sanity of dawning,
No chamber in my house brimful of horrors
But does not whisper of some dreadful prison,
Worse than all ships dithering through the ocean
Tottering like drunkards, arms upraised at sunset.

RICHARD III (a barman)

Vain derelict all avid for the sunset!
Shine out fair sun till you have bought new mirrors
That you may see your shadow pass the ocean,
And sunken no more pass our way at dawning,
But lie on the cold stone sea floor of some prison,
A chunk of sodden driftwood gnawed by horrors.

LEGION

At first I never looked on them as horrors;
But one day I was drinking hard near sunset,
And suddenly saw the world as a giant prison,
Ruled by tossing moose-heads, with hand mirrors,
And heard the voice of the idiot speak at dawning,
And since that time have dwelt beside the ocean.

EL UNIVERSAL (early edition)

Did no one speak of love beside the ocean,
Have you not felt, even among your horrors,
Granting them, there was such a thing as dawning,
A dawning for man whose star seems now at sunset,
Like million-sheeted scarlet dusty mirrors,
But one day must be led out of his prison?

LEGION

I see myself as all mankind in prison,
With hands outstretched to lanterns by the ocean;
I see myself as all mankind in mirrors,
Babbling of love while at his back rise horrors

Ready to suck the blood out of the sunset
And amputate the godhead of the dawning.

THE SWINE

And now the dawning drives us from our prison
Into the dawn like sunset, into the ocean,
Bereaving him of horrors, but leaving him his mirrors. . . .

Xochitepec

Those animals that follow us in dream
Are swallowed by the dawn, but what of those
Which hunt us, snuff, stalk us out in life, close
In upon it, belly-down, haunt our scheme
Of building, with shapes of delirium,
Symbols of death, heraldic, and shadows,
Glowering?—Just before we left Tlalpám
Our cats lay quivering under the maguey;
A meaning had slunk, and now died, with them.
The boy slung them half stiff down the ravine,
Which now we entered, and whose name is hell.
But still our last night had its animal:
The puppy, in the cabaret, obscene,
Looping-the-loop and soiling all the floor,
And fastening itself to that horror
Of our last night: while the very last day
As I sat bowed, frozen over mescal,
They dragged two kicking fawns through the hotel
And slit their throats, behind the barroom door. . . .

J. V. CUNNINGHAM

To What Strangers, What Welcome?: 4

You have here no otherness,
Unadressed correspondent,
No gaunt clavicles, no hair
Of bushy intimacy.
You are not, and I write here
The name of no signature
To the unsaid—a letter

At midnight, a memorial
And occupation of time.

I'll not summon you, or feel
In the alert dream the give
And stay of flesh, the tactile
Conspiracy.

The snow falls
With its inveterate meaning,
And I follow the barbed wire
To trough, to barn, to the house,
To what strangers, what welcome
In the late blizzard of time.

On the highway cars flashing,
Occasional and random
As pain gone without symptom,
And fear drifts with the North wind.
We neither give nor receive:
The unfinishable drink
Left on the table, the sleep
Alcoholic and final
In the mute exile of time.

DENIS GLOVER

The Magpies

When Tom and Elizabeth took the farm
　　　The bracken made their bed,
And *Quardle oodle ardle wardle doodle*
　　　The magpies said.

Tom's hand was strong to the plough
　　　Elizabeth's lips were red,
And *Quardle oodle ardle wardle doodle*
　　　The magpies said.

Year in year out they worked
　　　While the pines grew overhead,
And *Quardle oodle ardle wardle doodle*
　　　The magpies said.

But all the beautiful crops soon went
      To the mortgage-man instead,
And *Quardle oodle ardle wardle doodle*
      The magpies said.

Elizabeth is dead now (it's years ago)
      Old Tom went light in the head;
And *Quardle oodle ardle wardle doodle*
      The magpies said.

The farm's still there. Mortgage corporations
      Couldn't give it away.
And *Quardle oodle ardle wardle doodle*
      The magpies say.

REUEL DENNEY

To the Roman Bridge on Michigan Avenue

These urns beside the river are not full,
Brimmed with some meaning that the river sways
And swaps for dapple in the glint of days.
They are not empty either, ponderable
With space a spider measures in a cable
And the dead airs of wasps' delays
In covered conduit, sealed out of the blaze,
Held in a nest of dust that seems like wool.
The urns are solid concrete, through and through.
Inside like out the texture is the same,
The same thick pouring of the grey cement.
And this is why they seem the way they do:
Forms without content worthy of the name
And content that the form has never meant.

DOUGLAS STEWART

The Dosser in Springtime

That girl from the sun is bathing in the creek,
Says the white old dosser in the cave.
It's a sight worth seeing though your old frame's weak;

Her clothes are on the wattle and it's gold all over,
And if I was twenty I'd try to be her lover,
Says the white old dosser in the cave.

If I was twenty I'd chase her back to Bourke,
Says the white old dosser in the cave.
My swag on my shoulder and a haughty eye for work,
I'd chase her to the sunset where the desert burns and reels,
With an old blue dog full of fleas at my heels,
Says the white old dosser in the cave.

I'd chase her back to Bourke again, I'd chase her back to
      Alice,
Says the white old dosser in the cave.
And I'd drop upon her sleeping like a beauty in a palace
With the sunset wrapped around her and a black snake
      keeping watch—
She's lovely and she's naked but she's very hard to catch,
Says the white old dosser in the cave.

I've been cooling here for years with the gum-trees wet and
      weird,
Says the white old dosser in the cave.
My head grew lichens and moss was my beard,
The creek was in my brain and a bullfrog in my belly,
The she-oaks washed their hair in me all down the gloomy
      gully,
Says the white old dosser in the cave.

My eyes were full of water and my ears were stopped with
      bubbles,
Says the white old dosser in the cave.
Yabbies raised their claws in me or skulked behind the pebbles.
The water-beetle loved his wife, he chased her round and
      round—
I thought I'd never see a girl unless I found one drowned,
Says the white old dosser in the cave.

Many a time I laughed aloud to stop my heart from thumping,
Says the white old dosser in the cave.
I saw my laugh I saw my laugh I saw my laugh go jumping
Like a jaunty old goanna with his tail up stiff
Till he dived like a stone in the pool below the cliff,
Says the white old dosser in the cave.

There's a fine bed of bracken, the billy boils beside her,
Says the white old dosser in the cave.
But no one ever ate with me except the loathsome spider,
And no one ever lay with me beside the sandstone wall
Except the pallid moonlight and she's no good at all,
Says the white old dosser in the cave.

But now she's in the creek again, that woman made of flame,
Says the white old dosser in the cave.
By cripes, if I was twenty I'd stop her little game.
Her dress is on the wattle—I'd take it off and hide it;
And when she sought that golden dress, I'd lay her down
    beside it,
Says the white old dosser in the cave.

RANDALL JARRELL

A Sick Child

The postman comes when I am still in bed.
'Postman, what do you have for me to-day?'
I say to him. (But really I'm in bed.)
Then he says—what shall I have him say?

'This letter says that you are president
Of—this word here; it's a republic.'
Tell them I can't answer right away.
'It's your duty.' No, I'd rather just be sick.

Then he tells me there are letters saying everything
That I can think of that I want for them to say.
I say, 'Well, thank you very much. Good-bye.'
He is ashamed, and turns and walks away.

If I can think of it, it isn't what I want.
I want . . . I want a ship from some near star
To land in the yard, and beings to come out
And think to me: 'So this is where you are!

Come.' Except that they won't do,
I thought of them. . . . And yet somewhere there must be
Something that's different from everything.
All that I've never thought of—think of me!

Washing

On days like these
What doesn't blow away will freeze.
The washing flops on the line
In absolute torment—
And when the wind dies for a moment
The washing has the collapsed abject
Look of the sack of skin
Michelangelo made himself in his *Last Judgment.*

Its agonies
Are heartfelt as a sneeze.

When Mama wrung a chicken's
Neck, the body rushed around
And around and around the yard in circles.
The circles weren't its own idea
But it went on with them as if it would never stop.
The expression of its body was intense,
Immense
As this *Help! Help! Help!*
The reeling washing shrieks to someone, Someone.

But as old hens like to say,
The world isn't chickenhearted.
The washing inhabits a universe
Indifferent to the woes of washing,
A world—as the washing puts it—
A world that washing never made.

DYLAN THOMAS

A Refusal to Mourn the Death, by Fire,
of a Child in London

Never until the mankind making
Bird beast and flower
Fathering and all humbling darkness
Tells with silence the last light breaking
And the still hour
Is come of the sea tumbling in harness

And I must enter again the round
Zion of the water bead
And the synagogue of the ear of corn
Shall I let pray the shadow of a sound
Or sow my salt seed
In the least valley of sackcloth to mourn

The majesty and burning of the child's death.
I shall not murder
The mankind of her going with a grave truth
Nor blaspheme down the stations of the breath
With any further
Elegy of innocence and youth.

Deep with the first dead lies London's daughter,
Robed in the long friends,
The grains beyond age, the dark veins of her mother,
Secret by the unmourning water
Of the riding Thames.
After the first death, there is no other.

Do Not Go Gentle into That Good Night

Do not go gentle into that good night,
Old age should burn and rave at close of day;
Rage, rage against the dying of the light.

Though wise men at their end know dark is right,
Because their words had forked no lightning they
Do not go gentle into that good night.

Good men, the last wave by, crying how bright
Their frail deeds might have danced in a green bay,
Rage, rage against the dying of the light.

Wild men who caught and sang the sun in flight,
And learn, too late, they grieved it on its way,
Do not go gentle into that good night.

Grave men, near death, who see with blinding sight
Blind eyes could blaze like meteors and be gay,
Rage, rage against the dying of the light.

And you, my father, there on the sad height,
Curse, bless, me now with your fierce tears, I pray.
Do not go gentle into that good night.
Rage, rage against the dying of the light.

MARGARET WALKER

Childhood

When I was a child I knew red miners
dressed raggedly and wearing carbide lamps.
I saw them come down red hills to their camps
dyed with red dust from old Ishkooda mines.
Night after night I met them on the roads,
or on the streets in town I caught their glance;
the swing of dinner buckets in their hands,
and grumbling undermining all their words.

I also lived in low cotton country
where moonlight hovered over ripe haystacks,
or stumps of trees, and croppers' rotting shacks
with famine, terror, flood, and plague near by;
where sentiment and hatred still held sway
and only bitter land was washed away.

GWENDOLYN BROOKS

Old Mary

My last defense
Is the present tense.

It little hurts me now to know
I shall not go

Cathedral-hunting in Spain
Nor cherrying in Michigan or Maine.

Death from Cancer

This Easter, Arthur Winslow, less than dead,
Your people set you up in Phillips' House
To settle off your wrestling with the crab—
The claws drop flesh upon your yachting blouse
Until Longshoreman Charon come and stab
Through your adjusted bed
And crush the crab. On Boston Basin, shells
Hit water by the Union Boat Club wharf:
You ponder why the coxes' squeakings dwarf
The *resurrexit dominus* of all the bells.

Grandfather Winslow, look, the swanboats coast
That island in the Public Gardens, where
The bread-stuffed ducks are brooding, where with tub
And strainer the mid-Sunday Irish scare
The sun-struck shallows for the dusky chub
This Easter, and the ghost
Of risen Jesus walks the waves to run
Arthur upon a trumpeting black swan
Beyond Charles River to the Acheron
Where the wide waters and their voyager are one.

Concord

Ten thousand Fords are idle here in search
Of a tradition. Over these dry sticks—
The Minute Man, the Irish Catholics,
The ruined bridge and Walden's fished-out perch—
The belfry of the Unitarian Church
Rings out the hanging Jesus. Crucifix,
How can your whited spindling arms transfix
Mammon's unbridled industry, the lurch
For forms to harness Heraclitus' stream!
This Church is Concord—Concord where Thoreau
Named all the birds without a gun to probe
Through darkness to the painted man and bow:
The death-dance of King Philip and his scream
Whose echo girdled this imperfect globe.

Skunk Hour

(FOR ELIZABETH BISHOP)

Nautilus Island's hermit
heiress still lives through winter in her Spartan cottage;
her sheep still graze above the sea.
Her son's a bishop. Her farmer
is first selectman in our village;
she's in her dotage.

Thirsting for
the hierarchic privacy
of Queen Victoria's century,
she buys up all
the eyesores facing her shore,
and lets them fall.

The season's ill—
we've lost our summer millionaire,
who seemed to leap from an L. L. Bean
catalogue. His nine-knot yawl
was auctioned off to lobstermen.
A red fox stain covers Blue Hill.

And now our fairy
decorator brightens his shop for fall;
his fishnet's filled with orange cork,
orange, his cobbler's bench and awl;
there is no money in his work,
he'd rather marry.

One dark night,
my Tudor Ford climbed the hill's skull;
I watched for love-cars. Lights turned down,
they lay together, hull to hull,
where the graveyard shelves on the town. . . .
My mind's not right.

A car radio bleats,
"Love, O careless Love. . . ." I hear
my ill-spirit sob in each blood cell,
as if my hand were at its throat. . . .
I myself am hell;
nobody's here—

only skunks, that search
in the moonlight for a bite to eat.
They march on their soles up Main Street:
white stripes, moonstruck eyes' red fire
under the chalk-dry and spar spire
of the Trinitarian Church.

I stand on top
of our back steps and breathe the rich air—
a mother skunk with her column of kittens swills the garbage
      pail.
She jabs her wedge-head in a cup
of sour cream, drops her ostrich tail,
and will not scare.

Water

It was a Maine lobster town—
each morning boatloads of hands
pushed off for granite
quarries on the islands,

and left dozens of bleak
white frame houses stuck
like oyster shells
on a hill of rock,

and below us, the sea lapped
the raw little match-stick
mazes of a weir,
where the fish for bait were trapped.

Remember? We sat on a slab of rock.
From this distance in time,
it seems the color
of iris, rotting and turning purpler,

but it was only
the usual gray rock
turning the usual green
when drenched by the sea.

The sea drenched the rock
at our feet all day,

and kept tearing away
flake after flake.

One night you dreamed
you were a mermaid clinging to a wharf-pile,
and trying to pull
off the barnacles with your hands.

We wished our two souls
might return like gulls
to the rock. In the end,
the water was too cold for us.

The Scream

(derived from Elizabeth Bishop's story *In the Village*)

A scream, the echo of a scream,
now only a thinning echo . . .
As a child in Nova Scotia,
I used to watch the sky,
Swiss sky, too blue, too dark.

A cow drooled green grass strings,
made cow flop, *smack, smack, smack!*
and tried to brush off its flies
on a lilac bush—all,
forever, at one fell swoop!

In the blacksmith's shop,
the horseshoes sailed through the dark,
like bloody little moons,
red-hot, hissing, protesting,
as they drowned in the pan.

Back and away and back!
Mother kept coming and going—
with me, without me!
Mother's dresses were black
or white, or black-and-white.

One day she changed to purple,
and left her mourning. At the fitting,
the dressmaker crawled on the floor,

eating pins, like Nebuchadnezzar
on his knees eating grass.

Drummers sometimes came
selling gilded red
and green books, unlovely books!
The people in the pictures
wore clothes like the purple dress.

Later, she gave the scream,
not even loud at first . . .
When she went away I thought
"But you can't love everyone,
your heart won't let you!"

A scream! But they are all gone,
those aunts and aunts, a grandfather,
a grandmother, my mother—
even her scream—too frail
for us to hear their voices long.

The Mouth of the Hudson

(FOR ESTHER BROOKS)

A single man stands like a bird-watcher,
and scuffles the pepper and salt snow
from a discarded, gray
Westinghouse Electric cable drum.
He cannot discover America by counting
the chains of condemned freight-trains
from thirty states. They jolt and jar
and junk in the siding below him.
He has trouble with his balance.
His eyes drop,
and he drifts with the wild ice
ticking seaward down the Hudson,
like the blank sides of a jig-saw puzzle.

The ice ticks seaward like a clock.
A Negro toasts
wheat-seeds over the coke-fumes
of a punctured barrel.

Chemical air
sweeps in from New Jersey,
and smells of coffee.

Across the river,
ledges of suburban factories tan
in the sulphur-yellow sun
of the unforgivable landscape.

July in Washington

The stiff spokes of this wheel
touch the sore spots of the earth.

On the Potomac, swan-white
power launches keep breasting the sulphurous wave.

Otters slide and dive and slick back their hair,
raccoons clean their meat in the creek.

On the circles, green statues ride like South American
liberators above the breeding vegetation—

prongs and spearheads of some equatorial
backland that will inherit the globe.

The elect, the elected . . . they come here bright as dimes,
and die dishevelled and soft.

We cannot name their names, or number their dates—
circle on circle, like rings on a tree—

but we wish the river had another shore,
some further range of delectable mountains,

distant hills powdered blue as a girl's eyelid.
It seems the least little shove would land us there,

that only the slightest repugnance of our bodies
we no longer control could drag us back.

For the Union Dead

"Relinquunt Omnia Servare Rem Publicam."

The old South Boston Aquarium stands
in a Sahara of snow now. Its broken windows are boarded.
The bronze weathervane cod has lost half its scales.
The airy tanks are dry.

Once my nose crawled like a snail on the glass;
my hand tingled
to burst the bubbles
drifting from the noses of the cowed, compliant fish.

My hand draws back. I often sigh still
for the dark downward and vegetating kingdom
of the fish and reptile. One morning last March,
I pressed against the new barbed and galvanized

fence on the Boston Common. Behind their cage,
yellow dinosaur steamshovels were grunting
as they cropped up tons of mush and grass
to gouge their underworld garage.

Parking spaces luxuriate like civic
sandpiles in the heart of Boston.
A girdle of orange, Puritan-pumpkin colored girders
braces the tingling Statehouse,

shaking over the excavations, as it faces Colonel Shaw
and his bell-cheeked Negro infantry
on St. Gaudens' shaking Civil War relief,
propped by a plank splint against the garage's earthquake.

Two months after marching through Boston,
half the regiment was dead;
at the dedication,
William James could almost hear the bronze Negroes breathe.

Their monument sticks like a fishbone
in the city's throat.
Its Colonel is as lean
as a compass-needle.

He has an angry wrenlike vigilance,
a greyhound's gentle tautness;
he seems to wince at pleasure,
and suffocate for privacy.

He is out of bounds now. He rejoices in man's lovely,
peculiar power to choose life and die—
when he leads his black soldiers to death,
he cannot bend his back.

On a thousand small town New England greens,
the old white churches hold their air
of sparse, sincere rebellion; frayed flags
quilt the graveyards of the Grand Army of the Republic.

The stone statues of the abstract Union Soldier
grow slimmer and younger each year—
wasp-waisted, they doze over muskets
and muse through their sideburns . . .

Shaw's father wanted no monument
except the ditch,
where his son's body was thrown
and lost with his "niggers."

The ditch is nearer.
There are no statues for the last war here;
on Boylston Street, a commercial photograph
shows Hiroshima boiling

over a Mosler Safe, the "Rock of Ages"
that survived the blast. Space is nearer.
When I crouch to my television set,
the drained faces of Negro school-children rise like balloons.

Colonel Shaw
is riding on his bubble,
he waits
for the blessèd break.

The Aquarium is gone. Everywhere,
giant finned cars nose forward like fish;
a savage servility
slides by on grease.

Ballad for the Dead Ladies

(after Villon: Le grand testament)

Say in what land, or where
is Flora, the lovely Roman,
Andromeda, or Helen,
far lovelier,
or Echo, who would answer
across the brook or river—
her beauty was more than human!
Oh where is last year's snow?

Where is the wise Eloise,
and Peter Abelard
gelded at Saint Denis
for love of her?
That queen who threw Buridan
in a sack in the Seine—
who will love her again?
Oh where is last year's snow?

Queen Blanche, the fleur-de-lys,
who had a siren's voice,
Bertha Big Foot, Beatrice,
Arembourg, ruler of Maine,
or Jeanne d'Arc of Lorraine
the British burned at Rouen?
Where are they, where? Oh Virgin,
where is last year's snow?

Prince, do not ask this year
or next year, where they are;
or answer my refrain:
Oh where is last year's snow?

WILLIAM JAY SMITH

Morels

A wet gray day—rain falling slowly, mist over the valley, mountains dark
circumflex smudges in the distance—

Apple blossoms just gone by, the branches feathery still as if fluttering with half-visible antennae—

A day in May like so many of these green mountains, and I went out just as I had last year

At the same time, and found them there under the big maples—by the bend in the road—right where they had stood

Last year and the year before that, risen from the dark duff of the woods, emerging at odd angles

From spores hidden by curled and matted leaves, a fringe of rain on the grass around them,

Beads of rain on the mounded leaves and mosses round them,

Not in a ring themselves but ringed by jack-in-the-pulpits with deep egg-plant-colored stripes;

Not ringed but rare, not gilled but polyp-like, having sprung up over-night—

These mushrooms of the gods, resembling human organs uprooted, rooted only on the air,

Looking like lungs wrenched from the human body, lungs reversed, not breathing internally

But being the externalization of breath itself, these spicy, twisted cones,

These perforated brown-white asparagus tips—these morels, smelling of wet graham crackers mixed with maple leaves;

And, reaching down by the pale green fern shoots, I nipped their pulpy stems at the base

And dropped them into a paper bag—a damp brown bag (their color)—and carried

Them (weighing absolutely nothing) down the hill and into the house; you held them

Under cold bubbling water and sliced them with a surgeon's stroke clean through,

And sautéed them over a low flame, butter-brown; and we ate them then
  and there—

Tasting of the sweet damp woods and of the rain one inch above the
  meadow:

It was like feasting upon air.

Dachshunds

"The deer and the dachshund are one."
> —WALLACE STEVENS, "Loneliness in Jersey City"

The Dachshund leads a quiet life
  Not far above the ground;
He takes an elongated wife,
  They travel all around.

They leave the lighted metropole;
  Nor turn to look behind
Upon the headlands of the soul,
  The tundras of the mind.

They climb together through the dusk
  To ask the Lost-and-Found
For information on the stars
  Not far above the ground.

The Dachshunds seem to journey on:
  And following them, I
Take up my monocle, the Moon,
  And gaze into the sky.

Pursuing them with comic art
  Beyond a cosmic goal,
I see the whole within the part,
  The part within the whole;

See planets wheeling overhead,
  Mysterious and slow,
While Morning buckles on his red,
  And on the Dachshunds go.

Pictures of the Gone World: 2

Just as I used to say
                        love comes harder to the aged
because they've been running
                on the same old rails too long
  and then when the sly switch comes along
                            they miss the turn
    and burn up the wrong rail while
                  the gay caboose goes flying
      and the steamengine driver don't recognize
                       them new electric horns
and the aged run out on the rusty spur
                  which ends up in
         the dead grass where
   the rusty tincans and bedsprings and old razor
         blades and moldy mattresses
                    lie
   and the rail breaks off dead
              right there
    though the ties go on awhile
              and the aged
say to themselves
        Well
         this must be the place
        we were supposed to lie down
And they do
      while the bright saloon careens along away
  on a high
     hilltop
        its windows full of bluesky and lovers
    with flowers
        their long hair streaming
           and all of them laughing
      and waving and
           whispering to each other
   and looking out and
         wondering what that graveyard
   where the rails end
      is

The Iron Characters

The iron characters, keepers of the public confidence,
The sponsors, fund raisers, and members of the board,
Who naturally assume their seats among the governors,
Who place their names behind the issue of bonds
And are consulted in the formation of cabinets,
The catastrophes of war, depression, and natural disaster:
They represent us in responsibilities many and great.
It is no wonder, then, if in a moment of crisis,
Before the microphones, under the lights, on a great occasion,
One of them will break down in hysterical weeping
Or fall in an epileptic seizure, or if one day
We read in the papers of one's having been found
Naked and drunk in a basement with three high school boys,
Of one who jumped from the window of his hospital room.
For are they not as ourselves in these things also?
Let the orphan, the pauper, the thief, the derelict drunk
And all those of no fixed address, shed tears of rejoicing
For the broken minds of the strong, the torn flesh of the just.

RICHARD WILBUR

Museum Piece

The good gray guardians of art
Patrol the halls on spongy shoes,
Impartially protective, though
Perhaps suspicious of Toulouse.

Here dozes one against the wall,
Disposed upon a funeral chair.
A Degas dancer pirouettes
Upon the parting of his hair.

See how she spins! The grace is there,
But strain as well is plain to see.
Degas loved the two together:
Beauty joined to energy.

Edgar Degas purchased once
A fine El Greco, which he kept
Against the wall beside his bed
To hang his pants on while he slept.

Sonnet

The winter deepening, the hay all in,
The barn fat with cattle, the apple-crop
Conveyed to market or the fragrant bin,
He thinks the time has come to make a stop,

And sinks half-grudging in his firelit seat,
Though with his heavy body's full consent,
In what would be the posture of defeat,
But for that look of rigorous content.

Outside, the night dives down like one great crow
Against his cast-off clothing where it stands
Up to the knees in miles of hustled snow,

Flapping and jumping like a kind of fire,
And floating skyward its abandoned hands
In gestures of invincible desire.

Ballade for the Duke of Orléans

*who offered a prize at Blois, circa 1457, for the best ballade employing
the line "Je meurs de soif auprès de la fontaine."*

Flailed from the heart of water in a bow,
He took the falling fly; my line went taut;
Foam was in uproar where he drove below;
In spangling air I fought him and was fought.
Then, wearied to the shallows, he was caught,
Gasped in the net, lay still and stony-eyed.
It was no fading iris I had sought.
I die of thirst, here at the fountain-side.

Down in the harbor's flow and counter-flow
I left my ships with hopes and heroes fraught.

Ten times more golden than the sun could show,
Calypso gave the darkness I besought.
Oh, but her fleecy touch was dearly bought:
All spent, I wakened by my only bride,
Beside whom every vision is but nought,
And die of thirst, here at the fountain-side.

Where does that Plenty dwell, I'd like to know,
Which fathered poor Desire, as Plato taught?
Out on the real and endless waters go
Conquistador and stubborn Argonaut.
Where Buddha bathed, the golden bowl he brought
Gilded the stream, but stalled its living tide.
The sunlight withers as the verse is wrought.
I die of thirst, here at the fountain-side.

ENVOI

Duke, keep your coin. All men are born distraught,
And will not for the world be satisfied.
Whether we live in fact, or but in thought,
We die of thirst, here at the fountain-side.

Advice to a Prophet

When you come, as you soon must, to the streets of our city,
Mad-eyed from stating the obvious,
Not proclaiming our fall but begging us
In God's name to have self-pity,

Spare us all word of the weapons, their force and range,
The long numbers that rocket the mind;
Our slow, unreckoning hearts will be left behind,
Unable to fear what is too strange.

Nor shall you scare us with talk of the death of the race.
How should we dream of this place without us?—
The sun mere fire, the leaves untroubled about us,
A stone look on the stone's face?

Speak of the world's own change. Though we cannot conceive
Of an undreamt thing, we know to our cost
How the dreamt cloud crumbles, the vines are blackened by frost,
How the view alters. We could believe,

If you told us so, that the white-tailed deer will slip
Into perfect shade, grown perfectly shy,
The lark avoid the reaches of our eye,
The jack-pine lose its knuckled grip

On the cold ledge, and every torrent burn
As Xanthus once, its gliding trout
Stunned in a twinkling. What should we be without
The dolphin's arc, the dove's return,

These things in which we have seen ourselves and spoken?
Ask us, prophet, how we shall call
Our natures forth when that live tongue is all
Dispelled, that glass obscured or broken

In which we have said the rose of our love and the clean
Horse of our courage, in which beheld
The singing locus of the soul unshelled,
And all we mean or wish to mean.

Ask us, ask us whether with the worldless rose
Our hearts shall fail us; come demanding
Whether there shall be lofty or long standing
When the bronze annals of the oak-tree close.

PHILIP LARKIN

The Whitsun Weddings

That Whitsun, I was late getting away:
    Not till about
One-twenty on the sunlit Saturday
Did my three-quarters-empty train pull out,
All windows down, all cushions hot, all sense
Of being in a hurry gone. We ran
Behind the backs of houses, crossed a street
Of blinding windscreens, smelt the fish-dock; thence
The river's level drifting breadth began,
Where sky and Lincolnshire and water meet.

All afternoon, through the tall heat that slept
    For miles inland,
A slow and stopping curve southwards we kept.

Wide farms went by, short-shadowed cattle, and
Canals with floatings of industrial froth;
A hothouse flashed uniquely: hedges dipped
And rose: and now and then a smell of grass
Displaced the reek of buttoned carriage-cloth
Until the next town, new and nondescript,
Approached with acres of dismantled cars.

At first, I didn't notice what a noise
  The weddings made
Each station that we stopped at: sun destroys
The interest of what's happening in the shade,
And down the long cool platforms whoops and skirls
I took for porters larking with the mails,
And went on reading. Once we started, though,
We passed them, grinning and pomaded, girls
In parodies of fashion, heels and veils,
All posed irresolutely, watching us go,

As if out on the end of an event
  Waving goodbye
To something that survived it. Struck, I leant
More promptly out next time, more curiously,
And saw it all again in different terms:
The fathers with broad belts under their suits
And seamy foreheads; mothers loud and fat;
An uncle shouting smut; and then the perms,
The nylon gloves and jewellery-substitutes,
The lemons, mauves, and olive-ochres that

Marked off the girls unreally from the rest.
  Yes, from cafés
And banquet-halls up yards, and bunting-dressed
Coach-party annexes, the wedding-days
Were coming to an end. All down the line
Fresh couples climbed aboard: the rest stood round;
The last confetti and advice were thrown,
And, as we moved, each face seemed to define
Just what it saw departing: children frowned
At something dull; fathers had never known

Success so huge and wholly farcical;
  The women shared
The secret like a happy funeral;

While girls, gripping their handbags tighter, stared
At a religious wounding. Free at last,
And loaded with the sum of all they saw,
We hurried towards London, shuffling gouts of steam.
Now fields were building-plots, and poplars cast
Long shadows over major roads, and for
Some fifty minutes, that in time would seem

Just long enough to settle hats and say
   I nearly died,
A dozen marriages got under way.
They watched the landscape, sitting side by side
—An Odeon went past, a cooling tower,
And someone running up to bowl—and none
Thought of the others they would never meet
Or how their lives would all contain this hour.
I thought of London spread out in the sun,
Its postal districts packed like squares of wheat:

There we were aimed. And as we raced across
   Bright knots of rail
Past standing Pullmans, walls of blackened moss
Came close, and it was nearly done, this frail
Travelling coincidence; and what it held
Stood ready to be loosed with all the power
That being changed can give. We slowed again,
And as the tightened brakes took hold, there swelled
A sense of falling, like an arrow-shower
Sent out of sight, somewhere becoming rain.

Afternoons

Summer is fading:
The leaves fall in ones and twos
From trees bordering
The new recreation ground.
In the hollows of afternoons
Young mothers assemble
At swing and sandpit
Setting free their children.

Behind them, at intervals,
Stand husbands in skilled trades,

An estateful of washing,
And the albums, lettered
Our Wedding, lying
Near the television:
Before them, the wind
Is ruining their courting-places

That are still courting-places
(But the lovers are all in school),
And their children, so intent on
Finding more unripe acorns,
Expect to be taken home.
Their beauty has thickened.
Something is pushing them
To the side of their own lives.

HOWARD MOSS

Water Island

(To the memory of a friend,
drowned off Water Island, April, 1960)

Finally, from your house, there is no view;
The bay's blind mirror shattered over you
And Patchogue took your body like a log
The wind rolled up to shore. The senseless drowned
Have faces nobody would care to see,
But water loves those gradual erasures
Of flesh and shoreline, greenery and glass,
And you belonged to water, it to you,
Having built, on a hillock, above the bay,
Your house, the bay giving you reason to,
Where now, if seasons still are running straight,
The horseshoe crabs clank armor night and day,
Their couplings far more ancient than the eyes
That watched them from your porch. I saw one once
Whose back was a history of how we live;
Grown onto every inch of plate, except
Where the hinges let it move, were living things,
Barnacles, mussels, water weeds—and one
Blue bit of polished glass, glued there by time:
The origins of art. It carried them

With pride, it seemed, as if endurance only
Matters in the end. Or so I thought.

Skimming traffic lights, starboard and port,
Steer through planted poles that mark the way,
And other lights, across the bay, faint stars
Lining the border of Long Island's shore,
Come on at night, they still come on at night,
Though who can see them now I do not know.
Wild roses, at your back porch, break their blood,
And bud to test surprises of sea air,
And the birds fly over, gliding down to feed
At the two feeding stations you set out with seed,
Or splash themselves in a big bowl of rain
You used to fill with water. Going across
That night, too fast, too dark, no one will know,
Maybe you heard, the last you'll ever hear,
The cry of the savage and endemic gull
Which shakes the blood and always brings to mind
The thought that death, the scavenger, is blind,
Blunders and is stupid, and the end
Comes with ironies so fine the seed
Falters in the marsh and the heron stops
Hunting in the weeds below your landing stairs,
Standing in a stillness that now is yours.

A Swim off the Rocks

A flat rock is the best for taking off.
   Rafferty, the lawyer, with a cough,
      Goes first, head first—a dive
That makes us wonder how he's still alive.
The ballerina's next, and shames us all.
What grace in space! What an Australian crawl!

I'm next, and too self-conscious to be good.
   When I look back to where I stood,
      Miss Jones, a leather crafter,
Runs, jumps in, and makes it to the raft. Her
Body salty-white, she stares back at the shore, a
Lot like Lot's wife in Sodom and Gomorrah.

The ballerina knows how much restraint
   Enhances skill, and, with a little feint,

Spins away. Now Rafferty
Seems to be arguing a case at sea.
Splashing, gesticulating, he swims back,
And climbs, exhausted, onto the rock.

Miss Jones comes in—martyred, ill at ease,
    And towels carefully, even knees,
        While the lawyer fetches beer.
The dancer always seems to disappear.
Miss Jones, sotto-voice: "It's *said*, in *town*,
She's found a choreographer, all her own."

What *I* say, though, is let what *is* just be.
    Miss Jones and Mr. Rafferty,
        A hopeless combination,
Have my good wishes for a grand vacation.
The dancer needs no help, evidently.
And as for me, I simply like the sea.

JAMES DICKEY

The Performance

The last time I saw Donald Armstrong
He was staggering oddly off into the sun,
Going down, of the Philippine Islands.
I let my shovel fall, and put that hand
Above my eyes, and moved some way to one side
That his body might pass through the sun,

And I saw how well he was not
Standing there on his hands,
On his spindle-shanked forearms balanced,
Unbalanced, with his big feet looming and waving
In the great, untrustworthy air
He flew in each night, when it darkened.

Dust fanned in scraped puffs from the earth
Between his arms, and blood turned his face inside out,
To demonstrate its suppleness
Of veins, as he perfected his role.
Next day, he toppled his head off
On an island beach to the south,

And the enemy's two-handed sword
Did not fall from anyone's hands
At that miraculous sight,
As the head rolled over upon
Its wide-eyed face, and fell
Into the inadequate grave

He had dug for himself, under pressure.
Yet I put my flat hand to my eyebrows
Months later, to see him again
In the sun, when I learned how he died,
And imagined him, there,
Come, judged, before his small captors,

Doing all his lean tricks to amaze them—
The back somersault, the kip-up—
And at last, the stand on his hands,
Perfect, with his feet together,
His head down, evenly breathing,
As the sun poured up from the sea

And the headsman broke down
In a blaze of tears, in that light
Of the thin, long human frame
Upside down in its own strange joy,
And, if some other one had not told him,
Would have cut off the feet

Instead of the head,
And if Armstrong had not presently risen
In kingly, round-shouldered attendance,
And then knelt down in himself
Beside his hacked, glittering grave, having done
All things in this life that he could.

DENISE LEVERTOV

Resting Figure

The head Byzantine or from
Fayyum, the shoulders naked,
a little of the

dark-haired breast visible
above the sheet,

from deep in the dark head
his smile glowing
outward into the
room's severe twilight,

he lies, a dark-shadowed
mellow gold against
the flattened white pillow,
a gentle man—

strength and despair
quiet there in the bed,
the line of his limbs
half-shown, as under stone
or bronze folds.

LOUIS SIMPSON

Hot Night on Water Street

A hot midsummer night on Water Street—
The boys in jeans were combing their blond hair,
Watching the girls go by on tired feet;
And an old woman with a witch's stare
Cried "Praise the Lord!" She vanished on a bus
With hissing air brakes, like an incubus.

Three hardware stores, a barbershop, a bar,
A movie playing Westerns—where I went
To see a dream of horses called *The Star*. . . .
Some day, when this uncertain continent
Is marble, and men ask what was the good
We lived by, dust may whisper "Hollywood."

Then back along the river bank on foot
By moonlight. . . . On the West Virginia side
An owlish train began to huff and hoot;
It seemed to know of something that had died.
I didn't linger—sometimes when I travel
I think I'm being followed by the Devil.

At the newsstand in the lobby, a cigar
Was talkative: "Since I've been in this town
I've seen one likely woman, and a car
As she was crossing Main Street, knocked her down."
I was a stranger here myself, I said,
And bought the *New York Times,* and went to bed.

Frogs

The storm broke, and it rained,
And water rose in the pool,
And frogs hopped into the gutter,

With their skins of yellow and green,
And just their eyes shining above the surface
Of the warm solution of slime.

At night, when fireflies trace
Light-lines between the trees and flowers
Exhaling perfume,

The frogs speak to each other
In rhythm. The sound is monstrous,
But their voices are filled with satisfaction.

In the city I pine for the country;
In the country I long for conversation—
Our happy croaking.

VASSAR MILLER

Without Ceremony

Except ourselves, we have no other prayer;
Our needs are sores upon our nakedness.
We do not have to name them; we are here.
And You who can make eyes can see no less.
We fall, not on our knees, but on our hearts,
A posture humbler far and more downcast;
While Father Pain instructs us in the arts
Of praying, hunger is the worthiest fast.

We find ourselves where tongues cannot wage war
On silence (farther, mystics never flew)
But on the common wings of what we are,
Borne on the wings of what we bear, toward You,
Oh Word, in whom our wordiness dissolves,
When we have not a prayer except ourselves.

Bout With Burning

I have tossed hours upon the tides of fever,
Upon the billows of my blood have ridden,
Where fish of fancy teem as neither river
Nor ocean spawns from India to Sweden.
Here while my boat of body burnt has drifted
Along her sides crawled tentacles of crabs
Sliming her timbers; on the waves upwafted
Crept water rats to gnaw her ropes and ribs.
Crashing, she has dived, her portholes choking
With weed and ooze, the swirls of black and green
Gulping her inch by inch, the seagulls' shrieking
Sieved depth through depth to silence. Till blast-blown,
I in my wreck beyond storm's charge and churning
Have waked marooned upon the coasts of morning.

DONALD JUSTICE

Anniversaries

Great Leo roared at my birth,
The windowpanes were lit
With stars' applausive light,
And I have heard that the earth
As far away as Japan
Was shaken again and again
The morning I came forth.
Many drew round me then,
Admiring. Beside my bed
The tall aunts prophesied,
And cousins from afar,
Predicting a great career.

At ten there came an hour
When, waking out of ether
Into an autumn weather
Inexpressibly dear,
I was wheeled superb in a chair
Past vacant lots in bloom
With goldenrod and with broom,
In secret proud of the scar
Dividing me from life,
Which I could admire like one
Come down from Mars or the moon,
Standing a little off.

By seventeen I had guessed
That the "really great loneliness"
Of James's governess
Might account for the ghost
On the other side of the lake.
Oh, all that year was lost
Somewhere among the black
Keys of Chopin! I sat
All afternoon after school,
Fingering his ripe heart,
While boys outside in the dirt
Kicked, up and down, their ball.

Thirty today, I saw
The trees flare briefly like
The candles upon a cake
As the sun went down the sky,
A momentary flash,
Yet there was time to wish
Before the light could die,
If I had known what to wish,
As once I must have known,
Bending above the clean,
Candlelit tablecloth
To blow them out with a breath.

A Dream Sestina

I woke by first light in a wood
Right in the shadow of a hill

And saw about me in a circle
Many I knew, the dear faces
Of some I recognized as friends.
I knew that I had lost my way.

I asked if any knew the way.
They stared at me like blocks of wood.
They turned their backs on me, those friends,
And struggled up the stubborn hill
Along that road which makes a circle.
No longer could I see their faces.

But there were trees with human faces.
Afraid, I ran a little way
But must have wandered in a circle.
I had not left that human wood;
I was no farther up the hill.
And all the while I heard my friends

Discussing me, but not like friends.
Through gaps in trees I glimpsed their faces.
(The trees grow crooked on that hill.)
Now all at once I saw the way:
Above a clearing in the wood
A lone bird wheeling in a circle,

And in that shadowed space the circle
Of those I thought of still as friends.
I drew near, calling, and the wood
Rang and they turned their deaf faces
This way and that, but not my way.
They rose and danced upon the hill.

And it grew dark. Behind the hill
The sun slid down, a fiery circle;
Screeching, the bird flew on her way.
It was too dark to see my friends.
But then I saw them, and their faces
Were leaning above me like a wood.

Round me they circle on the hill.
But what is wrong with my friends' faces?
Why have they changed that way to wood?

To the Hawks

MCNAMARA, RUSK, BUNDY

Farewell is the bell
Beginning to ring.

The children singing
Do not yet hear it.

The sun is shining
In their song. The sun

Is in fact shining
Upon the schoolyard,

On children swinging
Like tongues of a bell

Swung out on the long
Arc of a silence

That will not seem to
Have been a silence

Till it is broken,
As it is breaking.

There is a sun now
Louder than the sun

Of which the children
Are singing, brighter,

Too, than that other
Against whose brightness

Their eyes seem caught in
The act of shutting.

The young schoolteacher,
Waving one arm in

Time to the music,
Is waving farewell.

Her mouth is open
To sound the alarm.

The mouth of the world
Grows round with the sound.

February, 1965

Variations for Two Pianos
For Thomas Higgins, pianist

There is no music now in all Arkansas.
Higgins is gone, taking both his pianos.

Movers dismantled the instruments, away
Sped the vans. The first detour untuned the strings.

There is no music now in all Arkansas.

Up Main Street, past the cold shopfronts of Conway,
The brash, self-important brick of the college,

Higgins is gone, taking both his pianos.

Warm evenings, the windows open, he would play
Something of Mozart's for his pupils, the birds.

There is no music now in all Arkansas.

How shall the mockingbird mend her trill, the jay
His eccentric attack, lacking a teacher?

Higgins is gone, taking both his pianos.
There is no music now in all Arkansas.

ALAN STEPHENS

The Vanishing Act
(syllabics for T. G.)

After he concluded that
he did not wish to raise his

voice when he spoke of such matters as the collapse of the

Something Empire, or of things
the folk suffer from, he simply set in words such meanings
as were there, and then, when he

finished the final verse, vanished in the blank below it:
he'll reappear only on
the next page (not written yet).

MAXINE KUMIN

The Pawnbroker

The symbol inside this poem is my father's feet
which, after fifty years of standing behind
the counter waiting on trade,
were tender and smooth and lay on the ironed sheet,
a study of white on white, like a dandy's shirt.
A little too precious; custom-made.
At the end of a day and all day Sunday they hurt.
Lying down, they were on his mind.

The sight of his children barefoot gave him a pain
—part anger, part wonder—as sharp as gravel
inside his lisle socks.
Polacks! he said, but meant it to mean
hod carriers, greenhorns, peasants; not ghetto Poles
once removed. *Where are your shoes? In hock?*
I grew up under the sign of those three gold balls
turning clockwise on their swivel.

Every good thing in my life was secondhand.
It smelled of having been owned before me by
a redcap porter whose ticket
ran out. I saw his time slip down like sand
in the glass that measured our breakfast eggs. At night
he overtook me in the thicket
and held me down and beat my black heart white
to make the pawnbroker's daughter pay.

On Saturday nights the lights stayed lit until ten.
There were cops outside on regular duty to let
the customers in and out.
I have said that my father's feet were graceful and clean.
They hurt when he turned the lock
on the cooks and chauffeurs and unlucky racetrack touts
and carwash attendants and laundresses and stock-
room boys and doormen in epaulets;

they hurt when he did up accounts in his head
at the bathroom sink
of the watches, cameras, typewriters, suitcases, guitars,
cheap diamond rings and thoroughbred
family silver, and matched them against the list
of hot goods from Headquarters,
meanwhile nailbrushing his knuckles and wrists
clean of the pawn-ticket stains of purple ink.

Firsthand I had from my father a love ingrown
tight as an oyster, and returned it
as secretly. From him firsthand
the grace of work, the sweat of it, the bone-
tired unfolding down from stress.
I was the bearer he paid up on demand
with one small pearl of selfhood. Portionless,
I am oystering still to earn it.

Not of the House of Rothschild, my father, my creditor
lay dead while they shaved his cheeks and blacked his mustache.

My lifetime appraiser, my first prince whom death unhorsed
lay soberly dressed and barefoot to be burned.
That night, my brothers and I forced
the cap on his bottle of twenty-year-old scotch
and drank ourselves on fire beforehand
for the sacrament of closing down the hatch,
for the sacrament of easing down the ways
my thumb-licking peeler of cash on receipt of the merchandise,
possessor of miracles left unredeemed on the shelf
after thirty days,
giver and lender, no longer in hock to himself,
ruled off the balance sheet,
a man of great personal order
and small white feet.

PAT WILSON

The Precious Pearl

The oyster shuts his gates to form the pearl.
He knows he has a saviour caught within him,
Poor fool, old Oyster. And it works against him,
An irritant that's locked within his shell,
A single-mindedness that thins his heart,
Turns it to narrow-heartedness. Yet he,
Poor foolish oyster, used to love the sea
In all its many forms, to every part
Open with tranquil, unassuming jaws.
Then that foul irritant was driven in,
And snap! the wounded tongue cherished its sin
Until at last by hard, immobile laws
    A shining, perfect pebble made from wrong—
    A perfect grievance—rolled from off the tongue.

PHILIP LEVINE

Lights I Have Seen Before

The children are off somewhere
  and when I waken
    I hear only
  the buzz of current
    in the TV
and the refrigerator

groaning against the coming
  day. I rise and wash;
    there is nothing
  to think of except
    the insistent push
of water, and the pipe's

cry against the water. I
  shave carefully,
    wanting to say
  something to someone,
    wanting to ease
myself away from the face

that is faintly familiar.
　　　Later, at my desk
　　　　a young girl
　　　cries against the past
　　　　and the new world
she is afraid to enter.

She puts her head down, trying
　　　to hide what I hear,
　　　　trying to ask
　　　for understanding
　　　　and quiets, and leaves,
And leaves the memory of

no word I can understand. On
　　　the way home houses
　　　　that are insane
　　　spread on my left hand
　　　　and on my right.
I drive on the road between.

Between the cry of matter
　　　and the cry of those
　　　　whose lives are here
　　　what is there to choose
　　　　but failure? What
can one say to oneself that

will make it believable?
　　　and I am on my
　　　　block, slowing for
　　　clusters of children
　　　　who hear nothing.
My next-door neighbor sees me

and waves as I pass and goes
　　　on chasing behind
　　　　the power mower
　　　in a spray of grass
　　　　and lights come on
where I have seen them before.

I tell time
by the sunlight's position
    on the bedroom wall:
it's 5:30, middle June.
    I rise, dress,
    assume my name

    and feel my
face against a hard towel.
    My mind is empty;
I see all that's here to see:
    the garden
    and the hard sky;

    the great space
between the two has a weight,
    a reality
which I find is no burden,
    and the height
    of the cot tree

    is only
what it has come to deserve.
    I have not found peace,
but I have found I am where
    I am by
    being only there,

    by standing
in the clouded presence of
    the things I observe.
What is it in the air or the
    water caught
    on the branches

    of the brown
roses hanging toward autumn?
    What is it that moves
when it's still, and strikes me dumb
    when it speaks
    of being alive.

Considering the Snail

The snail pushes through a green
night, for the grass is heavy
with water and meets over
the bright path he makes, where rain
has darkened the earth's dark. He
moves in a wood of desire,

pale antlers barely stirring
as he hunts. I cannot tell
what power is at work, drenched there
with purpose, knowing nothing.
What is a snail's fury? All
I think is that if later

I parted the blades above
the tunnel and saw the thin
trail of broken white across
litter, I would never have
imagined the slow passion
to that deliberate progress.

GEORGE STARBUCK

Bone Thoughts on a Dry Day

*Walking to the museum
over the Outer Drive,
I think, before I see them
dead, of the bones alive.*

How perfectly the snake smoothes over the fact
he strings sharp beads around that charmer's neck.

Bird bone may be breakable, but
have you ever held a cat's jaw shut?
Brittle as ice.

Take mice:
the mouse is a berry, his bones mere seeds:
step on him once and see.

You mustn't think that the fish
choke on those bones, or that chickens wish.

The wise old bat
hangs his bones in a bag.

Two chicks ride a bike,
unlike
that legless swinger of crutches, the ostrich.

Only the skull of a man is much of an ashtray.

Each owl
turns on a dowel.

When all the other tents are struck, an old
elephant pitches himself on his own poles.

But as for my bones—
tug of a toe, blunt-bowed barge of a thighbone,
gondola-squadron of ribs, and the jaw scow—
they weather the swing and storm of the flesh they plow,
out of conjecture of shore, one jolt from land.

I climb the museum steps like a beach.
There, on squared stone, some cast-up keels bleach.
Here, a dark sea speaks with white hands.

A Tapestry for Bayeux

I. RECTO

Over the
    seaworthy
cavalry
    arches a
rocketry
    wickerwork:
involute
    laceries
lacerate
    indigo
altitudes,

                    making a
                skywritten

filigree
    into which,
lazily,
    LCTs
sinuate,
    adjutants
next to them
    eversharp-
eyed, among
    delicate
battleship
    umbrages
twinkling an

anger as
    measured as
organdy.
    Normandy
knitted the
    eyelets and
yarn of these
    warriors'
armoring—
    ringbolt and
dungaree,
    cable and
axletree,

tanktrack and
    ammobelt
linking and
    opening
garlands and
    islands of
seafoam and
    sergeantry.
Opulent
    fretwork: on
turquoise and
    emerald,
red instants

accenting
  neatly a
dearth of red.
  Gunstations
issue it;
  vaportrails
ease into
  smoke from it—
yellow and
  ochre and
umber and
  sable and
out. Or that

man at the
  edge of the
tapestry
  holding his
inches of
  niggardly
ground and his
  trumpery
order of
  red and his
equipage
  angled and
dated. He.

II. VERSO

Wasting no
  energy,
Time, the old
  registrar,
evenly
  adds to his
scrolls, rolling
  up in them
rampage and
  echo and
hush—in each
  influx of
surf, in each

tumble of
  raincloud at

evening,
   action of
seaswell and
   undertow
rounding an
   introvert
edge to the
   surge until,
manhandled
   over, all
surfaces,

tapestries,
   entities
veer from the
   eye like those
rings of lost
   yesteryears
pooled in the
   oak of your
memory.
   Item: one
Normandy
   Exercise.
Muscle it

over: an
   underside
rises: a
   raggedy
elegant
   mess of an
abstract: a
   rip-out of
kidstuff and
   switchboards, where
amputee
   radio
elements,

unattached
   nervefibre
conduits,
   openmouthed
ureters,

              tag ends of
          hamstring and
              outrigging
          ripped from their
              unions and
          nexuses
              jumble with
          undeterred

          speakingtubes
              twittering
          orders as
              random and
          angry as
              ddt'd
          hornets. Step
              over a
          moment: peer
              in through this
          nutshell of
              eyeball and
          man your gun.

War Story

The 4th of July he stormed a nest.
He won a ribbon but lost his chest.
We threw his arms across the rest
        And kneed him in the chin.
        (You knee them in the chin
        To drive the dog-tag in.)

The 5th of July the Chaplain wrote.
It wasn't much; I needn't quote.
The widow lay on her davenport
        Letting the news sink in.
        (Since April she had been
        Letting the news sink in.)

The 6th of July the Captain stank.
They had us pinned from either flank.
With all respect to the dead and rank
        We wished he was dug in.

(I mean to save your skin
It says to get dug in.)

The word when it came was three days old.
Lieutenant Jones brought marigolds,
The widow got out the Captain's Olds
    And took him for a spin.
    (A faster-than-ever spin:
    Down to the Lake, and in.)

Pit Viper

A slow burn
in cold blood
is all snake
muscle does.
The nerves drone
their dull red
test pattern
for days. Days.

The eyes, black
pushbuttons,
are just that.
On each side
a fixed dish
antenna
covers the
infrared.

The ribs, like
a good set
of stiff twin
calipers,
lie easy
and don't take
measure of
what's not there.

The skin's dim
computer-
controlboard
arrangement

of massed lights
betrays no
least motion.
Take no joy.

A strike force
is no more
than its parts
but these parts
work. Dead-game
defensework
specialists,
they die well.

The point is
they don't choose
livings: they
don't choose Death.
God save them
they aren't small-
time haters
that joined up.

The Skindivers

Up and down the beach
gritty as grindstone pound
ball ball ball
heel and splay toe
of the beachball players.

Fitful as hot pigs
bedded into the sand
the red sunbathers drowse.
Ball Ball Ball
hoofs it over them all.

It's ball ball ball
in the beach-pavilion bars,
a polyrhythm riff
for washboard and brushed traps
thundering under the pier

and gone. The minuscule
ball ball ball
of our breaths arises. Still
deeper we settle, cool
and enraptured, a seed pearl

while up and down the beach
and over the waves and on
ball ball ball
throbs the dissolving call
of the beachball players.

MARK STRAND

The Tunnel

A man has been standing
in front of my house
for days. I peek at him
from the living room
window and at night,
unable to sleep,
I shine my flashlight
down on the lawn.
He is always there.

After a while
I open the front door
just a crack and order
him out of my yard.
He narrows his eyes
and moans. I slam
the door and dash back
to the kitchen, then up
to the bedroom, then down.

I weep like a schoolgirl
and make obscene gestures
through the window. I
write large suicide notes
and place them so he
can read them easily.

I destroy the living
room furniture to prove
I own nothing of value.

When he seems unmoved
I decide to dig a tunnel
to a neighboring yard.
I seal the basement off
from the upstairs with
a brickwall. I dig hard
and in no time the tunnel
is done. Leaving my pick
and shovel below,

I come out in front of a house
and stand there too tired to
move or even speak, hoping
someone will help me.
I feel I'm being watched
and sometimes I hear
a man's voice,
but nothing is done
and I have been waiting for days.

ROBERT MEZEY

Flights

F reeing your folded wings from girlhood's cell
O f sticky silk and twig, where will you go?
R ain hovers here, over your fluttering shell.

S ubmerged in dew's colostrum, you will know—
A scend and dip on the heavy blooms as they bend;
N o nectary suckled the nymph's dark embryo.
D amp softens the petal; dance softly where you land.
R est in the fragrant cup, perfectly still.
A nd, rising, scatter its powder upon the wind.

J uice from those buds churns in the delicate blood,
E phemeral, of the gaudy friends of moths;
A butterfly has wings of beaten gold,
N oiselessly beating sunward to its death.

W hen summer left, the butterflies fell down
I n the cold air, to the cold ground. I watched
T orn wings and withered thorax, as the wind
H urried their dry bodies to the woods.

L ong afterward, in winter, a bright ghost—
O r could it be I had not seen it die?—
V eered slowly downward, fluttering over the snow.
E verything slept except that butterfly.

The End of an Outing

Leaving the pond, she looks like someone I know,
glistening like hauled-up treasure, such as men lose,
and swinging her heavy auburn hair she comes to the blanket.

A pretty girl in a blue bathing suit.
Close to the seeping cloth, I squint at her shoulder and arm,
flushed, and palely freckled, and moist, and cold to the touch.

Behind the pines and cedars, the sun is falling,
casting their shadows deep on the empty beach
and the cold red water, suddenly unfamiliar.

In a few minutes, she will undress and sit
alone on the gritty bench of the bathhouse, in semi-dark,
slowly wiping her breasts with a damp towel.

MARY OLIVER

The Flute-Man

Under the plane trees cool and green as rain,
We hear the flute-man come across the morning,
Tapping his stick. Like him I only seem
To sing, so sweetly, for nothing.

How innocent of pain he stands and plays
Under the trees, like something lost from a choir;
Then tips his head towards silence and walks on,
Knowing it is deadly to implore.

I know his friend; burly and sly as hope
He trails behind. One must appear alone;
And yet there must be someone who at nightfall
Will see the little flute-man safely home.

Now through the leaves we watch him out of sight,
Warming his flute with fingers thin as threads.
Now if we catch him puzzling out his maps,
Who will blame him for the lie of blindness,

Or that his mind harbors a tradesman, wild
For bread, for warmth, for light?—oh, nothing new—
In solitude and longing to be valiant,
I lean across my songs; I sing to you.

R. H. W. DILLARD

Desert Fox
for C. W. Parker

The general knows. His maps
Spread on the table, creases
And all. And his pointer ceases
To make sense, just waggles up
And down. But he knows.

The grumble of the idling
Tanks below the window.
Their guns are muffled
Canvas in the dust.

"Must we always assault
From the rear, when most
Often a frontal thrust
Meets with the least
Opposition?" His heels
Click convulsively.
The colonels nod. His mind
Is clearly elsewhere.

Not there
But in the general's bed,
No Mata Hari, the English

Spy reclines. Miranda,
Pale and blue and yellow,
Her hair pressed to his
Pillow, her legs bare
Beneath the starched flat
Sheet, her breasts, arms,
Shoulders naked in the air,
His hollow room. Her teeth
Are small and round and sharp.

When will he move, arch a finger
On the map, alert the tanks
For a full advance? His eyes
Are closed, his pointer
Clatters to the floor. He sighs.

Her nervous tongue advances
The hollows of her lower
Lip, tips in and out.

A shout in the swirling sand,
The canvas rips as muzzles raise,
The general stalks the empty room.
His eyes lit, thoughts of the pass,
The plunging charge, the clash,
A grapple with the foe.

Bang, maps on the floor,
The double door snaps to,
A frightened aide,
The general in the sand
Who bellows in the wind,
Turns in the sand,
Stands in the turning sand.
He contemplates
A victory for the fatherland.

Her fingers tap his name
In Morse along her thigh,
Assault soon to begin,
Her job, his boots
Beyond the door.

A tank antenna whips
The wind.

Another win,
Another loss, toss
Of the sheets from head
To toe. He knows
The maps, lay of the land

As pale Miranda
Watches his advance
And nips her thumb.

An Alice for Annie

Blond Alice who looms large,
Miles high, must leave the court,
Grows into sunlight, so bright
Eyes close, she glows, and the sun
Shades in the dazzle of our love.

For love this Alice I do,
Who loves me, whom I have
Found, she me, alone,
Together, as that white rabbit
Humps high too as Stevens' king
Of ghosts, he tries to note
Our time upon his watch, fails
For forever is beyond his hands,
Not ours, and hops huge away.

We, Tweedledum and Tweedledee,
Like so alike, look, love alike,
We have no pool of tears to tread,
Are free, sway in those clouds around
The sun, shed joy, birds sing
As flowers on the ground so far below
Fold open in our light.

This Alice
Who is me as I am she, mine,
I am hers, I love, am loved,
We love, become two shining Cheshire grins.

Kanheri Caves

Over these blunted, these tormented hills,
Hawks hail and wheel, glissading down the sky:
It seems this green ambiguous landscape tilts
And teeters the perspective of the eye.
Only two centuries after Christ, this cliff
Was colonized by a mild antique race,
Who left us, like a faded photograph
Their memories that dry up in this place.

They left no ghosts. The rock alone endures.
Their drains and cisterns work: storms wrecked the stairs:
Blocks are fallen: sunlight cracks those floors
And fidgets in a courtyard where a pair
Of giant Buddhas smile and wait their crash;
Then temples, audience halls, a lonely tomb.
I touch its side. The stone's worn smooth as flesh.
A stranger dangles peaceful in that womb.

Worm he will be, if born: blink in the sun.
I'll crawl into his dark: perhaps he'll climb
Beyond the trippers to the final stone
Flat of the hillock, there to grow in Time.
Dry pubic ferns prickle the bitter sand.
Hawks in a hot concentric ecstasy
Of flight and shriek will wake his vision. And,
When the clouds lift, he'll glimpse the miles-off sea.

Jason

I was the captain of my ship.
At nightfall a disquieting shape
Would eddy on the steady breeze,
Each gold curl thick and separate.
So endlessly outpoured, the fleece
Tugged at me and I followed it.

After my watch I snuffed the wick.
I was young then, I slept and woke
Wrapped in my heavy need to find.

Through the ship's planks I heard the finned
Sea monsters thrash. I dreamt of the
Fleece running wild where our wake was.
My crew and I were beardless boys
But driven by a mystery.

Our raised bows cleaved to a charred land
With breasts of salt too soft to climb.
Then I was fifty, and had found
Nothing. A bald black pilot came
And told us that the fleece was there.
I combed my beard and climbed ashore.

Small crabs tacked through the ashy sand,
Nudging their fathers' fossils and
Going nowhere always, like my want.
Then in the seawind whose white paint
Had crusted my gold curls, I ran
Where the black pilot pointed. Then,
Drunk with the sun, I wept and laughed,
Though the bright fleece turned out no more
Than a burst quilt someone had left
To ooze its heart out on the shore.

MARVIN BELL

The All Girls Drill Team

Texas has nothing so abundant
as its chorus lines, it would appear
from attending intermissions
of all kinds.
Texas appears
in more stadiums, in more fieldhouses
than any other state, Alaska
appearing at this point to be too
wrapped up in itself.
Texas has more marching
girls than anything.
Texas has more drill
teams than anything.

I am not exactly against it.

Let the longhorny cow
boys watch the longhorny cow
girls, who, if they can
can-can, can
cater to us.
There is, as the stuck poet says, no description
for this vision, there is no believing
this distinct possibility:
a whole junior college at large
bending, waving and kicking their parts
according to such a score
as can be counted on.

Thus does Texas occasion
comparisons with one-sided states.
For Texas appears
to have steered itself into
a life-time of half-times,
and we love it.
What other state has within it
so much meat?
And turns to *art?*
Veritably, Texas
has everything
it brags about.

Travel

The park's trees have been growing all week.
We circle them, looking for signs.

Overhead, a kite, wanting,
bobs aimlessly.

The strain of the weekend relaxes,
the children give in to quiet.

Looking at the sun
I see myself drawn in.

If I shut my eyes,
I will dream of it as it happens.

Glossary

ACCENT When the stress on a syllable is greater than the stress on the surrounding syllables, that syllable is accented. See STRESS. For discussion and examples see Chapter 4.

ACCENTUAL LINE A line is accentual when throughout the poem there is a recurrent pattern of the number of accents in the line, but there is no recurrent pattern of the number of syllables in the line. See ACCENT. For discussion and examples see Chapter 4.

ACCENTUAL-SYLLABIC LINE A line is accentual-syllabic when throughout the poem there is a recurrent pattern of the number of accents and the number of syllables in the line, and for the most part the unaccented and accented syllables alternate in a recurrent pattern. See ACCENT. For discussion and examples see Chapter 4.

ALEXANDRINE A line of iambic hexameter is called an alexandrine. Pope both illustrates and criticizes the alexandrine in the second line of this couplet:

> A needless Alexandrine ends the song,
> That, like a wounded snake, drags its slow length along.

See IAMB and HEXAMETER.

ALLEGORY Allegory is extended metaphor in which the comparisons are to abstractions like *love, hope, goodness, evil*, etc. It is unlike symbolism in that what the symbol stands for is of secondary interest; in allegory the abstractions are of primary interest and the metaphor need not be interesting in and of itself. See META-PHOR and SYMBOL.

ALLITERATION Alliteration occurs whenever there are repetitions of sounds within lines. For discussion and examples see Chapter 6.

ALLUSION An allusion is a reference to a historical figure or event or to a literary work; often allusions are not identified in poems although the reader is expected to recognize them.

ANAPEST In accentual-syllabic lines, the unit which consists of two unaccented syllables followed by an accented syllable (- - /) is an anapestic foot. See ACCENTUAL-SYLLABIC LINE, FOOT. For discussion and examples see Chapter 4.

ANIMISM The idea that there is a soul or spirit in every physical thing is animism; this often becomes a device for poetry. See PERSONIFICATION.

ANTICLIMAX Anticlimax occurs when trivial or uninteresting details appear at a point when the reader is reasonably expecting the most dramatic or exciting details.

ANTITHESIS The figure of speech which includes strongly contrasting elements is antithesis. An example is the familiar "Man proposes, God disposes." See FIGURE OF SPEECH.

APOSTROPHE A figure of speech in which some person or idea is addressed directly is an apostrophe. See FIGURE OF SPEECH.

APPROXIMATE RHYME When rhyme is either assonance or consonance, it is often called approximate rhyme. See ASSONANCE and CONSONANCE.

ARCHETYPE The concept of the archetype grows out of the psychology of Jung. Archetypes are images, plots, or characters which reappear consistently enough to carry symbolic suggestions at their very mention, such as darkness symbolizing evil. See SYMBOL.

ASSONANCE Assonance is the kind of rhyme that occurs when the final consonant sounds differ, but the final vowel sounds which precede them are the same. See RHYME. For discussion and examples see Chapter 6.

AUDITORY IMAGERY Images which involve sound are auditory. See IMAGERY.

BALLAD A ballad is a poem, usually narrative, written in a song-like form. The traditional ballad stanza is a quatrain with the first and third lines tetrameter and the second and fourth lines trimeter, rhyming *abcb*. See COMMON METER. For discussion and an example see Chapter 5.

BALLADE The ballade is a French form with a strong refrain, usually consisting of three eight-line stanzas plus an envoy. See ENVOY. An example is "Ballad for the Dead Ladies," page 262.

BATHOS Bathos is usually the result of ineptitude. An unsuccessful attempt at elevation or an unintentional anticlimax can create bathos. See ANTICLIMAX.

BLANK VERSE Unrhymed iambic pentameter is known as blank verse. An example is "The Snow-Storm," page 124.

CACOPHONY Cacophony is the opposite of euphony. A cacophonous effect is one of harsh dissonant sounds. See EUPHONY.

CAESURA A pause or juncture in a line is a caesural pause; caesura may be used for variety and effect. The following lines illustrate caesura:

> Pure streams, // in whose transparent wave
> My youthful limbs // I wont to lave;
> No torrents strain // thy limpid source,
> No rocks impede // thy dimpling course.

CLOSED COUPLET A closed couplet is one in which the thought is completed at the end of the second line. An example is "Upon the Death of Sir Albert Morton's Wife," page 93.

COMMON METER A ballad stanza is often, but not always, in common meter, which consists of a quatrain with the first and third lines iambic tetrameter and the second and fourth lines iambic trimeter. See BALLAD. For discussion and an example see Chapter 5.

CONCEIT A conceit is a particularly involved or complicated metaphor, usually developed throughout a poem. The conceit is identified with the metaphysical poets of the seventeenth century. An example is "Housewifery," page 106.

CONNOTATION The emotions and feelings that words arouse in addition to their precise meanings are their connotations. For example, *famous* and *notorious* mean approximately the same things, but the first has a good connotation and the second a bad connotation. See DENOTATION.

CONSONANCE Consonance is the kind of rhyme that occurs when the final consonant sounds are the same, but the final vowel sounds which precede them differ. See RHYME. For discussion and examples see Chapter 6.

COUPLET A couplet consists of two lines rhyming *aa*. See STANZA. An example is "Upon the Death of Sir Albert Morton's Wife," page 93.

DACTYL In accentual-syllabic lines, the unit which consists of an accented syllable followed by two unaccented syllables (/- -) is a dactylic foot. See ACCENTUAL-SYLLABIC LINE, FOOT. For discussion and examples see Chapter 4.

DECORUM The classical concept of decorum is that there is harmony in a literary work which means that there is a tone and a style that are proper to a character, setting, or subject. See TONE.

DENOTATION The precise meaning of a word is its denotation. See CONNOTATION.

DIALECT To use dialect is to exactly imitate unconventional speech.

DICTION By the diction of a poem is meant the selection of words. The diction may be "high" if very formal words are chosen or "low" if informal words are chosen. See DECORUM and TONE.

DIDACTIC POETRY Poetry which attempts to teach a lesson is didactic.

DIMETER In accentual-syllabic poetry a dimeter line is one consisting of two feet. See ACCENTUAL-SYLLABIC LINE. For discussion see Chapter 4.

DOUBLE RHYME A double rhyme is one on two syllables. See RHYME. For discussion and examples see Chapter 5.

DRAMATIC IRONY Dramatic or poetic irony occurs in a poem when the reader can perceive something about the speaker's or a character's words or actions that the speaker or character cannot himself perceive. For discussion and examples see Chapter 7.

DRAMATIC MONOLOGUE A dramatic monologue is a poem in which the speaker seems to be conversing with someone, although the reader hears only one side of the conversation. An example is "Soliloquy of a Spanish Cloister," page 141.

DUPLE METER In an accentual-syllabic line, the use of two-syllable feet like iambic and trochaic feet is called duple meter. See IAMB and TROCHEE. For discussion and examples see Chapter 4.

ELEGY An elegy is a poem written to honor the memory of someone who has died. An example is "Elegy for Jane," page 239.

END-STOPPED LINE An end-stopped line is one which has no tension. See TENSION. For discussion and examples see Chapter 4.

ENGLISH SONNET The English sonnet is that variation of the sonnet used by Shakespeare. It consists of two parts: twelve lines followed by a summing-up couplet. See SONNET. For discussion and examples see Chapter 5.

ENJAMBMENT Enjambment occurs when a line ending does not occur at a point of punctuation. See TENSION.

ENVOY The concluding or dedicatory stanza which occurs at the end of fixed forms like the ballade is the envoy. See BALLADE.

EPIGRAM A short, pithy poem, usually satiric, is called an epigram. See SATIRE. An example is "Upon the Death of Sir Albert Morton's Wife," page 93.

EUPHONY Euphony is the opposite of cacophony. A euphonious effect is one of pleasant, melodious sounds. See CACOPHONY.

EXACT RHYME See TRUE RHYME.

EYE-RHYME Eye-rhyme is really not rhyme at all, but occurs when two words that do not sound alike are spelled alike except for the initial letter(s). Examples are *cough-through, love-move,* and *foot-hoot.* Since eye-rhyme cannot be heard, it is virtually useless in poetry. See RHYME.

FALLING METER In an accentual-syllabic line, falling meter occurs when the line consists of feet which begin on accented syllables like trochaic and dactylic feet. See TROCHEE and DACTYL.

FEMININE RHYME Feminine rhyme occurs when the rhyme is on an unaccented syllable. See RHYME. For discussion and examples see Chapter 6.

FIGURE OF SPEECH A departure from normal syntax or word use for effect is a figure of speech. See ANTITHESIS, APOSTROPHE, HYPERBOLE, IRONY, METONYMY, ONOMATOPOEIA, OXYMORON, PERSONIFICATION, and SYNECDOCHE.

FOOT The units by which accentual-syllabic lines are measured are called feet. See ACCENTUAL-SYLLABIC LINE, ANAPEST, DACTYL, IAMB, and TROCHEE. For discussion and examples see Chapter 4.

FREE VERSE Free verse is another name for the random line. See RANDOM LINE.

GENRE A literary work's genre is its particular type or category. Poetry may be called one genre and fiction another. Or, within poetry, the lyric may be called one genre and the epic another.

HAIKU A haiku is a three-line poem consisting of one line of five syllables, one line of seven syllables, and one line of five syllables. The form was developed in Japan. For discussion and example see Chapter 5.

HEPTAMETER In accentual-syllabic poetry a heptameter line is one consisting of seven feet. See ACCENTUAL-SYLLABIC LINE. For discussion see Chapter 4.

HEROIC COUPLET A heroic couplet is a closed couplet written in iambic pentameter. See CLOSED COUPLET.

HEXAMETER In accentual-syllabic poetry a hexameter line is one consisting of six feet. See ACCENTUAL-SYLLABIC LINE. For discussion see Chapter 4.

HYPERBOLE The figure of speech which consists of exaggeration is hyperbole. See FIGURE OF SPEECH. An example is the second stanza of "The Canonization," page 4.

IAMB In accentual-syllabic lines, the unit which consists of one unaccented syllable followed by an accented syllable (- /) is an iambic foot. See ACCENTUAL-SYLLABIC LINE, FOOT. For discussion and examples see Chapter 4.

IMAGERY Descriptive passages in poems appeal to the senses; the mental pictures of the way things look, smell, sound, taste, or feel to touch are images. See AUDITORY IMAGERY, OLFACTORY IMAGERY, TACTILE IMAGERY, TASTE IMAGERY, and VISUAL IMAGERY. For discussion see Chapter 2.

INTERNAL RHYME When a rhyme pattern includes rhymes within the line, internal rhyme occurs. See RHYME. An example is "The Raven," page 134.

IRONY The common term for dramatic irony is irony. Irony also refers to the figure of speech in which the actual intent is expressed in words which appear to mean the opposite; in other words, irony occurs when the speaker says one thing but means another. See DRAMATIC IRONY and FIGURE OF SPEECH.

ITALIAN SONNET The Italian sonnet is the original sonnet form as used by Petrarch. It consists of two parts: eight lines and six lines. See OCTET, SESTET, and SONNET. For discussion and examples see Chapter 5.

LIGHT VERSE Light verse is poetry that is essentially humorous in intent. An example is "On a Honey Bee," page 113.

LIMERICK A limerick is a light verse form consisting of five lines, usually accentual-syllabic in triple meter, with the first, second, and fifth lines trimeter and the third and fourth lines dimeter, rhyming *aabba*, usually double rhyme. See TRIPLE METER and DOUBLE RHYME. For discussion and an example see Chapter 5.

LINE The basic constructional unit of a poem is the line. It is indicated either by placing the lines one under the other or by placing a virgule (/) between the lines. For discussion and examples see Chapters 1 and 4.

LYRIC A lyric is a short poem, usually subjective and emotional, often offering a fresh perception of something familiar. Originally a lyric was a poem written to be set to music, but recently the term has been used to describe almost any non-narrative poem.

MASCULINE RHYME Masculine rhyme occurs when the rhyme is on an accented syllable. See RHYME. For discussion and examples see Chapter 6.

METAPHOR A metaphor is a comparison, an analogy which identifies one object with another. For discussion and examples see Chapter 2.

METER The accentual-syllabic system of organizing lines is often called meter. Sometimes meter is used to refer to the rhythm of the line, no matter how the line is organized. See ACCENTUAL-SYLLABIC LINE and RHYTHM. For discussion and examples see Chapter 4.

METONYMY The figure of speech in which the name of an object closely related to the intended word is used instead of the word itself. For example, one might say "the crown" instead of "the king." See FIGURE OF SPEECH.

MONOMETER In accentual-syllabic poetry a monometer line is one consisting of one foot. See ACCENTUAL-SYLLABIC LINE. For discussion see Chapter 4.

NEAR-RHYME When rhyme is either assonance or consonance, it is often called near-rhyme. See ASSONANCE and CONSONANCE.

OBJECTIVE CORRELATIVE According to T. S. Eliot, the inventor of the term, the objective correlative is "a set of objects, a situation, a chain of events which shall be the formula of that *particular* emotion, such that when the external facts, which must terminate in sensory experience, are given, the emotion is immediately evoked." For discussion and examples see Chapter 2.

OCTAMETER In accentual-syllabic poetry an octameter line is one consisting of eight feet. See ACCENTUAL-SYLLABIC LINE. For discussion and examples see Chapter 4.

OCTAVE A stanza consisting of eight lines is an octave. See ITALIAN SONNET and STANZA.

OCTET The octave that is the first part of an Italian sonnet is often referred to as the octet. See ITALIAN SONNET and OCTAVE.

ODE An ode is a lyric poem of irregular form which treats a dignified subject in an exalted manner. An example is "To Autumn," page 122.

OFF-RHYME When rhyme is either assonance or consonance, it is often called off-rhyme. See ASSONANCE and CONSONANCE.

OLFACTORY IMAGERY Images which involve smells are olfactory. See IMAGERY.

ONOMATOPOEIA The figure of speech in which words are used to imitate sounds is onomatopoeia. See FIGURE OF SPEECH.

OTTAVA RIMA An octave rhyming *abababcc* in iambic pentameter is known as ottava rima. See OCTAVE and STANZA. An example is "Among School Children," page 182.

OXYMORON The figure of speech which combines two seemingly contradictory words is oxymoron. An example is "eloquent silence." See FIGURE OF SPEECH.

PARADOX A statement which seems to contradict itself is a paradox. An example is lines 25–26 of "The Canonization," page 4.

PARAPHRASE A paraphrase of a poem is a prose summary of the literal content of the poem.

PENTAMETER In accentual-syllabic poetry a pentameter line is one consisting of five feet. See ACCENTUAL-SYLLABIC LINE. For discussion and examples see Chapter 4.

PERSONIFICATION The figure of speech that consists of assigning human qualities to non-human objects is personification. See FIGURE OF SPEECH.

PETRARCHAN SONNET See ITALIAN SONNET.

POETRY Poetry is discourse arranged in lines. For discussion see Chapter 1.

PUN To pun on a word is to use the word so that it has at least two meanings, both of which are appropriate to the content. An example is the use of the word *die* in "The Canonization," a discussion of which is in Chapter 1.

PYRRHIC FOOT Students of poetry have sometimes predicated the existence in accentual-syllabic poetry of a foot consisting of two unaccented syllables (- -) called the pyrrhic foot. However, since it is impossible in English not to put more stress on one of the syllables, the pyrrhic foot does not actually exist.

QUATRAIN A quatrain is a stanza consisting of four lines. See STANZA.

RANDOM LINE A line is random when throughout the poem there is no recurrent pattern either of the number of accents or of the number of syllables in the line. For discussion and examples see Chapter 4.

REFRAIN A refrain is a line which is repeated regularly throughout the poem. An example is in "War Story," page 293.

RHYME Rhyme is the repetition of the final sounds of lines. See TRUE RHYME, ASSONANCE, and CONSONANCE. For discussion and examples see Chapter 6.

RHYME ROYAL Rhyme royal is a stanza consisting of seven lines of iambic pentameter, rhyming *ababbcc*. See STANZA. An example is "They Flee from Me," page 88.

RHYME SCHEME In poems in which rhyme is patterned, the representation of that pattern (as *abab cdcd*, etc.) is called the rhyme scheme. For discussion and examples see Chapters 5 and 6.

RHYTHM The pattern of the variation of accented and unaccented syllables is the poem's rhythm; the rhythm can be very regular or irregular. See ACCENTUAL LINE, ACCENTUAL-SYLLABIC LINE, RANDOM LINE, and SYLLABIC LINE. For discussion and examples see Chapter 4.

RISING METER In an accentual-syllabic line, rising meter occurs when the line consists of feet which begin on unaccented syllables like iambic and anapestic feet. See ANAPEST and IAMB.

RUN-ON LINE A line which does not end at a point of punctuation is a run-on line. See TENSION.

SATIRE The ridiculing of someone or something is satire; satire is usually humorous but its purpose is often serious. An example is "The All Girls Drill Team," page 303.

SCANSION The visual representation of the pattern of accented and unaccented syllables in poetry is called scansion. For discussion and examples see Chapter 4.

SENTIMENTALITY Sentimentality as a critical term results from demanding an emotion greater than is merited by the material. "The Solitary Reaper," page 117, comes dangerously close to sentimentality.

SESTET A stanza consisting of six lines is a sestet. See ITALIAN SONNET and STANZA.

SESTINA The sestina is an old Italian form. For discussion and an example see Chapter 5.

SHAKESPEAREAN SONNET See ENGLISH SONNET.

SIMILE A metaphor introduced by *like* or *as* is sometimes called a simile. See META-PHOR.

SLANT-RHYME When rhyme is either assonance or consonance, it is often called slant-rhyme. See ASSONANCE and CONSONANCE.

SONNET A fourteen-line form developed in Italy, the sonnet has become one of the most-used forms in English poetry. See ENGLISH SONNET and ITALIAN SONNET. For discussion and examples see Chapter 5.

SPENSERIAN STANZA A stanza of nine lines, rhyming *ababbcbcc*, with the first eight lines iambic pentameter and the last iambic hexameter is a Spenserian stanza. An example is the following stanza from Byron's "Childe Harold":

> Roll on, thou deep and dark blue Ocean—roll!
> Ten thousand fleets sweep over thee in vain;
> Man marks the earth with ruin—his control
> Stops with the shore; upon thy watery plain
> The wrecks are all thy deed, nor doth remain
> A shadow of man's ravage, save his own,
> When for a moment, like a drop of rain,
> He sinks into thy depths with bubbling groan,
> Without a grave, unknelled, uncoffined, and unknown.

See STANZA.

SPONDEE Students of poetry have sometimes predicated the existence in accentual-syllabic poetry of a foot consisting of two accented syllables (/ /) called a spondee. However, since it is impossible in English not to put more stress on one of the syllables, the spondee does not actually exist.

SPRUNG RHYTHM Gerard Manley Hopkins called the line he developed sprung rhythm. Actually, the line is accentual. See ACCENTUAL LINE.

STANZA A unit in a poem, roughly corresponding to a paragraph in prose, made up of a group of lines and indicated by a space before and after is a stanza. For discussion and examples see Chapter 5.

STRESS Stress is the relative differences in the amount of energy expended in pronouncing syllables. For discussion and examples see Chapter 4.

SYLLABIC LINE A line is syllabic when throughout the poem there is a recurrent pattern of the number of syllables in the line, but there is not recurrent pattern of the number of accents in the line. For discussion and examples see Chapter 4.

SYMBOL Whenever an object in a literary work can be viewed as representative of an abstraction as well as operating in its literal context, it becomes a symbol. See Chapter 7.

SYNECDOCHE The figure of speech in which the part is used to indicate the whole is synecdoche, as when one says "the bow cut the water" meaning that "the ship moved forward." See FIGURE OF SPEECH.

SYNTAX The study of sentence constructions and word order is the study of syntax.

TACTILE IMAGERY Images which involve the sense of touch are tactile. See IMAGERY.

TANKA A tanka is a five-line poem consisting of one line of five syllables, one line of seven syllables, one line of five syllables, and two lines of seven syllables. The form was developed in Japan. For discussion and an example see Chapter 5.

TASTE IMAGERY Images which involve the sense of taste are taste images. See IMAGERY.

TENSION Tension exists when a line break occurs where there is no juncture in normal speech patterns. For discussion and examples see Chapter 4.

TERCET A stanza which contains three lines is a tercet. See STANZA.

TERZA RIMA Originated by Dante, terza rima indicates three-line stanzas linked by rhyme in the following manner: *aba bcb cdc ded* etc. An example is "Acquainted with the Night," page 75.

TETRAMETER In accentual-syllabic poetry a tetrameter line is one consisting of four feet. See ACCENTUAL-SYLLABIC LINE. For discussion and examples see Chapter 4.

THEME The abstraction about the world or the human condition to which a poem can sometimes be reduced is its theme. For discussion and examples see Chapter 7.

TONE The general emotional context of a poem is its tone. See CACOPHONY, EUPHONY, and OBJECTIVE CORRELATIVE. For discussion and examples see Chapter 2.

TRIMETER In accentual-syllabic poetry a trimeter line is one consisting of three feet. See ACCENTUAL-SYLLABIC LINE. For discussion and examples see Chapter 4.

TRIPLE METER In an accentual-syllabic line, the use of three-syllable feet like anapestic and dactylic feet is called triple meter. See ANAPEST and DACTYL. For discussion and examples see Chapter 4.

TROCHEE In accentual-syllabic lines, the unit which consists of one accented syllable followed by an unaccented syllable (/ -) is a trochaic foot. See ACCENTUAL-SYLLABIC LINE. For discussion and examples see Chapter 4.

TRUE RHYME True rhyme is the kind of rhyme that occurs when the final consonant sounds and the final vowel sounds which precede them are the same, or when there are no final consonant sounds and the final vowel sounds are the same. See RHYME. For discussion and examples see Chapter 6.

VARIABLE FOOT William Carlos Williams called the line he developed the variable foot. Actually, the line is random. See RANDOM LINE.

VERS LIBRE Vers libre is another name for the random line. See RANDOM LINE.

VILLANELLE The villanelle is an old French form. For discussion and an example see Chapter 5.

VISUAL IMAGERY Images which involve sight are visual. See IMAGERY.

Index of Authors, Titles, and First Lines

[Authors' names are printed in capital letters, titles are printed in italics, and first lines are printed in roman type. Poems which are discussed in Part I are marked with an asterisk (°).]

313